STRATEGIES FOR INCLUDING CHILDREN WITH SPECIAL NEEDS IN EARLY CHILDHOOD SETTINGS

M. DIANE KLEIN, Ph.D.

RUTH E. COOK, Ph.D.

ANNE MARIE RICHARDSON-GIBBS, M.A.

DELMAR

THOMSON LEARNING™

Australia Canada Mexico Singapore Spain United Kingdom United States

DELMAR

™

THOMSON LEARNING

Strategies for Including Children with Special Needs in Early Childhood Settings
by M. Diane Klein, Ruth E. Cook, Anne Marie Richardson-Gibbs

Business Unit Director:
Susan L. Simpfenderfer

Editorial Assistant:
Alexis Ferraro

Executive Marketing Manager:
Donna J. Lewis

Acquisitions Editor:
Erin O'Connor Traylor

Executive Production Manager:
Wendy A. Troeger

Channel Manager:
Nigar Hale

Developmental Editor:
Melissa Riveglia

Project Editor:
Amy E. Tucker

Cover Design:
Tom Cicero

Executive Editorial Assistant:
Amy Simcik

Production Editor:
J.P. Henkel

For permission to use material from this text or product, contact us by
Tel   (800) 730-2214
Fax   (800) 730-2215
www.thomsonrights.com

Library of Congress Cataloging-in-Publication Data
Klein, M. Diane
    Strategies for including children with special needs in early childhood settings / M. Diane Klein, Ruth E. Cook, Anne Marie Richardson-Gibbs.
        p. cm.
Includes bibliographical references and index.
    ISBN 0-8273-8352-5
    1. Handicapped children--Education (Early childhood)--United States. 2. Inclusive education--United States. I. Cook, Ruth E. II. Richardson-Gibbs, Anne Marie. III. Title.

LC4019.3 .K54 2000
371.9'046--dc21   00-064503

NOTICE TO THE READER

Contents

Preface

This book is intended to be a resource to early childhood educators working in a variety of community-based settings, including child care, Head Start, and preschool programs in which young children with special needs are included. Recent changes in the federal special education law, or IDEA, have strengthened the mandate for inclusion of young children with special needs in typical and natural environments where they have opportunities to interact with their peers and to participate as equal members of their community. This access to inclusive environments is a precious, hard-fought right.

As this access to community-based settings increases, the responsibility for meeting the needs of young children with special needs is no longer the exclusive purview of special educators and therapists. It is increasingly shifting to early childhood educators. This book is an immediately applicable resource that can provide both an introduction to working with young children with special needs for students in early childhood education, and a usable resource and problem-solving guide to early childhood education (ECE) practitioners and paraprofessionals. The book can also be useful for parents whose young children are placed in inclusive settings, for therapists and disability specialists who serve children in inclusive settings, and for early childhood special education personnel who provide inclusion support to young children with special needs.

CONCEPTUAL APPROACH

As access to inclusive environments becomes more widely available, and more and more young children with special needs (including children with significant and complex needs) are served in typical early childhood settings, teacher trainers in the field of disability and early childhood special education have an obligation. They must provide training and resources to early childhood educators that will enable them to expand their skill base and confidence in working with young children who have significant learning and behavior challenges.

The book assumes that the reader already has a solid base of knowledge and at least beginning level experience in early childhood education. This is an important assumption because it is upon this foundation that effective early childhood *special* education must be built. This knowledge base includes understanding child development across the domains of social and emotional development, language and cognition, adaptive skills, and emergent literacy. It also includes a solid knowledge of developmentally appropriate practice and a strong commitment to understanding and meeting the needs of children and families from culturally diverse backgrounds. Without this essential foundation, ECE professionals cannot effectively meet the needs of children with disabilities. Indeed, the special needs and circumstances of many children require knowledge and skills above and beyond this level.

The content and scope of this book are far from exhaustive. Rather, this guide is intended as an immediately useful introduction to understanding and accommodating young children with special needs in group settings. This includes an introduction to the nature of specific disabilities, useful teaching strategies, planning and intervention issues in daily activities, and an approach to working with parents, paraeducators, and specialists.

ORGANIZATION

The book is organized in three parts. Part I, Special Education Foundations: Understanding Special Needs and Generic Instructional Strategies, includes basic information related to working with children with special needs. Chapter 1 describes several essential teaching techniques that can enhance the learning of all children. Chapter 2 includes basic descriptions of some of the most challenging disabilities, including Down syndrome, autism, visual impairment, hearing loss, and cerebral palsy. Chapter 3 discusses considerations for designing the classroom environment in ways that best meet the needs of children who have various types of disabilities. Chapter 4 provides a basic understanding of behavior disorders in children with special needs and an overview of practical strategies and techniques for both preventing behavior problems, and managing them once they occur. Part I ends with Chapter 5 on monitoring children's progress; it explains the IFSP and IEP and provides simple suggestions for ongoing monitoring of children's progress toward specific goals and objectives.

Part II, Adapting Daily Activities in Inclusive Early Childhood Settings, includes several chapters devoted to the particular challenges posed by different daily activities. These include arrival and departure, transitions, free play, circle time, tabletop activities, outside activities, snack, music and rhythm, and emergent literacy activities. Each chapter provides general suggestions for designing these activities in ways that will be most supportive of children with special needs. Also included are notes, labeled "Helpful Hint," related to special adaptations for children with specific disabilities.

Part III, Working with the Early Childhood Special Education Team, includes two chapters. Chapter 14 provides the early childhood educator with important information about the challenges often faced by parents of children with special needs. It addresses the importance of establishing partnerships with families. Chapter 15 describes the roles and contributions of specialists and therapists and the ways in which paraeducators and one-to-one assistants can best support children with special needs. Also included in this chapter is a brief overview of collaborative teaming and problem-solving processes.

SPECIAL FEATURES

Each chapter contains several helpful features. These include:

- Chapter-at-a-Glance introductions that highlight key points.
- Real-life examples of key points throughout each chapter.
- A Case Study that demonstrates key ideas at the end of each chapter.
- End of chapter Helpful Resources, References, and Key Terms defined in a glossary at the end of the book.
- Helpful Hints, which address challenges and adaptations specific to different disabilities, are inserted throughout the text.

ABOUT THE AUTHORS

Dr. M. Diane Klein, lead author of the book, has a background in speech pathology and audiology from Western Michigan University. She received her Ph.D. in developmental psychology from Michigan State University. She has had a wide range of experiences with children with special needs, including children with severe and multiple disabilities. Dr. Klein has years of experience as a university instructor and clinical supervisor in both communication disorders and special education. She is currently a professor of early childhood special education and Chair of the Division of Special Education at California State University, Los Angeles. She has coordinated the credential, M.A., and certificate programs in early childhood special education. These programs emphasize the training of early intervention personnel to work in urban multicultural environments.

Dr. Klein has directed numerous federal personnel preparation and outreach grants, including the current Project Support, which develops training models and materials related to inclusion support training in early childhood special education. She has conducted research in the area of mother-infant communication and has developed early intervention programs to serve high-risk families from multicultural backgrounds, including the Mother Infant Communication Project.

In addition to her work at the university, Dr. Klein frequently conducts in-service training in the area of communication skills for children with special needs, curriculum development in early childhood special education, and inclusion support strategies. She also serves on numerous boards and committees related to early intervention services in the state of California and as the Executive Director of Centro de Niños y Padres Early Intervention Program.

Dr. Ruth E. Cook is a professor and director of special education and director of the early intervention specialist personnel preparation program at Santa Clara University in Santa Clara, California. Dr. Cook received her Ph.D. with an emphasis in developmental psychology from the University of California at Los Angeles. Her interest in inclusion of young children with special needs developed while serving as director of the Early Childhood Center at Southern Illinois University at Edwardsville, and the Child Development Center at Mount Saint Mary's College in Los Angeles.

She has directed several federal training grants in early childhood special education. Currently she consults widely in the areas of family-professional relationships and strategies for effective inclusion, and serves as program consultant in ECSE for the Department of Teaching and Learning at the University of San Diego.

Anne Marie Richardson-Gibbs is an early childhood special educator. She has worked with young children with special needs since the late 1970s. Ms. Richardson-Gibbs holds a masters degree in child development and two special education credentials. Currently, she is the Program Director of Centro de Niños y Padres, an early intervention program that provides services to young children with special needs and their families from the multicultural community of East Los Angeles.

For the past eight years Ms. Richardson-Gibbs has provided inclusion support for young children with disabilities in community-based programs, and she conducts early childhood inclusion training and consultation. She has also worked as a statewide early intervention program specialist for the California Department of Education, and she is currently the training coordinator for Project Support, which trains early childhood inclusion support personnel.

ACKNOWLEDGMENTS

First and foremost, we would like to acknowledge the children and their families who have helped us understand disabilities and the challenges and solutions of successful inclusion. We gratefully acknowledge the teachers and staff of Children's Center at Cal Tech, Pasadena, CA; Scott Child Development Center, Pasadena, CA; El Monte City School District Head Start and State Preschool programs; Options Head Start, San Gabriel Valley, CA; All Saints Children's Center, Pasadena, CA; Covina First Baptist Child Development Center; and the San Bernardino County West End Early Childhood Centers.

Special gratitude is extended to the children and families at Centro de Niños, for teaching us so much about children with special needs; to the lead teachers Caroline, Kirsten, and Naree; and veteran assistant teachers Amanda, Hilda, Evelyn, Emma, Beatrice, and Elizabeth. We also wish to thank Centro de Niños for its contributions to the photos included throughout the book. Another important contribution to this book has been the feedback from our own university students in early childhood special education and our Project Support inservice participants. They have helped us learn how to teach the most critical elements of the knowledge and skill base necessary to support young children with special needs in community-based programs.

We would also like to thank our wonderful colleagues Dr. Sherry Best, Dr. Jamie Dote-Kwan, Dr. Nancy Hunt, and Dr. Deborah Chen for their willingness, over many years and many projects, to share their knowledge of low-incidence disabilities, and Sharon Kilpatrick who generously shared her experiences and expertise and served as our all-purpose sounding board and cheerleader. Also thanks to many other colleagues in the field, for their ideas and encouragement, especially Dr. Shirley Sparks, Whit Hayslip, Paula Miller, Carole Dale, and Victoria Bridges. Thanks also to Delmar, and particularly to Amy Simcik, without whose persistence this book never would have been published.

The authors and Delmar wish to extend gratitude to the following reviewers who provided valuable insight throughout the development of this book:

Alice Beyrent, Department Chair
Hesser College, Manchester, NH

Blanche Jackson Glimps
Kentucky Christian College, Grayson, KY

Ann Higgins Hains, Ph.D.
University of Milwaukee, Milwaukee, WI

Mary Henthorne
Western Wisconsin Tech College, La Crosse, WI

Melinda Lindsey, Ph.D.
Boise State University, Boise, Idaho

Jan Powell, M.A.
Mt. San Jacinto College, Mt. San Jacinto, CA

Eugene Scholten, Ph.D.
Grand Valley State University, Allendale, MI

Vicki D. Stayton, Ph.D.
Western Kentucky University, Bowling Green, KY

Patti Zaske
Modesto Junior College, Modesto, CA

Finally, we would like to acknowledge all the current and future early childhood educators who willingly open their classrooms and their hearts to young children with disabilities. We hope this book contributes to making your work a joyful and satisfying endeavor.

DEDICATION

We dedicate this book to Dr. Annette Tessier who has provided the wisdom, the humor, and the inspiration for the training of hundreds of early childhood special educators over the past 30 years, and to Centro de Niños y Padres early intervention program, a program that, like Annette, continues to enhance the lives of children, families, staff and students. It will always reflect her values and her spirit.

Centro de Niños photos taken by Anne Marie Richardson-Gibbs and Tina Arora.

Introduction

Since 1975, with the passage of Public Law 94–142 (The Education for all Handicapped Children Act), the United States has had laws in place that mandate educational services for school-age children with disabilities. In 1986 Public Law 99–457 (Education of the Handicapped Act Amendments) extended this law to include preschool-age children and encouraged states to develop comprehensive services for infants from birth to age three. In 1990 the 1975 law was further amended, and the name was changed to The Individuals with Disabilities Education Act (IDEA) Amendments, which replaced the term *handicapped children* with the "person-first" phrase *individuals with disabilities*. This new educational legislation reflected the values of the Americans with Disabilities Act (ADA), also adopted in 1990, which assures reasonable accommodations to all individuals with disabilities. This includes the right of access and accommodation in preschool and child care centers.

Beginning with the IDEA Amendments in 1990, a series of several additional amendments were made. Most recently in 1997, IDEA has been further amended by Public Law 105–17. These recent amendments strengthened the mandate for placement of preschool and school-age children in the "least restrictive environment" and the provision of services for infants and toddlers in "natural environments," such as child care centers. As a result, toddlers and preschoolers, regardless of the severity of their disability, will increasingly be served in nonspecial education settings. Families are beginning to realize that their children have the right to receive appropriate services to address the needs created by their disabilities in typical community-based environments. See the box on page xx for a summary of federal legislation.

KEY LEGISLATION AFFECTING YOUNG CHILDREN WITH DISABILITIES

1968 *Public Law 90–538: Handicapped Children's Early Education Assistance Act* Established experimental early education programs through Handicapped Children's Early Education Program (HCEEP).

1972 *Public Law 92–424: Economic Opportunity Act Amendments* Established preschool mandate that required that not less than 10 percent of the total number of Head Start placements be reserved for children with disabilities.

1975 *Public Law 94–142: Education for All Handicapped Children Act* Provided free appropriate public education to all school-age children (preschool services not mandated).

1986 *Public Law 99–457: Education of the Handicapped Act Amendments of 1986* Extended P.L. 94–142 to include three- to five-year-olds; provided incentives to states to develop comprehensive systems of services for infants and toddlers from birth to three with disabilities and their families.

1990 *Public Law 101–336: The Americans with Disabilities Act (ADA)* Assures full civil rights to individuals with disabilities, including access and accommodations in preschools and child care centers.

1990 *Public Law 101–476: Individuals with Disabilities Education Act (IDEA)* Reauthorization of P.L. 94–142. Uses "person-first" language, that is, "individuals with. . . ." rather than "handicapped."

1997 *Public Law 105–17: Individual with Disabilities Education Act Amendments of 1997* Reauthorization of IDEA. Preschool services included under Part B; infants and toddlers included under Part C strengthens mandates for inclusion in the least restrictive environment for preschoolers and provision of services in "natural environments" for infants and toddlers.

Serving young children in the least restrictive and natural environments requires a major shift in the roles and responsibilities of professionals and in how early intervention and special education services are delivered. This shift also creates the potential for increasing the responsibilty of child care workers and early childhood educators for the early care and education of children with significant needs and challenges. Many early childhood personnel, whose jobs are already extremely demanding, may not feel ready to take on this new role.

The purpose of this book is to help provide early childhood personnel with a basic and practical understanding of the characteristics and effects of disabilities on young children's learning. It suggests simple ways of adapting the early childhood setting and activities so these children can participate with their peers. Equally important, the book describes the knowledge and skills that can be provided by the many specialists who work in the disabilities field.

It is our hope that this book will help early childhood educators realize that their job is not to *fix* the child or to meet all the child's needs. Rather, we hope the information in this book will inspire and encourage early childhood educators to welcome children with special needs into the early childhood centers. We want to help these educators gain the confidence to not only recognize the many skills and intuitions they already have, but also to draw upon the information and supports that can be provided by family members, special educators, and disability specialists. We also hope that by gaining understanding of the nature of various disabilities—of how children experience the world around them and what they find engaging—that early childhood educators will celebrate each child's uniqueness and appreciate the gifts this *specialness* can bring to the early childhood setting.

Part I

Special Education Foundations: Understanding Special Needs and Generic Instructional Strategies

1

Generic Instructional Strategies Supporting the Inclusion of Young Children with Special Needs

Chapter-at-a-Glance

A number of strategies are generic in that they can be used effectively with any child who has special needs. These strategies will be discussed in this chapter:

- **Getting children's attention.** The role of motivation and the importance of identifying high-preference activities are essential factors in optimizing learning for children with special needs.
- **Working in the learning zone.** The use of social mediation of the environment (e.g., *scaffolding*) can help guide the teacher in providing just the right amount of support.
- **Doing it again and again.** Repetition, routines, and predictable environments are key to learning and successful inclusion of young children with special needs.
- **Teaching one step at a time.** Perhaps one of the most tested strategies for helping children learn is the use of task analysis to break skills into small steps.
- **Talking to children.** The role of adult language input and communicative interactions in supporting the development of language and cognition is well documented. These strategies must be built into the curriculum and must be part of the child's ongoing experience.
- **Using an ounce of prevention.** A strategy called *positive behavior support* can significantly assist children with behavior disorders and can prevent the development of inappropriate behaviors.

3

INTRODUCTION

Increasingly the early childhood teacher is faced with the inclusion of young children with special needs and challenges in the classroom or child care facility.

The purpose of this book is to provide information and specific activities to support the optimal participation of young children with special needs in early childhood centers and programs. The field of early childhood special education (ECSE) embraces the philosophy of developmentally appropriate experiences in the least restrictive environment. However, experience has shown us that to ensure success early childhood education (ECE) teachers and ECSE consultants must also learn the specific strategies and techniques that are the necessary tools for accommodating and supporting children with special needs in community-based settings.

This chapter will present an overview of these techniques and strategies. ECE teachers will discover that while the focus of this book is on meeting the needs of children with special needs, many of the practices described will also significantly enhance the development of *all* children. ECE teachers will also realize that as a result of their training and experience and their dedication to children and families, they have already developed many of the skills and strategies described in this book.

Perhaps the greatest difference between ECE and ECSE is the extent to which the teacher plays an active and direct role as intervenor or social mediator of children's experiences. The role of the ECE teacher is to organize and manage the environment and materials and to encourage children to participate in those environments. To ensure that children with special needs fully benefit from the early childhood environment, the teacher may need to orchestrate children's experiences more directly. For some ECE teachers this may require taking a more active role than they otherwise might.

GETTING THEIR ATTENTION: CHALLENGES IN MOTIVATING YOUNG CHILDREN

Children cannot learn if they are not paying attention and are not engaged. Children pay attention to things that interest them. One of the challenges of working with children with special needs is that it is sometimes difficult to identify what motivates them (see Figure 1–1).

Specific Challenges

Some children, such as some of those with autism, may be interested in things that are not typically interesting to other children. They may engage in repetitive sensory experiences, such as watching a flickering light or rocking back and forth.

Figure 1–1   Teacher encouraging child to be engaged in activity.

Other children, such as those with cognitive delays, may be interested in activities appropriate for much younger children, such as throwing, banging, or mouthing objects. Still others may have difficulty sustaining attention long enough to become engaged and motivated by an activity.

Difficult-to-Read Cues

Children with severe or multiple disabilities are often difficult to *read*. Teachers often miss or misunderstand their cues of interest.

- Children may not look directly at a toy or event. They may use peripheral rather then central vision, thus giving the impression of not visually attending.
- Children with special needs may not reach or point, even though they are interested. This could be due to motor difficulties and/or visual impairment.
- Some children with special needs do not smile often or may have a rather flat facial expression. This may be a characteristic of children with very low muscle tone or visual impairment, or it may be a symptom of an emotional disorder. Other children may lack a social smile but may smile unpredictably. This is sometimes a characteristic of children with autism.

PREFERENCE INVENTORY		
Activity/Item/Person	Response to Presentation	Response to Removal
1. Barney tape	Became very still	Cried
2. Placed on tricycle	Smiled, rocked a bit	No response
3. Grandmother enters room	Raised arms	Cried when she left room
4. Placed on potty	Cried	Stopped crying
5.		

Figure 1–2   Sample Preference Inventory Recording Sheet.

Conducting a High-Preference Inventory

As a result of these kinds of differences, it may be helpful for the ECE teacher to identify motivators for a specific child by conducting a **high-preference inventory.** Information for the inventory is collected via a number of sources, including caregiver interviews and direct observations of the child at the center. (See Figure 1–2 for example of an inventory recording sheet.)

Unique Ways of Expressing Interest and Attention

An advantage of conducting the high-preference inventory, in addition to identifying motivating objects and activities, is that it provides an opportunity to carefully observe and better understand the child's unique ways of expressing interest and attention. For example, the child may:

- become very still and quiet when she is interested in something but may not be looking at or even facing the object.
- flap arms and hands excitedly when interested in something.
- stiffen and extend arms and legs, or turn head away even though she is interested. In other children this reaction may be a sign of rejection or disinterest. The story of Jorge provides an example.

Jorge's Music

Jorge is a little boy with severe physical disabilities. He does not talk and has little facial expression. Mrs. Muniz, his teacher, is concerned because he does not seem to enjoy any of the activities in the child-care center. She asked the ECSE consultant for some help in motivating Jorge. The consultant joined Mrs. Muniz in carefully observing Jorge several times during the day.

They noticed that when someone turned on the tape player during free play and again during song time, Jorge stiffened a bit and extended his arms. Mrs. Muniz said she always assumed that he was uncomfortable when he did this. They decided to check with Jorge's mother. They learned from her that this extension is often an indication of excitement or pleasure. The mother also commented that Jorge loves listening to CDs when his older sister is home.

This helped Mrs. Muniz realize that music was one of Jorge's passions. She was able not only to acknowledge this and increase opportunities for him to listen to music, but she could use music as a reward for Jorge's participation in other activities, such as finger painting, which he had previously resisted. Gradually, Mrs. Muniz realized that Jorge was becoming interested in many more activities.

WORKING IN THE LEARNING ZONE: UNDERSTANDING THE ZONE OF PROXIMAL DEVELOPMENT

One theory that has proven helpful in working with young children with special needs has to do with the importance of assisting children's learning through *social mediation of the environment.* The Russian psychologist L. S. Vygotsky developed the concept of the **zone of proximal development.** (Vygotsky, 1980) Explained simply, this is the range of performance within which a child can function if she has support from another individual. As portrayed in Figure 1–3, area A would be the range within which the child can function independently and does not need assistance. Area C is probably much too difficult for the child; in this range the child would need almost total support to perform the task. Area B is the range within which the child can achieve *with some support.* After receiving such support, the child can eventually advance to independence, and the zone of proximal development would move along the continuum to a level of greater difficulty.

Area A	{ Area B }	Area C
Child already can perform independently	Zone of Proximal Development: Adult assistance most effective within this range	Too difficult

Figure 1–3   The Zone of Proximal Development.

Scaffolding

The term used to refer to the provision of just the right amount of support within the zone is **scaffolding** (Bruner, 1982). The term is derived from the structure that supports a painter or window washer working on a tall building. The scaffold is the support necessary for the worker to perform successfully. Adults who can read children's cues can determine just the right amount and type of support necessary for children to perform the task. Adults then gradually reduce this support until the children can perform independently. The example of Jason may help demonstrate this concept:

Jason's Puzzle

Jason can independently complete his shape puzzle, which contains just three separate noninterlocking shapes: a square, a circle, and a triangle. He is interested in another puzzle that has pieces in the shape of a simple scene containing a tree, a house, and a car. He tries to do this puzzle but is unsuccessful because he is not used to placing the pieces in just the right position relative to other pieces. His teacher notices his frustration and moves in to assist him.

- She scaffolds and mediates this experience by helping him rotate the pieces slightly so they will fit.
- She does this several times, waiting each time to see at what point he needs assistance.
- She gradually reduces her assistance until he can perform this new puzzle independently.

Many teachers scaffold each day without giving it much thought. They already use this technique to help children learn difficult tasks. By being more aware of scaffolding as a specific strategy and matching it carefully to the child's existing skill, it can be very effective as a support for a child with special needs.

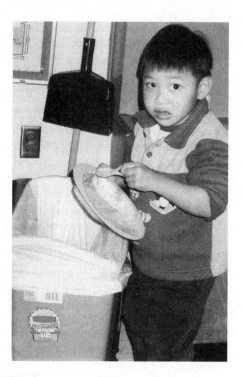

Figure 1–4　Child cleaning his plate.

DOING IT AGAIN AND AGAIN: THE IMPORTANCE OF REPETITION AND ROUTINE

Two strategies, predictable routines and planned transitions, can foster a learning environment for children with special needs.

Creating Predictable Routines

For children with special needs, consistency in daily routines makes it much easier to learn than a chaotic, unpredictable schedule. In addition, unpredictable environments may contribute to children's anxiety and insecurity. This is true not only for children with special needs but also for children who have been in unstable or abusive home situations.

Similarly, frequent repetition of activities develops a sense of comfortable familiarity and mastery, which not only helps children learn but builds self-esteem (see Figure 1–4).

Children with special needs will be most successful within a predictable routine that is consistent and varies only when there is a special event or activity. Novel events are best appreciated against a backdrop of familiar routine. The following is an example of a daily schedule that works well for a half-day structured toddler program:

9:00 Arrival and free play
9:40 Cleanup
9:45 Opening circle and welcome song
10:00 Rhythm/dancing activity
10:10 Art centers
10:30 Outside activity
10:50 Toileting and handwashing
11:05 Snack
11:20 Cleanup, tooth brushing
11:40 Goodbye circle
11:50 Departure

Planning Transitions

Also important are clear cues that signal transitions from one activity to the next. Children with special needs often find transitions stressful and difficult. They may be unsure about what is happening next. They may have difficulty stopping an enjoyable activity. They may find the relative *busyness* of a transition frightening.

Creating routines for transitions can be helpful for children who have difficulty with transitions from one activity to another. These examples of consistent cues may help create transition routines.

- turning lights off and on to signal the end of free play and cleanup time
- playing the song "Hi Ho, Hi Ho, It's off to work we go" when transitioning to centers
- ringing a bell to signal the end of outside play
- singing a goodbye song before going to cubbies to prepare for departure

ONE STEP AT A TIME: MAKING SKILLS EASIER TO LEARN THROUGH TASK ANALYSIS

Skills and tasks that seem simple for typically developing children may be too complex for children who have special needs. This does not mean they cannot learn the task; it simply means the task needs to be broken down into smaller steps. The strategy of **task analysis** can often be helpful. Task analysis is particularly beneficial in teaching skills that can be analyzed into a sequence of observable behavioral steps.

Analyzing the Sequence

For example, most children have little difficulty learning to dispose of their empty lunch containers and utensils in the trash or sink. However, for some children with special needs, this may be difficult to learn. Simple repetition of the task each day may not be sufficient learning support. The teacher can perform a simple task analysis of the sequence of behaviors, sometimes referred to as a **behavior chain,** as follows:

Task analysis of taking dishes to the sink

Step 1: Stand up from table; push chair in.
Step 2: Pile empty cup, spoon, and napkin on plate.
Step 3: Carry items to trash container.
Step 4: Place paper items in trash.
Step 5: Move to sink.
Step 6: Place washable items (spoon and cup) in sink.
Step 7: Walk to bathroom.

The more severe the disability, the smaller the steps may need to be. For example, Step 2 above may need to broken into separate training for each item—the cup, spoon, and napkin.

Training Each Step

The teacher teaches one step at a time, using the principles of scaffolding and the zone of proximal development for each step. Sometimes it is effective to begin by teaching the *last* step and work backward, referred to as **backward chaining.** These steps refer to the previous example.

1. **First training objective:** The teacher provides total assistance to get the child over to the sink and then encourages the child to *place washable items in the sink* by herself and *move away from the sink to the bathroom.*
2. **Second training objective:** After the child learns to do this, she is taught to sort the paper items from the washable items, place them in the trash, and then proceed to the sink
3. **Third training objective:** Once she is handling the tasks in the second objective independently, the teacher works on getting the child to walk without assistance from the table to the trash, while carrying her utensils. The child then independently completes the steps in the first and second objectives, thus completing the chain.

Depending on the nature of the child's special needs, she may never be able to perform some steps in a behavior sequence independently without some kind of assistance or environmental adaptation. The teacher will work with the disability specialist to modify the task to achieve maximum independence for the child with minimum demands on the teacher.

TALKING TO CHILDREN MAKES A DIFFERENCE

One of the most interesting discoveries in recent years is the extent to which adult communication can play an important role in children's development. For children with learning challenges, adult communicative input can often make or break the child's chances for optimizing learning potential. (A nicely condensed summary of this research appeared in the Spring/Summer 1997 *Newsweek* Special Edition and in an earlier issue of *Life* (Grunwald & Goldberg, 1993). The following adult communicative strategies have been demonstrated to support the development of language and cognition in young children.

Follow the Child's Lead

Probably the single most important communication strategy is to respond to the child's attempts to communicate and to talk about things that interest the child, as this interaction demonstrates:

Child (tugging at teacher's sleeve): *Buh! Buh!*
Teacher (not understanding): *What, Shelley? What are you trying to tell me?*
Child points to a bluebird sitting on the windowsill.
Teacher: *Oh! You see the bird. It's a bluebird. He likes to sit on our windowsill.*

Use Progressive Matching

Progressive matching, also called *expansion,* is a simple strategy based on the principle that the child learns best from an adult language model that is just slightly more complex than the child's current capabilities. For example, if a child is just beginning to use two-word combinations, the adult uses simple, short sentences and phrases. If a child is using simple sentences, the adult can model more complex structures. The adult can also add additional information in addition to modeling slightly more complex structure. This is referred to as **expatiation,** or **semantic extension.**

Child: Bird window.
Teacher: Yes. The bird is in the window!
Child: Rock sinking. Rock too heavy?
Teacher: Do you think the rock is sinking *because* it's too heavy?

Use Labels and Specific Descriptors

Children cannot develop vocabulary and concepts if they do not hear the specific names of things, actions, and characteristics. Compare these two examples. Each teacher is commenting on the child's attempt to brush the doll's hair.

Ms. Ramirez: Oh she looks very pretty now doesn't she. How nicely you're doing that!

Mr. Jones: Oh I see you're *brushing* the *baby's hair.* Her *hair* looks very pretty now that you've *brushed* it.

Note that Ms. Ramirez, while following the child's lead and talking about what the child is interested in, does not use specific vocabulary. She does not label key actions and objects. Mr. Jones, on the other hand, specifically labels the most salient aspects of the child's activity: *brush, baby,* and *hair.* This is sometimes referred to as **mapping language onto experience.** In this way the child not only learns key vocabulary and concepts, but also learns that language is a way of representing the world around us in precise ways, like a road map. This in turn supports the child's cognitive development by helping her develop complex internal representations of complex relationships among objects, events, and characteristics.

Repeat Key Words and Phrases

All individuals, young and old, need some degree of repetition when learning a new task or word. Children with special needs often need many more repetitions than their same-aged peers. Thus it is important for teachers to develop the habit of repeating key words and phrases to assist children in processing and remembering what is said.

Teacher, (talking about the body parts of a baby chick): *Here is the chick's mouth. We call this a beak. A beak. The chick's mouth is called a beak.*
Child: *A buh?*
Teacher: *That's right. Beak. It's a beak.*

Use Appropriate Pacing

Pacing refers to the rate of speaking and the length of pause between sentences. Teachers who vary their pace can create different moods and add interest to their spoken language. Many children with disabilities have difficulty processing rapidly incoming information. Their comprehension and interest can often be enhanced by slowing down the pacing of complex or new information.

We vary widely in how fast we speak. Some people just naturally talk quickly, while others may speak very slowly. Teachers may wish to audio tape themselves to determine whether their typical speaking rate in the classroom is unusually fast. If so, they can significantly assist young children with language learning difficulties—as well as children whose first language is not English—by simply slowing down their speaking rate.

Give Children Ample Time to Respond

This strategy is somewhat related to pacing. Many children with special needs not only have difficulty processing what they hear, but it also may take them longer to organize and encode what they want to say. A common phenomenon observed among children with special needs is called **learned helplessness.** This refers to a pattern of extreme passivity and lack of initiative. There are many reasons why children may develop this characteristic. A common reason is that some adults do not allow sufficient time for children to respond.

Create the Need to Communicate

Children with limited or no communication skills must be *motivated* to communicate. One simple way to do this is to create a situation in which the child must initiate communication in some way to obtain something she wants. For example, a favorite toy or music tape can be kept out of the child's reach. The child must learn to initiate a request for the desired object.

An even simpler technique is called a **request for more** strategy. The teacher simply interrupts a pleasurable activity, such as swinging or listening to music, and waits for the child to respond, using prompts and cues if necessary. The following examples illustrate this strategy.

Jessica and Pokemon: Creating a Need to Communicate

Jessica has Down syndrome and does not use speech. She is able to make a few noises and she can point and use directed eye gaze. Her mother reports that she loves watching Pokemon™ on TV at home. The teacher usually makes sure to give Jessica the Pokemon™ puzzle during free play times. Jessica has mastered this puzzle, and it is clearly one of her preferred toys. The teachers decides to encourage Jessica to communicate more by leaving the puzzle in view, but on a shelf Jessica cannot reach. Initially the teacher shows Jessica where the puzzle is and prompts her to point and vocalize to get the puzzle. The next time Jessica wants the puzzle, the teacher waits and does not prompt her. Jessica walks to the teacher, makes a sound to get her attention, then points to the puzzle. The teacher responds quickly, saying, "Oh, Jessica, you want the Pokemon™ puzzle. Let me get it for you."

Interrupting the Ride

Juan Carlos loves being pushed in the swing at the park. The teacher helps him get seated into the swing and starts pushing him. Suddenly the teacher stops the swing. She then waits until Juan Carlos indicates he wants more swinging by saying "Go!" The teacher then says, "Oh, you want to swing some more? Okay, here we go." And starts pushing the swing again. Eventually, by using this technique on a regular basis, the teacher helps Juan Carlos learn to use a short sentence, "More swing please," rather than just a single word.

DEVELOPING VOCABULARY AND CONCEPTS

Follow the child's lead: Talk about and elaborate upon what the child is interested in.

Use appropriate pacing and rate of speaking: Some children have difficulty processing rapid speech. Some adults may need to slow down a bit.

Encourage conversational turn-taking: Be sure to wait long enough to give the child plenty of time to respond to your comments or questions.

Carefully label things and actions: for example, "We call that a *'taxi'* and "See how I'm *copying* the letter."

Carefully describe characteristics of things and events at developmental level of the child: for example, "You have five big blocks in your tower, and one tiny one on top!"

Use repetition and redundancy: "You have five blocks in your tower. Five blocks: one, two, three, four, five. Can you count the five blocks?"

For more advanced children ask open-ended questions: "Why did that fall down?" "How can we fix it?" Closed questions: "What is that called?" "What color is that?"

Encourage understanding of relationships between events and effects: "What do you think will happen if we add the water now? Yes, if we add the water, then it will bubble up." "The paint turned orange because we added the red to the yellow."

DEVELOPING SENTENCE STRUCTURE

Model "expansions" of child's utterance: Produce a slightly longer, more complex version of what the child said. For example, the child says "Johnny ball?" Teacher responds, "Yes, that is Johnny's ball."

Model complex sentence structure: "If we add another block, then it will fall down." "After we eat lunch, then we will go outside." "The paint dried out because we left the top off."

Figure 1–5 Communicative interaction strategies that facilitate language development.

Examples of how the strategies described in this section can be used to develop vocabulary and sentence structure are listed in Figure 1–5.

USING AN OUNCE OF PREVENTION: MANAGING BEHAVIOR PROBLEMS

The most common child characteristic that results in failed placements in inclusive settings is disruptive behavior. (Chapter 4 will address this topic in some detail.) While any child can develop problem behaviors, children with special needs are more likely to present challenging behaviors. Characteristics of certain disabilities may be more likely to lead to the development of behavior problems if they are not handled effectively. For example, children who have neurological impairments or attention deficits may have difficulty learning to regulate impulses and control aggression. Children with autism may be highly sensitive to certain sounds or to generally overstimulating environments and may have a tantrum or run away in an attempt to escape this sensory overload.

Generic Strategies to Head Off Behavior Problems

Certain preventive strategies can be incorporated into any classroom. While these strategies will not prevent all behavior problems, they will go a long way in minimizing the development of challenging behaviors. These preventive strategies include many of the strategies already discussed in this chapter.

- using a consistent, predictable schedule with clear transition cues
- allowing adequate time to complete tasks
- reducing frustration tolerance by breaking new or difficult tasks into small steps
- identifying *triggers* such as loud music or being crowded by other children
- reducing sensory overload
- providing some alternative communication mode such as pictures or signs for a child who cannot express wants and needs
- establishing and enforcing consistent, clear rules (preferably no more than three or four), with consistent consequences
- providing extra attention and adult support *before* a child demands it or engages in inappropriate behavior

Some children with disabilities may develop problem behaviors despite these measures, and some may enter your classroom with already well-established behavior challenges. For these children various strategies and interventions may be necessary. But for many children "an ounce of prevention" is definitely more effective than "a pound of cure"!

GENERIC INSTRUCTIONAL STRATEGIES FOR CHILDREN WITH MILD TO MODERATE DISABILITIES

Chapter 2 will deal with the characteristics and needs of children with specific types of disabilities, often referred to as **low-incidence disabilities** because they affect relatively small proportions of the population. Such disabilities as visual impairment, severe cognitive disability, or autism often present unique and complex challenges.

It should be noted, however, that many—perhaps most—children with special needs who are included in early childhood settings can be characterized as having **high-incidence disabilities,** sometimes referred to as **mild to moderate disabilities.** These occur with greater frequency but tend to require less intensive interventions. Mild to moderate disabilities include such characteristics as learning disabilities, attention deficit disorders, mild cognitive disability (mental retardation), mild speech and language delay, and noncompliant behaviors.

For children with mild to moderate disabilities, careful and thoughtful implementation of the generic strategies described in this chapter will often be sufficient to support their successful inclusion in the early childhood setting. The addition of frequent and careful observation of the child's behavior in light of specific goals and objectives can ensure not only access to the inclusive environment but also the successful achievement of desired outcomes for that child.

SUMMARY

The generic instructional strategies included in this chapter can assist and enhance the learning of *all* young children. For children who have special needs, these strategies are essential supports for efficient learning. For children with mild to moderate disabilities, careful use of these strategies may be sufficient to support their successful inclusion in the early childhood classroom. For children with low-incidence disabilities who have more significant challenges, these strategies are necessary but not sufficient. Chapter 2 will present an overview of the characteristics of specific disabilities and some additional strategies that may be useful to early childhood educators who find these children included in their classroom or program.

CASE STUDY

Helping Manuel Adjust

When Mrs. Jackson learned that a child with special needs would be placed in her Head Start classroom, she was not concerned. Manuel was described as a "four-year-old child with Down syndrome, recently placed in foster care." Mrs. Jackson had worked with two other children who had Down syndrome and found them to be delightful. They were easygoing and affectionate.

After Manuel's first week in her classroom, however, Mrs. Jackson began to worry. Manuel was unexpectedly active and aggressive. His only word was "No!" which he used often as he pushed away any child who came within reach. His favorite activities seemed to be playing in water—wherever he could find it, especially in the toilet!—and dumping things out of containers.

Mrs. Jackson contacted the Head Start special needs coordinator for her program and asked for some assistance. After observing Manuel in the classroom and at home, Mrs. Jackson, the special needs coordinator, and the foster mother arranged a meeting to talk about possible interventions. The foster mother indicated that Manuel had only been with her for one

(continued)

month; his biological mother had recently been incarcerated for selling drugs, and no other family members were available to care for Manuel.

Several changes were identified that Mrs. Jackson could fairly easily incorporate into her classroom. Because she realized Manuel was dealing with many unexpected changes in his life, her first goal was to *increase the predictability* of the daily schedule. She tried to be a bit more consistent about the sequence of the major activities of the day, and she was careful to signal clearly the end of one activity and the transition to a new activity. She also assigned the assistant who seemed to have the best relationship with Manuel to be his primary caregiver. These adaptations created a safer environment for Manuel and seemed to reduce his overall levels of anxiety and aggression.

Another strategy incorporated his *high-preference activities* of water play and dumping. When Mrs. Jackson read Manuel's file, she realized that his developmental level was below that of a two-year-old and that the activities that motivated him were not so atypical when viewed in that light. She began to use the water table more often in the classroom and outside activities. She tried to think of center activities that could incorporate water in more appropriate ways, such as food coloring, soap and water, and water and cornstarch. Mrs. Jackson also asked an older child to help Manuel learn to play Dumptruck. This involved loading a large dumptruck with Legos™, pushing the truck a little ways, then dumping the plastic building blocks into a container. A volunteer helped encourage the peer helper to *repeat* this activity over and over until Manuel began to be able to do it himself —loading and driving the truck to the container, not just dumping its contents. Initially Manuel would only do the dumping. By beginning at this level, the volunteer and the peer were able to *scaffold the activity* until Manuel could do it independently.

These strategies provided more opportunities for Manuel to focus on the same activities in which the other children were participating. Because he was highly motivated by the activities, he gradually became less bothered by other children in his space. Within one month he was no longer aggressive with the other children and seemed well settled into the daily routine. Staff then began focusing on his needs in the area of language development. Mrs. Jackson reminded them to *emphasize and label key words,* especially the words for things that interested him most, and repeat the words in short sentences or phrases. Manuel began immediately to try to imitate the key words and gradually began using the words spontaneously, especially to request a favorite food or toy.

Case Study Questions

1. *What aspects Manuel's life created challenges for his adjustment to the Head Start Center?*
2. *What steps could Mrs. Jackson take in the future when new children are referred to her program to make their transition to the center-based program easier?*
3. *What generic instructional strategies did Mrs. Jackson use? Can you think of additional strategies or adaptations that might be helpful for Manuel?*

KEY TERMS

backward chaining
behavior chain
expatiation
high-incidence disabilities
high-preference inventory
learned helplessness
low-incidence disabilities
mapping language onto experience

mild to moderate disabilities
pacing
progressive matching
request for more
scaffolding
semantic extension
task analysis
zone of proximal development

HELPFUL RESOURCES

Organizations

Consortium on Inclusive Schooling Practices, Web site:
<www.asri.edu/CFSP/brochure/abtcons.htm>
Council for Exceptional Children, Division for Early Childhood (DEC),
(303) 620-4579, e-mail: dec_execoff@ceo.cudenver.edu, Web site:
<www.dec-sped.org>
National Early Childhood Technical Assistance System (NECTAS),
(Provides resources and technical assistance for programs serving
infants and young children with disabilities. Excellent resource for early
childhood inclusion materials.) 500 Nations Bank Plaza, 137 East
Franklin St., Chapel Hill, NC 27514, (919) 962-2001, e-mail:
nectas@unc.edu, Web site:
National Information Center for Children and Youth with Disabilities
(NICHCY), Web site:
Zero to Three: National Center for Infants, Toddlers and Families, Web site:
<www.zerotothree.org>

Projects

The Early Childhood Research Institute on Inclusion (ECRII), Box 328,
Peabody College, Vanderbilt University, Nashville, TN 37203, Web site:
<www.inform.umd.edu/EDUC/Depts/ecrii/>
NECTAS. (1999). *Guide to early childhood project materials supporting inclusion.*
Chapel Hill, NC: Author.
Project Support, (OSEP funded project to develop training model for early
childhood inclusion support personnel), Division of Special Education,

Charter School Of Education, California State University, Los Angeles, CA (323) 343-4400, e-mail: dklein@calstatela.edu.

Legal Resources

Brown, W. (1994). *Early intervention regulation: Annotation and analysis.* Horsham, PA: LRP Publications.

Child care centers and the Americans With Disabilities Act (ADA), Web site: <www.usdoj.gov/crt/ada/adahom1.htm.> or <www.usdoj.gov/crt/ada/chcing.pdf>

Kids Together, Inc. (1996). Rights to regular education. Web site: <www.kidstogether.org/right-ed.htms>

National Early Childhood Technical Assistance System (NECTAS), Web site:

Rab, V. Y., & Wood, K. I. (1995). *Child care and the ADA: A handbook for inclusive programs.* Baltimore, MD: Paul H. Brookes.

Turnbull, H. R., & Turnbull, A. P. (1998). *Free appropriate public education.* Denver, CO: Love Publishing.

Articles and Books

Bredekamp, S., & Rosegrant, T. (Eds.). (1992). *Reaching potentials: Appropriate curriculum and assessment for young children.* Washington, DC: National Association for the Education of Young Children.

Bricker, D. (1998). *An activity-based approach to early intervention.* Baltimore, MD: Paul H. Brookes.

Cavallaro, C., & Haney, M. (1999). *Facilitating inclusion in early childhood programs.* Baltimore, MD: Paul H. Brookes.

Chandler, P. A. (1994). *A place for me: Including children with special needs in early care and education settings.* Washington DC: National Association for the Education of Young Children.

Cook, R., Tessier, A., & Klein, M. D. (2000). *Adapting early childhood curricula for children in inclusive settings* (5th ed.). Columbus, OH: Merrill/Prentice Hall.

Davis, M. D., Kilgo, J. L., & Gamel-McCormick, M. (1998). *Young children with special needs: A developmentally appropriate approach.* Boston: Allyn and Bacon.

Division for Early Childhood, Council for Exceptional Children. (1993). *DEC recommended practices: Indicators of quality in programs for infants and young children with special needs and their families.* Reston, VA: Author.

Grunwald, L., & Goldberg, J. (1993, July). The amazing minds of infants. *Life.*

Jones H. A., & Rapport M. J. (1997). Research-to-practice in inclusive early childhood education. *Teaching Exceptional Children, 30*(2), 57–61.

Linder, T. W. (1993). *Transdisciplinary play-based intervention: Guidelines for developing a meaningful curriculum for young children.* Baltimore, MD: Paul H. Brookes.

O'Brien, M. (1997). *Inclusive child care for infants and toddlers.* Baltimore, MD: Paul H. Brookes.

Odom, S., & McLean, M. E. (Eds.). (1996). *Early Intervention/early childhood special education: Recommended Practices.* Austin, TX: Pro-Ed.

Peck, C., Odom S., & Bricker, D. (Eds.). (1993). *Integrating young children with disabilities into community programs.* Baltimore, MD: Paul H. Brookes.

Wolery, M., & Wilbers, J. (Eds.). (1994). *Including children with special needs in early childhood programs.* Washington, DC: National Association for the Education of Young Children.

Periodicals

Infants and Young Children, Aspen Publications, 7201 McKinney Circle, Frederick, MD 21701.

Journal of Early Intervention, Division for Early Childhood, Council for Exceptional Children, 1920 Association Drive, Reston, VA 22091.

Topics in Early Childhood Special Education, PRO-ED, 8700 Shoal Creek Boulevard, Austin, TX 78758.

REFERENCES

Bruner, J. (1982) The organization of action and the nature of the adult-infant transaction. In E. Tronick (Ed.) *Social intercharge in infancy: Affect, cognition and communication* (pp 23–35) Baltimore, MD: University Park Press.

Grunwald, L. & Goldberg, J. (1993, July). The amazing minds of Infants. *Life* p 46–60.

MacDonald, J. D. (1998). Becoming partners with children: From play to conversation. San Antonio, TX: Special Press.

Vygotsky, L. (1980). *Mind in Society: The development of higher psychological processes.* Cambridge, MA: Harvard University Press.

Your child: From Birth to Three (1997 Spring/Summer). Special Issue *Newsweek.*

2

Adaptations for Children with Specific Disabilities

Chapter-at-a-Glance

In this chapter we will discuss strategies and adaptations for use with children with specific mild to severe disabilities:

- **Moderate to severe cognitive delays.** One of the most common disabilities characterized by cognitive delay is Down syndrome. Children with Down syndrome have identifiable physical features. Their developmental progression has much in common with typically developing children, but milestones are achieved at a slower pace.
- **Autism.** Autism is characterized by atypical social and communicative behaviors. Children with autism often avoid social interaction and can be easily overstimulated by sound and touch.
- **Visual impairment and blindness.** Children with visual impairment may range from having limited vision (e.g., some light perception only) to having some functional vision under certain conditions or within a very circumscribed visual field. Visual impairment restricts the development of mobility and the understanding of many concepts.
- **Hearing loss.** Children with mild to moderate hearing loss can usually be accommodated in the inclusive setting with simple adaptations and a good understanding of the components and function of the hearing aid. Children with more severe losses will require a team approach. The ECE teacher will need to be informed as to the preferred mode of communication, manual sign or speech.
- **Cerebral palsy.** The most common motor disability is cerebral palsy, which interferes in various ways with children's voluntary muscle movement and postural control. ECE teachers will need to obtain information and demonstration

(continued)

23

regarding how to position the child for maximum comfort and performance and how to adapt toys and utensils.

- **High-incidence disabilities.** High-incidence disabilities occur with greater frequency than other conditions and are often characterized by less intensive needs. These include children at risk for learning disability, children who have speech and language delay or disorder, and children with mild cognitive delays.

INTRODUCTION

While the teaching strategies described in Chapter 1 will be useful with all children, many children have special needs that require specific adaptations. It is imperative that the ECE professional initially obtain the services of the appropriate disability specialist to understand the specific dimensions of the child's disability. However, access to these specialists is often limited. Thus, the information presented in this chapter will identify some of the most critical needs and strategies for use with children with the following conditions: Down syndrome, visual impairment, hearing impairment, cerebral palsy, and autism. While there are many other specific disabilities and conditions, these are some of the most common.

The first section describes the low-incidence disabilities most likely to be represented in inclusive settings. These disabilities are readily diagnosed early in life and have many clear and distinct characteristics. They often require the support of a number of specialists. High-incidence disabilities, such as learning disabilities, speech and language difficulties, or mild cognitive delays, are more common but may be more difficult to diagnose and may have less distinct characteristics. A section at the end of this chapter includes a brief discussion of high-incidence disabilities.

CHILDREN WITH DOWN SYNDROME: A COMMON EXAMPLE OF SIGNIFICANT COGNITIVE DISABILITIES

Children who have cognitive delays or disabilities are developmentally younger than their chronological age. Thus, their reasoning ability, language skills, emotional and behavioral maturity, and independence may be like that of a much younger child. One of the most common disorders characterized by significant cognitive disability is **Down syndrome.**

Physical and Health Characteristics

Physical Features. Because this is a chromosomal condition, children with Down syndrome typically present identifiable physical features. These usually (but not always) include short stature, low muscle tone (hypotonia), loose joint ligaments that sometimes make arms and legs seem *floppy*, and short fingers with atypical crease patterns in the palms of the hands. Children with Down syndrome often have almond shaped eyes, a wide nasal bridge, and a small mouth cavity, which sometimes encourages a protruding tongue.

Health Problems. Children who have Down syndrome are more likely to have certain health problems. These sometimes include heart malformations, frequent upper respiratory infections, chronic mouth breathing, and mild to moderate hearing loss.

A rare but dangerous condition that is more common in children with Down syndrome than in the normal population is **spinal subluxation.** This is a partial dislocation of one of the upper spinal vertebrae. The condition exists in approximately 15 percent of children who have Down syndrome. In approximately 1 percent of these children, the dislocation leads to a serious condition of spinal cord compression. Even though it is rare, teachers should be aware of the symptoms of this spinal cord compression:

- head tilt to one side
- increased clumsiness
- limping or refusal to walk
- weakness of one arm

Some medical professionals suggest that every child who has Down syndrome should be x-rayed to determine whether spinal subluxation—and thus the potential for spinal compression—exists (Roizen 1997). In the absence of this diagnostic information, teachers may want to limit gymnastic activities such as somersaults.

Developmental Characteristics

Cognition. While the *average* range of cognitive ability for children with Down syndrome is in the moderate range, it should be noted that there is a very wide range of cognitive levels in this population, from severe to mild cognitive disability.

Motor. Though gross motor development is typically somewhat delayed as a result of low muscle tone, most children with Down syndrome walk by age two years.

Social. Children with Down syndrome are often responsive and prefer social interactions over interactions with objects. However, it is important to note that this has become somewhat of a stereotype, that all children with Down syndrome are good natured and love people. In fact there are many exceptions to this typical temperament.

Learning Style. Children with Down syndrome achieve many of the same developmental milestones as typically developing children; however, they usually do so at a slower pace. In addition, their rate of response is often rather slow, and they need many repetitions to master a task.

Children with Down syndrome may be much more interested in people than in objects. In addition, they often demonstrate low **task persistence.** That is, they are not motivated by the challenge of a difficult or lengthy task. They are more likely to be motivated by the praise and encouragement of their significant others, rather than by task mastery and achievement.

Teaching Strategies for Children with Down Syndrome

Pacing. It is helpful for teachers to slow down the pace of activities in the classroom. While this may not be necessary for every activity, if the child with Down syndrome appears to be having difficulty learning a particular task or routine, slowing down your demonstration or presentation will help the child learn the task more easily.

Pacing involves both the rate of speaking and moving—how fast the teacher talks or performs a task or activity—as well as how long the teacher *waits* for the child to respond or complete a task. One teacher made the following comment: "Counting to five silently before giving the child a prompt or providing assistance really has helped me slow down and give kids plenty of time to respond."

Helpful Hint

A slower pace can be a helpful strategy for many children, not just children with Down syndrome. For example, children who are learning English as a second language will comprehend better and learn English faster if the teacher avoids speaking too quickly. Similarly, children who have learning disabilities and language delays may also benefit from a slower speech rate.

Task Analysis. It is important to break tasks into small steps (as discussed in Chapter 1) and assist the child in learning one step at a time.

Jose Learns to Clean up after Snack

Jose is having trouble cleaning up his dishes after snack. He plays with leftover food, and because he likes playing in water, he goes directly to the sink rather than throwing paper items in the trash His teacher, Mr. Chee, has to help him with nearly every step each day. Mr. Chee can first do a task analysis. This involves analyzing the task into its component parts or steps. These would include:

1. piling up the dishes on his tray
2. standing up

3. picking up the tray
4. walking to the counter
5. placing the tray on the counter
6. throwing the paper items in the trash
7. placing dishes in the sink
8. placing the tray on the stack

By learning one step at time, Jose will eventually be able to complete the entire task on his own.

Helpful Hint

It is often more effective to start at the *end* of the sequence and work backward. In Jose's example, Mr. Chee would begin working on teaching Jose to place the tray on the stack of trays first, then work on placing the dishes in the sink, and so on, until he can do the whole sequence.

Repetition. One of the most effective, yet simplest, techniques for supporting the learning of children with cognitive disabilities is repetition. Simply repeating key words or movements an extra time or two can significantly increase the child's opportunity to learn. Compare the two samples that follow. Two different teachers describe what happens when water is added to flour

Use of Repetition: Comparing Mrs. Moore and Mrs. Reston

Mrs. Moore: Look. When you pour the water in, it gets really sticky. See? OK, does someone else want a turn mixing the dough?

Mrs. Reston: First *pour* the *water* into the *flour.* OK, you *poured* the *water* into the *flour.* Now feel how *sticky* it is. The *water* and the *flour* are *sticky* now. You *poured* the *water* into the *flour* and made *sticky dough!*

While the content of the two comments is similar, Mrs. Reston's language includes more repetition and recasting of the key words describing the activity.

CHILDREN WITH AUTISM

Autism offers significant challenges to educators and families alike. It is a rare disorder (although there is evidence that the incidence is increasing), that is much more prevalent in boys than in girls.

Since the disorder was first identified in the 1930s by Leo Kanner there have been numerous theories about its cause. Early on it was considered a psychiatric disorder with an emotional origin. Specifically, it was often theorized that autism was caused by rejecting caregivers. This theory has been clearly debunked. Today, as a result of several different research efforts related to the neurophysiology of the disorder, we realize that autism is related to atypical structure and/or neural transmission processes of the brain. However, the exact nature of these central nervous system differences—as well as the causes—are still not well understood.

Even more painful for parents, the best intervention methods for children with autism are also not well understood. Recent years has seen a virtual explosion of treatment approaches. Most have some anecdotal testimonials from parents attesting to their effectiveness. Almost none have reliable research or clinical evidence to support their claims.

The following is a summary of the characteristics of autism, current theory as to the neurological basis of the disorder, and some consistently effective intervention strategies.

Characteristics of Autism

The hallmark of the disorder is a pervasive failure of the development of social communication. The most recent *Diagnostic and Statistical Manual of Psychological Disorders* (DSM IV, 1994) classifies autistic disorder under the category of "Pervasive Developmental Disorders." Common to all of these is the poor development of social skills. While we will not go into detail here regarding the diagnostic criteria, it is important to note that to be diagnosed with autism, the child must exhibit significant delay in social communication and symbolic skills prior to the age of three years and must demonstrate characteristics in the following three areas: (1) significant delay or inappropriate use of language; (2) failure to develop normal social relationships and interactions; and (3) demonstration of obsessive or ritualistic, repetitive behaviors such as spinning objects or insistence on exact repetitions of sequences of nonfunctional behavior. One currently accepted theory is that many children with autism demonstrate *neurological hyperresponsivity.* They are also described as having extremely acute sensory abilities, particularly in the areas of hearing and touch. Thus they are hypersensitive to certain sensations. For example, sounds that may be barely audible to most individuals, such as a faraway siren, may be distracting or irritating. Moderately loud sounds, such as a typical preschool classroom, are often painful or overwhelming to the child with autism.

This sensitivity may extend to the area of touch. A child may find the tags on the inside of his shirt to be unbearable. As a result of this tactile defensiveness, an infant with autism quickly finds ways to avoid certain kinds of touch. He may not mold easily to his mother's body when held. As he gets older, he may constantly move away from potential body contact.

Most children with autism avoid making direct eye contact. They prefer to use their peripheral vision. As a result they often appear not to be paying attention because they do not look directly at the object or person.

One of the ironic and mysterious characteristics of children with autism is that while they avoid many sensations, they have an intense craving for others—particularly when they can control it themselves. For example, a child may stare at bright lights, listen obsessively to a certain song, or engage in continuous self-stimulatory or self-injurious behavior.

Children with autism are also described as having serious motor planning difficulties. They have difficulty initiating behavior. They also have a hard time changing a behavior once it is underway. Recent studies have also demonstrated that children with autism use few nonverbal communication gestures, such as pointing, directed reaching, or facial expressions. Figure 2–1 summarizes common characteristics of autism.

Intervention/Treatment Approaches

A complete inventory of even the most common treatment approaches is far too lengthy to include here. These treatments range from drugs and special diets to specific auditory training regimens to behavior modification. A few of the most common approaches are described here.

COMMON CHARACTERISTICS OF CHILDREN WITH AUTISM

- Avoidance of social interaction, or inappropriate social interaction: may avoid eye gaze, walk away when approached, or approach/touch adult as an inanimate object rather than a person.
- Inability to establish *joint reference,* or shared attention, directed by an adult, to an object or event.
- Absence of language, or use of bizarre or nonfunctional language; use of *echolalia,* repetition of same phrase or sentence over and over; use of unusual sounds.
- Hypersensitivity to certain sensory stimuli, especially sound and touch: may seek to avoid or escape; may refuse to touch certain textures; may appear *not* to hear; may cover ears or scream in response to certain sounds; may notice sounds too quiet for anyone else to hear.
- Insistence on sameness: child may react with extreme anxiety or agitation when daily schedule or physical environment is changed.
- Repetitious, self-stimulatory behavior, such as spinning toy car wheels, twirling piece of string or a bent stick, rocking, and hand flapping.
- Preference for use of peripheral (side) vision rather than direct eye gaze, especially when looking at people.
- Noncompliant behavior.
- Poor self-help skills, though not due to motor problems.
- More common in boys than girls.

Figure 2–1   Common characteristics of children with autism.

Lovaas's Discrete Trial Approach. This traditional behavioral approach is highly structured and often uses tangible reinforcers (e.g., candy or tokens) for specific behavior (e.g., eye contact or naming objects).

The **discrete trial approach** typically requires approximately 30 to 40 hours per week of intensive one-on-one specific response training (McEachin, Smith, & Lovaas, 1993).

Functional Behavior Analysis. Employing a different behavioral approach, educators using **functional behavior analysis** carefully analyze the child's current behavior repertoire and teach appropriate functional behaviors, particularly focusing on language and social skills (Koegel, & Koegel, 1995).

TEACCH. The Treatment and Education of Autistic and Communication Handicapped Children (TEACCH) model is a specially designed, highly structured, classroom program that specifically adapts the activities and environment of the classroom to mitigate those factors that interfere with learning. It supports the development of appropriate behavior and communication patterns and teaches basic academic skills (Mesibov, Schopler, & Hearsey, 1994).

Sensory Integration Therapy. This model first assesses the extent to which sensory processing and integration difficulties are interfering with normal development. **Sensory integration therapy** then implements specific therapeutic procedures to ameliorate abnormalities in sensory integration. This approach should be planned and carried out only by a trained **sensory integration (SI) therapist,** most often an occupational therapist (Williamson & Anzolone, 1997). See Chapter 15.

Floor Time. This approach, developed by child psychiatrist Stanley Greenspan, is becoming increasingly popular among early interventionists working with two- and three-year-olds who demonstrate difficulties with self-regulation and symptoms of autism. **Floor time** focuses on the interactive relationship between the caregiver and child, attempting to enhance and increase turn taking and responsive interaction cycles through open-ended play activities (Greenspan & Weider, 1998).

PECS (Picture Exchange Communication System). Children with autism often handle visual/graphic information more easily than auditory/verbal information, although many children with autism may prefer use of peripheral vision to central vision. One successful approach to developing communication behaviors is the use of the **picture exchange communication system (PECS)** further described in Chapter 13. This fairly simple approach requires the child to select a picture card, approach the adult, and hand the adult the card to make a request or comment. This approach has several advantages for children with autism:

- It focuses on *functional* communication.
- It requires little interaction and exchange.
- It relies more on visual information than on auditory.

- It provides an acceptable replacement behavior for children whose communicative behaviors have become disruptive and inappropriate.

The many other approaches to autism are too numerous to mention here. Unfortunately, there is no *magic bullet* or cure and there is much disagreement among professionals as to the most effective intervention.

Managing Behavior Challenges in Children with Autism

While the social communication difficulties are at the core of the disability of autism, the characteristic most likely to interfere with successful inclusion is inappropriate behavior. Often because of the communication difficulty and/or hypersensitivity to certain stimuli, children with autism may present extremely challenging behaviors. Examples of these behaviors include:

- Repetitive, self-stimulatory actions such as rocking, spinning, and hand flapping. (Occasionally these behaviors may involve self-mutilation, such as head banging or skin picking.)
- Rigid, ritualistic patterns such as touching all the pictures on the wall upon arrival at school or racing along the playground fence in a repeated pattern.
- Absence of social responsiveness and extreme difficulty with compliance.
- Escape behaviors such as running away (with little warning), crawling into small spaces, covering ears, and screaming.

While some children with autism respond positively to various drug therapies, the most common and most effective interventions at the time of this writing appear to be the use of functional behavior analysis and the use of an approach referred to as *positive behavior support*. The topic of behavior management is addressed in Chapter 4 of this book.

Teaching Strategies for Children with Autism

Several strategies have proven to be consistently helpful for the early childhood teacher.

Work Closely with the Child's Parents. Typically parents of children with autism are extremely well informed about the disorder as well as the specific characteristics of their children.

Complete a High-Preference Inventory. Interview the child's parents to determine those objects and activities that the child really likes and those that he most dislikes. Often these may be unusual fixations—either positive or negative. It is important for the teacher to understand the child's fears and cravings.

Jason's Unexplained Tantrums

In a discussion with Jason's mother, his teacher, Rhonda, was surprised to learn that Jason has an extreme fear of fans or anything that sounds like a fan. This helped her realize that Jason's seemingly random temper might be related to the air conditioner turning on in the classroom. Jason's mother also told Rhonda that although Jason is very sensitive to light touch or tickling, that he often finds a deep massaging type of touch very calming.

Create a Well-Organized, Predictable Classroom. This is probably the single most important strategy. Areas of the classroom should be well marked. The daily schedule should be consistent. And transitions from one activity to the next should be very clear. Turn the lights off and on or use a bell or certain song as a cue.

Try to Reduce the Noise Level of the Classroom to the Extent Possible. If the room is highly resonant, consider adding area rugs and wall hangings made of absorbent materials or fabric. Avoid meaningless background music. If possible, use incandescent and natural lighting rather than fluorescent.

Use Firm Pressure Touch, When Touching the Child, Rather than Light Touch. While light, fleeting touch may be annoying to the child, firm pressure, especially applied to the chest and back, may be calming or at least easier to tolerate. Provide some kind of anticipatory cue so the child knows you are going to touch him and is not startled by the contact.

Be Consistent about Consequences for Unacceptable Behavior. For example, if the child bites other children, all staff should respond to this behavior in the same way, such as promptly removing the child from the play area. Even more importantly, try to determine exactly what triggers the behavior and change the environment to reduce the likelihood of reoccurrence.

Use Visual Communication Systems. Many children with autism respond better to visual stimuli such as pictures or printed words rather than to speech. Pictures can be used during transitions to cue what is happening next. Pictures can also be used by the child to indicate wants and needs.

Speak in a Quiet Voice. Some children with autism are particularly sensitive to certain voice qualities or too loud speech. Loud shrill voices may be particularly annoying.

Request Support from Specialists. In addition to support from an early childhood special educator, in some cases it may be helpful to obtain specialized support. A **behavior specialist** may be able to determine the cause of and interventions for certain disruptive behaviors. In some cases an evaluation by a SI therapist (usually an occupational therapist) may be helpful in understanding sensory overload and processing problems. See Chapter 15 for a more complete discussion on consulting specialists.

CHILDREN WITH CEREBRAL PALSY

Cerebral palsy is a neurological disorder that significantly affects the child's ability to control movement. It is generally the result of some insult to the brain which occurs either in utero or at the time of birth.

Characteristics of Children with Cerebral Palsy

Persistence of Primitive Reflexes. One of the reasons children with cerebral palsy have difficulty controlling their voluntary movements is that involuntary movements and postures caused by certain reflexes persist and cannot be overridden by voluntary movement. An example of such a persistent reflex would be the *rooting reflex*. This reflex enables the infant to automatically turn to the mother's breast when that side of the face is stimulated. While this reflex is helpful to the newborn, it normally disappears as higher level control centers of the brain take over and establish voluntary patterns, such as grasping a bottle at midline.

The child who has cerebral palsy, however, may continue to reflexively turn his head to the side touched well past infancy. Thus if you are helping the child eat and touch the side of his face to move it toward midline, he will actually resist your touch and turn toward the side you are touching rather than to midline. It is easy to mistake the child's resistance for rejection or noncompliance. It is important to realize the child has no control over this movement.

Another common reflex pattern seen in children who have cerebral palsy is referred to as the **asymmetric tonic neck reflex (ATNR)** (see Figure 2–2). This reflex is triggered by certain movements of the head and neck and results in a sort of *fencing* position with the arm and leg on one side of the body flexed, and the other arm and leg extended. Positioning to inhibit this reflex is essential because the ATNR inhibits voluntary use of arms and hands and interferes with trunk control and stability. Be sure to check with a physical therapist and parent regarding how to position the child to inhibit this reflex.

Thus, the child with cerebral palsy has difficulty initiating and controlling voluntary movements, as well as difficulty *inhibiting* involuntary movements as reflected in the example of Chung Lee.

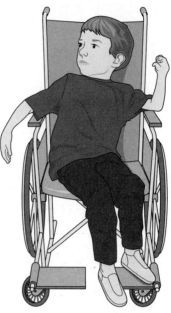

Child with ATNR poorly positioned

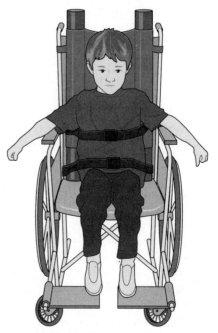

Child seated with supports that inhibit ATNR

Figure 2–2 Positioning to inhibit asymmetric tonic neck reflex.

> **Chung Lee's ATNR**
>
> Chung Lee has cerebral palsy. She is included in a Head Start program. Her teacher, Ms. Torelli, noticed that at lunch time when the assistant was feeding Chung Lee, she often turned her head away from her. Ms. Torelli assumed that this meant Chung Lee wasn't hungry.
>
> However, after talking with her physical therapist, Ms. Torelli realized that this was a reflex that occurred when Chung Lee tried to move her head forward and open her mouth. The physical therapist showed Ms. Torelli how to position her and stabilize her head to avoid the head-turning reflex (ATNR). This intervention was successful and allowed Chung Lee to eat more easily.

Muscle Tone. The movements of children with cerebral palsy may be either **hypotonic** or **hypertonic.** These terms refer to the tone of the muscles. Muscles described as low tone or floppy are hypotonic. They lack strength, and intense movements of any duration are difficult. Muscles that are tense often cause the limbs to either extend or contract into extreme positions. Muscles with increased tone or tension are hypertonic. Many children with cerebral palsy actually demonstrate both high and low tone in different parts of their body. Also, some children have constantly alternating tone, which produces a sort of writhing movement. This is referred to as **athetosis.**

The extent to which cerebral palsy interferes with the child's development of movement, or **motor control,** depends upon the severity of the condition and the affected parts of the body. Thus the degree of disability may range from mild involvement, which may be most noticeable in fine motor tasks, to involvement of both upper and lower extremities as well as the neck and trunk. If only the legs are affected and not the upper body, the condition is referred to as **diplegia.** Involvement of both arms and legs on only one side of the body is referred to as **hemiplegia.** Involvement of the trunk and all four limbs is referred to as **quadriplegia.** When there is severe involvement of both arms and legs, the child is likely to need a wide range of adaptive equipment, such as a wheelchair, other adapted seating, and standers.

Cognitive Level. Cognitive abilities in children with cerebral palsy can range from severe impairment of overall cognitive ability to normal intellectual function. Cognitive level may be difficult to assess accurately in children who have cerebral palsy. This is primarily due to significant limitations of both spoken language and nonverbal communication such as pointing, nodding, and use of facial expressions. Without some reliable means of communication it is very difficult to assess cognitive skills accurately. Parents are often the most knowledgeable regarding cognitive skills of young children with cerebral palsy. The early childhood educator can make certain informal observations that may provide clues as to cognitive level in the preschool age child who has severe cerebral palsy. For example, a sense of humor, quick social response, learning something after only a few repetitions, and use of directed eye gaze to communicate wants and needs may be indicators of cognitive ability. *It is crucial that teachers not associate severe motor involvement with low cognitive ability.* It is possible for a child with severe spastic quadriplegia who has very little voluntary muscle control to be extremely bright.

Even when cognitive level is normal, the child with cerebral palsy may have learning disabilities related to perceptual difficulties such as auditory and visual processing difficulties or visual-motor (eye-hand) coordination problems.

Communication Skills. This is often the most important area of support and intervention for the child who has cerebral palsy. If the motor involvement interferes with the intelligible production of speech, it is essential that some form of **augmentative or alternative communication (AAC)** be established. Parents and some professionals may believe that use of an AAC system, such as a communication board, interferes with the child's development of speech. In fact just the opposite may be the case. Speech development can be enhanced by providing an alternative means of communication.

It is critical that the early childhood teacher work closely with other specialists (such as a speech and language specialist, physical therapist, or physical disabilities itinerant teacher) to design an AAC system. If no resources appear to be immediately available, teachers can develop simple communication systems, such as picture cards, that take advantage of the child's existing repertoire of voluntary movements. Such movements might include directed eye gaze, reaching, or pointing with the head.

Mobility and Postural Control. Two areas related to the child's motor control difficulty must be understood: mobility and postural control. **Mobility** is the child's ability to move his body, either to ambulate from one place to another or to move and manipulate objects by using his arms and hands.

Postural control refers to the child's ability to maintain a stable position. Achieving a stable position often requires environmental adaptations such as special chairs which support the optimal position of the child's body. If the child is not in a secure, comfortable, balanced position, he is not free to work on controlling body movements or paying attention to things going on around him. His energy and attention are focused on maintaining balance.

Also important is positioning the child in ways that will inhibit certain primitive reflex patterns such as ATNR. Persistence of positions caused by these reflexes will be detrimental to the child because they may place extra stress on certain joints or muscles, or they may result in maladaptive compensatory movements or postures.

The early childhood teacher must work closely with a physical therapist or an educational specialist in the area of physical disabilities to determine the child's positioning and equipment needs. Parents are also helpful resources regarding these adaptations.

Nutrition. Providing adequate nutrition may be a challenge for children with severe physical disabilities. Because of fine motor difficulties, children may have trouble eating independently. Poorly developed chewing and swallowing patterns may interfere with eating certain textures of food. The child with cerebral palsy cannot swallow correctly if the head is tilted back. The head should be in a neutral position or slightly forward. Finally, children with cerebral palsy may experience frequent stomach upset and constipation.

Teaching Strategies for Children with Cerebral Palsy

These strategies apply to children with cerebral palsy and those with other significant motor disorders.

Provide Ample Wait Time for Child to Respond. Children with cerebral palsy often have difficulty organizing a response. For example, if you ask the child to point to the toy he wants, it may take him quite a long time to respond even if he understands the task. If the teacher assumes that the child cannot respond or has not understood and does not offer enough time for the child to respond, he will soon become discouraged and stop trying to respond (learned helplessness).

Be Aware of Involuntary Movements. It is important to understand that some of the child's movements may be unintentional. For example as the child attempts to open his mouth to vocalize, this may trigger an involuntary reflex of turning his head to side. It may appear that he is trying to avoid looking at you. You may not realize that he is trying to vocalize, but he is unable to inhibit other movements. Sometimes proper positioning will help the child inhibit these extraneous movements. Consult with a physical therapist or educational specialist about positioning and other strategies for each child.

Position the Child for Maximum Participation. Consultation with physical and occupational therapists will be important to determine the positions and adaptive equipment that may be necessary to ensure that the child can participate in early childhood activities. Figure 2–3 is an example of the use of adaptive equipment to increase participation.

Enable Child to Participate in Some Way in All Activities. As a general rule, children should be positioned so that hips and knees are bent at 90-degree angles, feet are not dangling but resting flat on some surface, and the child is seated squarely on buttocks not on the tail bone. An example of a child seated in a stable position is shown in Figure 2–4. For some children, shoulders and head may also need stabilization or support.

It is important to figure out some way for the child with a severe physical disability to participate and not just observe the activity. One way of participating is to allow the child to activate a switch to turn on a tape player, radio, TV, battery-operated toy, or food blender. Not only does this allow the

Figure 2–3   Child placed in stander to increase his ability to participate in tabletop activity.

child to participate more actively, but it also provides important switch activation practice for eventually operating a computer or electronic communication device. See Figure 2–5 for an example of a switch.

The child can also point to a card indicating the song or storybook he would like during circle time (see Figure 2–6). Again, this not only aids participation but also supports the development of literacy skills. Jenny's example demonstrates both of these strategies.

Figure 2–4 Child seated in stable position with simple adaptations.

Figure 2–5 Child using a switch to access participation in an activity.

Figure 2–6   Song selection board.

Jenny's Favorite Song

Jenny has spastic quadriplegia. As a result she has limited voluntary control of her arms and legs, and she cannot speak. She has fairly good control of her head, and she often uses directed eye gaze to indicate what she wants. At music time her teacher presents choices of three songs. Picture cards representing the song choices are attached with velcro to a large board. When it is Jenny's turn to choose a song, she simply uses her eye gaze to select a song card. The cards are spaced far enough apart so that it is easy to determine which one Jenny is indicating.

Her favorite song is "The Wheels on the Bus." She especially likes the verse "The horn on the bus goes *beep beep beep.*" Since Jenny has fairly good head control, her physical disabilities consultant suggests constructing a head switch that allows Jenny to turn on a tape recorder by simply moving her head to the right. The tape recorder has a loop tape that repeats the sound of a loud horn going "beep beep beep" each time the switch is activated. Now when the children get to Jenny's favorite verse of the song Jenny can independently make an important contribution. Jenny feels very much like a real participant in this activity even though her physical ability is extremely limited. The other children think the loud beeping of the tape recorder is great fun. They are also learning to read the names of the songs printed on each card.

CHILDREN WITH VISUAL DISABILITIES

While inclusion of a child with total blindness may be rare, children with **low vision** or whose visual disability is combined with other disabilities are increasingly participating in inclusive settings. Visual disability is a technical and complex field that requires the expertise of a visual impairment (VI)

Central visual field loss

Peripheral visual field loss
with decreased central
sensitivity

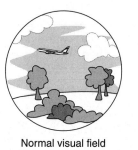

Normal visual field

Multiple "blind spots"
in the visual field

Loss of the left visual field

Figure 2–7 Examples of restricted visual fields.

consultant. However, early childhood educators should find the following foundational information helpful.

Characteristics of Visual Disabilities

There are many types of visual impairment. This may be the child's only disability or it may accompany other conditions, such as Down syndrome or cerebral palsy. Diseases of the eye and various visual conditions affect not only visual acuity (i.e., how accurately the child can see at close and far ranges) but also may affect the visual field (i.e., where the child can see). For example, one child may see only a narrow central field (tunnel vision), while another child may use peripheral vision, and yet another can see only an area in one corner of the visual field. See Figure 2–7.

The itinerant vision specialist can conduct a functional vision assessment. This assessment provides information regarding how the child is actually using his or her vision. The results of the functional vision assessment will provide the teacher with information and recommendations about such things as:

- optimal distance of objects
- visual field preference

- use of light sources
- color preferences
- creation of optimal contrasts

It is important to realize that few individuals are totally blind. Nearly all children who have visual impairment have some usable vision. These children are referred to as having **partial sight,** or low vision. Even children with total blindness may see shadows and movement. Furthermore, children can *learn* to use their residual sight just as children who have hearing loss can learn to use their residual hearing. When visual information is consistently paired with other sensations such as touch or sound, eventually the vision may acquire meaning. Umberto's example demonstrates this possibility.

Umberto Learns to Use His Vision

Umberto has a significant visual disability. He has light perception and vaguely perceives shapes. Umberto's mother has told the teacher that his favorite food is bananas. His mother often sends a small container of mashed bananas in his lunch. The teacher asks his mother to send the whole banana, rather than mashing it ahead of time. Each time Umberto has a banana, his teacher shows him the banana before peeling and mashing it. The first few times she shows him the banana, it appears as a meaningless blotch of yellow. But each time the banana is presented, Umberto holds it and feels his teacher peel it. He smells it, tastes it, and hears the word *banana.* Eventually he can actually recognize the banana, and he has a very thorough understanding of all its characteristics.

General Categories of Vision Disabilities

The pathology and characteristics of all types of visual impairment are much too extensive to describe here. However, the early childhood educator should be aware of the difference between total blindness and low vision, as well as the condition referred to as **cortical visual impairment.**

Only about 25 percent of all individuals who have visual impairment are totally blind. Another 25 percent have some light perception. The remaining 50 percent have enough usable vision that with proper enhancement they can see large print. Thus they are said to have low vision (Chen & Dote-Kwan, 1995).

Total Blindness. While an individual who is *legally blind* may have considerable vision, the educational definition of *total blindness* refers to a total absence of vision or the ability to perceive only light (Hunt & Marshall, 1994). Such individuals learn primarily through other senses, such as hearing and touch.

Low Vision. Children who have low vision have some residual vision that with proper intervention, adaptation, and training can become functional. In addition to using a variety of sensory cues, the child who has low vision will also learn how to use and enhance residual vision. The early childhood educator can work closely with a VI specialist to learn about specific strategies, such as lighting and contrast, and adaptive equipment (e.g., print enlargers).

Cortical Visual Impairment. Some children with severe neurological disorders may have a complex condition known as cortical visual impairment. This condition often accompanies multiple disabilities, including seizure disorders and cerebral palsy. In this case the problem is not with the structure and function of the eye itself but rather with the brain's ability to process and make sense of incoming visual information. It is a common misconception that this condition cannot be improved. These children often have some fleeting functional vision; however, it is somewhat unpredictable.

Strategies for Working with Children with Visual Impairments

Use of Sensory Cues. Children who are blind or who have only light perception must rely on other sensory cues for information about objects and experiences. Most useful sensory cues should be offered *prior* to an event to help the child *anticipate it.* For example, prior to presenting the child with finger paint, it might be helpful for the child to smell the paint and hear the teacher repeat "finger paint."

The most common cues are **auditory** and **tactile cues.** Most teachers are intuitively aware of the need to use verbal and sound cues for children with visual disabilities and to provide opportunities for the child to touch and feel various properties of an object. However, it is also important to be aware of other important sensory cues.

Olfactory cues. These are cues related to the odor or fragrance of an object. It is important to realize that *all* objects have an odor. Thus you can encourage the child to smell any object to obtain additional information about that object. For example, encourage the child to smell food items, paints, lotions, and flowers. Equally important might be the opportunity to smell such less fragrant items as dirt, paper towels, soiled clothing, and the fish bowl!

Kinesthetic cues. These cues incorporate movement. For example, before placing a child in a swing, tell him what you're about to do and then move him in a brief swinging motion before placing him in the swing. If you want the child to begin finger-painting, you could move his hands in circles on the paper before giving him the paint.

Strategies to Enhance Low Vision. Using lighting, contrast, distance, and position to optimal effect can help make the most of low vision.

Lighting. Use of proper lighting can enhance vision. Should the object be lit from behind or from the side? Which lighting is best, natural, incandescent, or fluorescent? Is the child light sensitive, in which case he might do

---

TIPS FOR ADAPTING ILLUMINATION FOR CHILDREN WITH LOW VISION

Note: *Always consult vision specialist to determine best adaptations (For example, some children with visual impairment are extremely* <u>sensitive</u> *to light, and these suggestions may not be appropriate.)*

1. Avoid creating glare or light directed at child's face.
2. When interacting with adult, child's back should be toward the light source so adult's face is illuminated.
3. Overhead lighting in classroom should be bright.
4. Lighter colored walls maximize light.
5. It may be helpful to illuminate play materials directly.

Figure 2–8   Tips for adapting Illumination for children with low vision. (Adapted from Dote-Kwan (2000), Project Support).

Figure 2–9   Example of visual contrast.

better in low light conditions using a spot light on the object? These are questions that can best be answered in consultation with a vision specialist. For children who are not light sensitive, Figure 2–8 lists some specific suggestions for enhancing illumination.

Contrast. Maximum contrast helps the child with low vision optimize his functional use of sight. For example, dark-colored objects should be placed on a light background, such as a dark blue bowl on a white placemat. Place light-colored objects on dark backgrounds; for example, a white and yellow jack-in-the box can be placed on a black blanket on the floor. See Figure 2–9 for examples of visual contrast.

Distance and position. If the child is nearsighted, objects need to be brought closer to the child, and printed material needs to be enlarged. For the child who has a narrow visual field, or **tunnel vision,** it may be easier to see objects that are further away; the child may see small objects and pictures better than larger ones (Chen & Dote-Kwan, 1995). The optimal position of objects and materials will depend on the nature of a child's field loss.

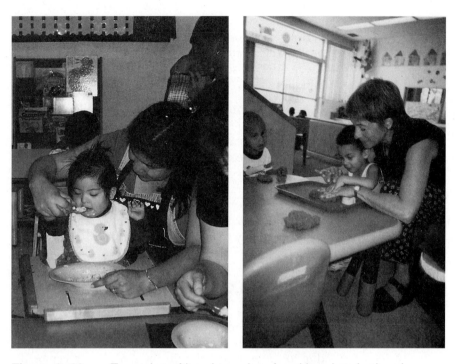

Figure 2–10   Examples of hand-over-hand and hand-under-hand guidance.

Use of Hand-Over-Hand Guidance. Use of hand-over-hand or hand-under-hand techniques are common when working with children with limited vision (Chen, 1999). With **hand-over-hand technique** the adult manipulates the child's hands to perform a task such as pushing a switch. **Hand-under-hand guidance,** on the other hand, may be more effective for children who resist having their hands manipulated or who are tactually defensive, such as for a task like finger painting. See Figure 2–10 for examples.

Real Objects in Meaningful Contexts. Keep in mind that the child with low vision and the child who is blind will have difficulty understanding *replicas* of real things. For example, understanding that a stuffed animal is a representation of a real animal is a slow process. If the child is unfamiliar with real cats, it will be impossible for him to understand what a toy cat is. Also, functional contexts will offer the most meaning for the child with a visual disability. Introduce new words and concepts in natural and logical situations first. For example, trying to pretend to wash dishes or put a doll to bed in dramatic play will not be meaningful if the child has never washed dishes or experienced putting a real baby to bed.

Strategies for Working with Children Who Have Cortical Visual Impairment. Strategies that may be helpful for children with cortical visual impairment are quite different from those used with children with low vision. For example, these children may actually see better with their peripheral vision rather than central vision. Thus they may see objects better by looking *away* from them rather than directly at them. Chen and Dote-Kwan (1995) also suggest the following strategies for children with cortical blindness.

- Reduce multi-sensory stimulation, allowing the child to concentrate on the visual input.
- Allow the child to touch objects while looking at them.
- Place objects far apart; avoid visual crowding.
- Bring objects fairly close to child.
- Use contrasting colors, especially yellow and red (rather than black and white) to highlight objects.
- Understand that the child may be able to use peripheral vision more effectively than central vision.

CHILDREN WITH HEARING LOSS

Many young children have some degree of hearing loss. Hearing losses vary in severity, ranging from mild to profound, and in type of loss (e.g., a loss due to some obstruction in the middle ear versus damage to the auditory nerve). Children with mild to moderate hearing loss can usually be accommodated in the early childhood setting with fairly simple adaptations related to using visual cues, seating the child close to the speaker, and learning how to perform daily checks on the function of the child's hearing aid. Working closely with the child's parents is essential. Children with more severe hearing loss will need greater support in the ECE setting. The ECE teacher will need to obtain important information and assistance from not only parents, but perhaps the audiologist and a speech pathologist or teacher of the Deaf. The following summarizes some of the key issues in working with children with hearing loss.

Understanding Different Types of Hearing Loss

To understand the type of hearing loss the child has we must consider:

- The *severity* or extent of the loss, which is measured in **decibels,** a measure of loudness.
- The *pitch range* or **frequencies** (e.g., high or low) most affected.
- The site along the auditory pathway that causes the loss (e.g., the bones of the middle ear, the cochlea, or the nerve that connects the ear to the brain.)

Information regarding the type of hearing loss a child has can be obtained from the child's parent, from an audiogram often included in the child's file, or from the child's audiologist.

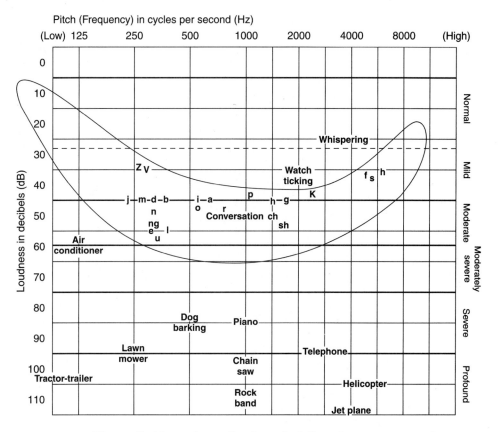

Figure 2–11 Acoustic characteristics of common sounds.

Loudness Threshold and Pitch Range. Very few children are totally deaf. Most children with hearing loss have some **residual hearing.** It is important to ask certain questions about this residual hearing. Is it in the high frequencies or low frequencies? Figure 2–11 provides information about the intensity (or loudness) and the frequency range (pitch) of common environmental sounds. For example, the roar of a truck is a fairly loud, low frequency sound at around 100 decibels. A whisper, on the other hand, is fairly quiet at less than 30 decibels but is a higher pitch sound. A rock band is in the middle of the pitch range, but is very loud at 110 decibels.

Helpful Hint

The average conversational voice is at about 50 to 60 decibels. The quietest sound most individuals can detect is around 0 to 10 decibels, and the pain threshold is around 120 decibels.

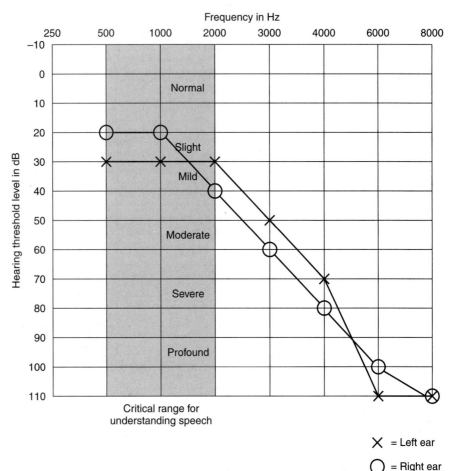

Figure 2–12   Sample audiogram for a child with a bilateral high frequency hearing loss.

Also, what is the **threshold** of this hearing? In other words, how loud does a sound have to be for the child to hear it? Figure 2–12 presents an audiogram on which a child's hearing threshold is recorded for each pitch, with the lowest pitch (250 Hz) on the left and the highest pitch (8,000 Hz) on the right.

Note that this child has near normal hearing in both ears for low pitch sounds, but hearing thresholds are much worse in the higher frequencies, especially in the right ear (marked with circle).

Most children with a significant hearing loss wear a hearing aid. The audiological report will contain information regarding the child's **aided hearing,** or how well the child hears with the hearing aid on. With the hearing aid on, the child may have significantly improved thresholds for loud-

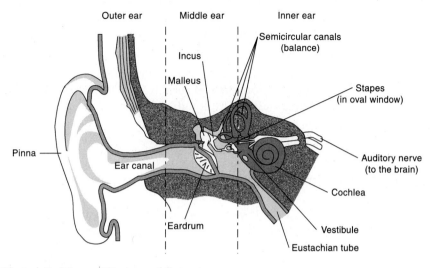

Figure 2–13 Diagram of the ear.

ness, but he may still experience significant distortion of sounds. This will be particularly true if the child has significantly worse hearing in the high frequencies than the low, as compared with the child who has a more *flat* audiogram, with the loss about the same for all pitches. When sounds are distorted, they remain unclear even when they are made louder.

Conductive Versus Sensorineural Hearing Loss. The audiological report will also indicate whether the loss is a **conductive** or a **sensorineural hearing loss.** This difference is related to where the problem is that has caused the hearing loss. Figure 2–13 is a diagram of the hearing mechanism.

A problem or obstruction in the outer or middle ear will cause a conductive loss. Examples of conditions that cause conductive loss include:

- middle ear infections
- ruptured tympanic membrane (ear drum)
- otosclerosis (calcification of the middle ear bones)
- foreign objects placed in the ear canal
- congenital atresia, or narrowing of the ear canal

Conductive losses are never at the profound level of severity. Usually a conductive loss will not exceed around 60 decibels. Also, conductive losses can often be improved through surgery, such as replacing bones in the middle ear, or medication, including antibiotics for an ear infection.

Losses that result from problems in the cochlea in the inner ear, or along the auditory nerve which leads to the auditory areas in the temporal lobe of the brain are referred to as *sensorineural*. Common causes of sensorineural hearing losses in children include:

- diseases such as meningitis or cytomegalovirus (CMV)
- heredity

- ototoxic drugs, such as high doses of aspirin
- head injury that severs the auditory nerve

For the most part sensorineural losses are permanent, although more children are receiving cochlear implants. Not long ago this surgical procedure, which approximates certain functions of the cochlea, was considered quite experimental. Although still not a widely performed procedure, the performance of children with cochlear implants is often impressive (Hunt & Marshall, 1994).

Issues Related to Preferred Communication Modes: Signing versus Speech

For as long as there have been individuals with hearing loss, there has been controversy about the best communication system to use. Put simply, some people believe that children with hearing loss must live in a *hearing world* and thus must learn speech or *spoken English* as their primary mode of communication. Others strongly believe that sign language should be taught as the primary language of persons with significant hearing loss. Many children with hearing loss have great difficulty learning spoken English. Thus, proponents of manual communication systems argue that the opportunity to learn an effective communication system should not be delayed or compromised by struggling to learn speech when American Sign Language, the sign system preferred by most members of the Deaf Community, can be learned early and with little difficulty, if children have good models.

It is critical that the ECE teacher discuss the approach being used by the child's family. If the family is using an **oral approach,** procedures for enhancing speech development and use of residual hearing should be incorporated into the classroom. If the family prefers a **manual approach,** the ECE staff will need to learn a basic signing vocabulary. (See Figure 2–14 for a selection of beginning signs.) Some families will prefer a **total communication approach,** which attempts to combine the two approaches.

Learning Styles and Characteristics of Children with Hearing Loss

Language Development. For children with significant hearing loss the greatest challenge is in the area of the development of communication skills, including both receptive and expressive language. In the early years the development of symbolic communication is often significantly delayed, unless the child has been exposed to sign language from an early age. The development of language and literacy will continue to be major challenges throughout the school years.

Cognitive Skills. Children whose only disability is hearing loss do not have impairment of cognitive skills. However, often children have multiple disabilities, including hearing loss. When this is the case, significant cognitive delay may be compounded by the hearing loss. One key to informal assess-

Sick Hurt Help Play Toilet Want Water More Eat

Figure 2–14 Commonly used beginning signs.

ment of cognitive abilities in a child with hearing loss is to observe carefully the child's play and problem-solving skills. It is important not to confuse language skills with cognitive skills. Children will demonstrate normal play activities in those areas that do not require language, such as block building and drawing. Also, children who have significant hearing loss but normal cognition will often find effective nonverbal ways of communicating through gestures and facial expression.

Social Skills. Because of the typical delay in speech and language, social skills may be affected at the preschool level. The ECE teacher can significantly alleviate this problem by explaining the nature of the child's communication difficulty, by teaching a basic sign vocabulary to hearing peers in the class, and by encouraging participation of hearing peers in the activities preferred by the child with a hearing loss.

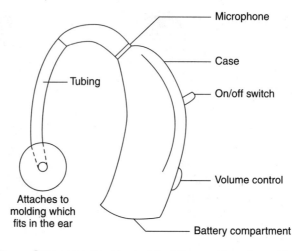

Figure 2–15　　Components of a behind-the-ear hearing aid.

Teaching Strategies for Children with Hearing Loss

Seat the Child Close to the Sound Source. Make sure the child is positioned near the teacher, the stereo speaker, or musical instruments.

Help the Child Develop Residual Hearing. Identify interesting environmental sounds, such as an airplane, telephone ringing, and air conditioner.

Make Sure Child Can See Your face. Don't cover your mouth with your hand. Be aware of lighting glare, which might interfere with the child's sight. Finally, face the child, preferably at eye level.

Speak Clearly at a Good Volume. However, do not exaggerate your speech.

Use the Child's Name to Get His Attention. You may also need to touch the child. Wait for him to be looking at you before giving directions.

Work Collaboratively with Parents. Also, consult with other professionals, including an audiologist, speech pathologist, and/or deaf and hard-of-hearing specialist.

Include Visual and Tactile Cues. These cues will assist the child's comprehension of language. Also when possible, demonstrate what you want the child to do.

Learn about the Child's Hearing Aid. It is critical that early childhood educators obtain training related to the child's hearing aid (see Figure 2–15). Parents are often a good resource for this information:

- how to set the hearing aid controls
- how to check the battery and function of the aid
- how to clean the earmold

**TIPS FOR INCLUDING CHILDREN WITH HEARING LOSS
IN LARGE GROUP ACTIVITIES**

- Use music! Even silent children will often vocalize during music and singing.
- Use music with heavy bass sound; vibro-tactile, low pitch is easier to hear and sense.
- Use preferential seating for children to make the most use of their hearing.
- Seat children away from ongoing noises, such as heaters, electrical equipment, and outdoor windows, so that hearing aids don't pick up this ambient noise.

Figure 2–16   Tips for including children with hearing loss in group activity.

- how to insert the aid in the child's ear
- how to assist the child in managing his hearing aid independently

Make Sure You and Other Speakers Are Close Enough. Be aware that the further the speaker is from the hearing aid, the more distorted (i.e., less clear) the speech signal will be.

Reduce Ambient Noise. Be aware of the effect of the acoustics in your room. Rooms that are highly *resonant* tend to create difficult auditory environments for children with hearing aids. Use rugs, cloth wall hangings, and soft furniture to reduce resonance. Also wherever possible, eliminate or reduce background (ambient) noise such as fans, music, and traffic. See a list of tips in Figure 2–16 for including children with hearing loss in large group activities:

HIGH-INCIDENCE DISABILITIES

The disabilities described so far in this chapter are considered low-incidence disabilities because they occur relatively rarely in the general population. While children with low-incidence disabilities may be less common in the ECE classroom, they often present significant challenges and have distinct needs and characteristics.

More common are the high-incidence disabilities, which are more prevalent and are often considered to be *milder,* requiring less intense interventions. However, this is not always the case.

Some high-incidence disabilities present a greater diagnostic challenge and are often not identified until the child approaches school age. While characteristics of these disabilities often overlap and may be much more variable and more difficult to define, the following is a simplified attempt at characterizing them.

Learning Disability

The term **learning disability** covers a wide range of neurologically based difficulties or *brain differences* that affect the ways in which a child processes and organizes visual and auditory information. These neurological differences can interfere significantly with learning to read and write. Most professionals are uncomfortable with the use of this term prior to school age since interference with academic performance is considered part of the definition. The federal definition of learning disability requires that there be a *discrepancy* between intellectual ability and academic achievement (Hunt & Marshall, 1994).

Children with learning disabilities often have difficulties with impulse control and behavior regulation, difficulty sustaining and focusing attention, and difficulty with language development. Children with learning disabilities often demonstrate inconsistent and variable skills and performance. For example, they may have great difficulty in one skill area, but excel in another. Or, they may perform a task perfectly one day, and appear to have forgotten it the next.

It is important to determine each child's unique learning and processing characteristics. That is, via conversations with parents and specialists, try to determine which learning modes (e.g., visual, auditory, tactile) are preferred by the child, as well as whether there are certain situations or sensory experiences which the child finds stressful. It will also be important to determine the effects of any medications the child may be taking.

Speech and Language Disorder

Language skills refer to the ability to learn vocabulary, to put words together into complete sentences, and to understand when others speak. Children with language disorders may also have difficulty with **pragmatics,** or the appropriate and effective use of language in social communication. **Speech skills** refer to the ability to produce the sounds, or **phonemes,** that make up words. While many children have difficulty with both speech and language, it is possible to have difficulty with just one or the other. In early childhood it is sometimes difficult to differentiate between speech and language *delays,* which suggest that child may eventually catch up, versus speech and language *disorders,* which require intensive speech or language therapy.

Teachers must realize that children who attempt to communicate but who cannot make themselves understood can experience a great deal of frustration. As a result children may develop behavior problems, either as an attempt to communicate their needs or simply as an expression of frustration. When the child's speech is extremely difficult to understand it may be helpful to use some nonverbal strategies suggested in other chapters to reduce frustration. (See for example, suggestions regarding AAC earlier in this chapter and the use of picture communication in this chapter and Chapter 13.)

In Chapter 1 the strategies for communicative interactions include some of the most effective and easily implemented strategies that the ECE teacher can use to support and enhance language development, such as following the child's lead, expanding and recasting the child's utterance, and repetition of key words. Speech disorders require therapeutic interventions with a speech-language specialist. Simple strategies that can support the speech specialist's efforts include phoneme awareness activities, avoidance of too rapid speech rate, teacher's repetition of key words, and rhyming and sound imitation games.

Mild Cognitive Delay

Some children, while they do not have an identifiable condition that affects overall cognitive development, such as Down syndrome, may demonstrate immaturity and slower rates of intellectual and social development. Children with mild cognitive delays are perhaps best understood as simply functioning like younger children in earlier developmental stages. They can be well supported by determining their present level of function and building on those existing skills. Careful, conscious use of the generic strategies described in Chapter 1 can be effective in enhancing development and learning.

SUMMARY

Children can experience learning and developmental challenges from a number of different causes. Many conditions and anomalies create challenges for young children and their caregivers. This chapter has attempted to familiarize the early childhood educator with the characteristics most frequently associated with certain disabilities.

CASE STUDY

Ryan's Day at School

Ryan is a five-year-old with a severe vision impairment and cerebral palsy, which affects his speech and motor development. He attends his neighborhood kindergarten class five mornings each week. Ryan has a 1:1 aide to help him participate in all kindergarten activities with his peers.

During large group times, Ryan sits on the floor with his classmates facing the teacher. He sits to her right because he has partial sight in his right eye. His aide makes sure that Ryan is always seated so that he can use the partial sight he has. When the teacher reads a book, Ryan is given small *props* that represent the concrete elements of the story. If the teacher is reading *If You Give a Mouse a Cookie*, for example, the aide gives Ryan a cup, and cookie. Ryan's peers take turns giving Ryan these objects so he can *see* with his hands what they are seeing with their eyes. During songs, Ryan's aide helps him clap or move his legs and body to the beat. During counting exercises and the calendar portion of group time, Ryan either claps as the children count or uses an adapted calendar from the American Printing House for the Blind.

(continued)

During work times, Ryan moves around the room with help from his aide or peers. He moves by crawling or using a stander/walker. He can get into and out of regular chairs very slowly, so his teacher usually dismisses him first to give him time to find and sit at the appropriate work area. With assistance from the itinerant teacher for students with visual impairments, the teacher provides Ryan with modified lessons that the aide helps him complete. All lessons focus on Ryan's use of his hands and other senses. A bright light and a light box are also used for appropriate lessons to help Ryan use his partial sight. The itinerant specialist has spent several hours in the classroom during the first month to model how to best assist Ryan and then support the teacher, peers, and aide by coaching them as they gradually take over more of the direct assistance. She continues to meet with the kindergarten teacher on a weekly basis to provide ideas and adaptations for lesson plans and visits the classroom when requested by teacher or aide.

When it is time for recess, Ryan selects what he wants to do from a list of choices that the aide offers him, using hand signals and line drawings for Ryan to feel. He is offered the swing, sand box, or bicycles. Ryan enjoys all of these activities and will alternate his choices throughout the week. Gradually the aide has reduced his reliance on concrete props and simply asks Ryan, "What do you want to do today?" Ryan has also become oriented to the physical layout of the playground and can gesture toward the desired area as he verbally communicates what he wants.

Lunch time is an opportunity for Ryan to work on self-help skills in a noisy environment. He is learning to move his wheelchair on his own and maneuvers it through the cafeteria line with some help from his aide. He reaches for his eating utensils and food and places them on his wheelchair tray. A **Dycem mat,** which is made of a sticky substance to help keep objects stationary, is provided to help keep his plate from slipping around as he uses his spoon or fork and hand to find his food, scoop, and eat it. Ryan sits with classmates at the end of the table where his wheelchair fits. Although the cafeteria is noisy, Ryan appears comfortable as the same routine is followed each day.

Case Study Questions

1. *What are the specific strategies that help accommodate Ryan's low vision status?*
2. *What specific strategies are used to accommodate his motor disability?*
3. *What kinds of adaptations do you think might be helpful for Ryan at recess?*

KEY TERMS

aided hearing
asymmetric tonic neck reflex (ATNR)
athetosis
auditory cue
augmentative or alternative
  communication (AAC)

behavior specialist
conductive hearing loss
cortical visual impairment
decibels
diplegia
• discrete trial approach

Down syndrome
Dycem mat
floor time
frequencies
functional behavior analysis
hand-over-hand technique
hand-under-hand guidance
hemiplegia
hypertonic
hypotonic
language skills
learning disability
low vision
manual approach
mobility
motor control
oral approach

partial sight
phonemes
picture exchange communication
   system (PECS)
postural control
pragmatics
residual hearing
quadriplegia
sensorineural hearing loss
sensory integration therapy
speech skills
spinal subluxation
tactile cue
task persistence
threshold
total communication approach
tunnel vision

HELPFUL RESOURCES

Articles and Books

Batshaw, M. L. (Ed) (1997). *Children with disabilities.* (4th Ed.) Baltimore, MD: Paul H. Brookes.

Blackman, J. A. (Ed.). (1997). *Medical aspects of developmental disabilities in children birth to three.* Rockville, MD: Aspen Systems.

Chen, D. (Ed.). (1999). *Essential elements in early intervention: Visual impairment and multiple disabilities.* New York: AFB Press.

Chen, D., & Dote-Kwan, J. (1995). *Starting points: Instructional practices for young children whose multiple disabilities include visual impairment.* Los Angeles, CA: Blind Children's Center.

Clarke, K. (1988). Barriers or enablers? Mobility devices for visually impaired multi-handicapped infants and preschoolers. *Education of the Visually Handicapped, 20,* 115–132.

Cole, E. (1992). *Listening and talking: A guide to promoting spoken language in young hearing impaired children.* Washington, DC: A.G. Bell Association for the Deaf.

American Psychiatric Association. (1994). *Diagnostic and statistical manual of mental disorders (DSM-IV),* Washington, DC: Author.

Finnie, N. (1975). *Handling the young cerebral palsied child at home.* New York: Penguin.

Flexer, C. (1994). *Facilitating hearing and listening in young children.* Washington, DC: A.G. Bell Association for the Deaf.

Geralis, E., & Ritter, T. (Eds.). (1997). *Children with cerebral palsy: A parent's guide.* Rockville, MD: Woodbine House.

Greenspan, S. I., & Weider, S. (1998). The child with special needs: Encouraging intellectual and emotional growth. Reading, MA: Addison-Wesley.

Janzen, J. E. (1996). *Understanding the nature of autism.* San Antonio, TX: Therapy Skill Builders.

Klein, M. D. Richardson-Gibbs, A. M., Kilpatrick, S., & Harris, K. (2000). *Project Support : A practical guide for early childhood inclusion support providers.* Los Angeles: California State University, Los Angeles

Koegel, R. L., & Koegel, L. K. (Eds.). (1995). *Teaching children with autism: Strategies for initiating positive interactions and improving learning opportunities.* Baltimore, MD: Paul H. Brookes.

McCormick, L., Loeb, D., & Schiefelbusch, R. L. (1997). *Supporting children with communication difficulties in inclusive settings.* Boston: Allyn & Bacon.

McEachin, J., Smith, T., & Lovaas, O. I., (1993). Long-term outcomes for children with autism who received early intensive behavioral treatment. *American Journal on Mental Retardation, 98,* 359–372.

Mesibov, G. B., Schopler, E., & Hearsey, K. A. (1994). Structured teaching. In E. Schopler and G. Mesibov (Eds.), *Behavioral Issues in autism* (pp. 195–210). New York: Plenum Press.

Nussbaum, D. *There's a hearing impaired child in my class.*

Pogrund, R. L., Fazzi, D. L., & Lampert, J. S. (Eds.). (1992). *Early focus: Working with young blind and visually impaired children and their families.* New York: American Foundation for the Blind.

Thompson, B., et al. (1992). *Handbook for the inclusion of young children with severe disabilities.* Laurence, KS: Learner Managed Designs.

Tokes, J. (Ed.). (1999). *Hearing impaired infants: Support in the first eighteen months.* Baltimore, MD: Paul H. Brookes.

Webster, A., & Ellwood, J. (1985). *The hearing-impaired child in the ordinary school.* New York: Routledge Kegan & Paul.

Williamson, G. G., & Anzalone, M. E. (1997). Sensory integration: A key component of the evaluation and treatment of young children with severe difficulties in relating and communication. *Zero-to-three, 17,* 29–36.

Curricula

Blind Children's Center. (1993). *First steps: A handbook for teaching young children who are visually impaired.* Los Angeles: Author.

Bricker, D. D., & Waddell, M. (1996). *AEPS Curriculum for three to six years.* Baltimore, MD: Paul H. Brookes.

Johnson-Martin, N. M., Attermeier, S. M., & Hacker, B. J. (1996). *The Carolina curriculum for preschoolers with special needs.* Baltimore, MD: Paul H. Brookes.

Odom, S., et al. (1988). *The integrated preschool curriculum.* Seattle, WA: University of Washington Press.

VORT Corporation. (1985). *HELP activity guide for special preschoolers.* Palo Alto, CA: Author.

Organizations

American Foundation for the Blind, 11 Pen Plaza, Suite 300, New York, NY 10001, (800) 232-5463.

Assistive Technology Education Network Web site: <www.webable.com>

Autism, Web site: <www.web.syr.edu/jmwobus/autism/>

Council on Education of the Deaf, Web site: <www.edu.kent.edu/deafed/home.htm>

Deaf Blind Link, Web site: <www.tr.wosc.osshe.edu/dblink/index.htm>

Epilepsy Foundation, Web site: <www.epilepsy-socalif.org>

National Association for Down Syndrome, Web site: <www.nads.org>

National Organization for Rare Diseases (NORD), Web site: <www.rarediseases.org>

Special Education Resources on the Internet, Web site: <www.hood.edu/seri/>

United Cerebral Palsy, Web site: <www.ucpa.org>

Journals

Augmentative and Alternative Communication, Decker Publishing, Inc., One James T. South, P.O. Box 620, L.C.D. 1, Hamilton, Ontario l8N3K7, Canada.

Focus on Autism and other Developmental Disabilities, Pro-Ed, 8700 Shoal Creek Blvd., Austin, TX 78757.

Journal of the Association for Persons with Severe Handicaps, Association for Persons with Severe Handicaps, 29 West Susquehanna Ave., Suite 210, Baltimore, MD 21204.

RE:view, Association for the Education and Rehabilitation of the Blind and Visually Impaired (AER), 4600 Duke Street, Suite 430, Alexandria, VA 22304.

Topics in Language Disorders, Aspen Publishers, Inc., 200 Orchard Ridge Drive, Gaithersburg, MD 20878.

The Volta Review, Alexander Graham Bell Association for the Deaf, 3417 Volta Place, N.W., Washington D.C. 20007.

Catalogs for Adaptive Equipment

AbleNet, Inc., 1081 Tenth Ave. S.E., Minneapolis, MN 55414, (800) 322-0956.

Crestwood Company, Communication Aids, 6625 N. Sydney Place, Milwaukee, WI 53209, Web site: <www.communcationaids.com>

Guide to toys for children who are blind or visually impaired. American Toy Institute, Inc., Toy Manufacturers of America, Inc., 200 Fifth Ave., Suite 740, New York, NY 10010, (212) 675-1141.

Rifton, P.O. Box 901, Rifton, NY 12471-0901, (800) 777-4224.

Tumbleforms, J.A. Preston Corporation, (800) 631-7277.

Videos

Communication/Therapy Skill Builders, 3830 E. Bellevue, P.O. Box 42050, Tuscon, AZ 85733.

Functional Vision: Learning to Look, BVD Promo Services, P.O. Box 930182, Verona, VI 53593-0182.

Getting there: A look at mobility skills of four young blind children, Blind Babies Foundation, 1200 Gough Street, San Francisco, Ca 90410.

Let's eat: Feeding a child with a visual impairment, Blind Children's Center, 4120 Marathon Street, Los Angeles, CA 90029.

Positioning for infants and young children with motor problems, Learner Managed Designs, 2201 K W. 25th St., Lawrence, KS 66046.

Special Needs Project (videos on feeding, potty training and sensory integration), 3463 State St., Suite 282, Santa Barbara, CA 93105.

Visually Impaired Preschool Services, 1215 South 3rd St., Louisville, KY 40203.

What can baby see? American Foundation for the Blind, 11 Penn Plaza, Suite 300, New York, NY 10001.

REFERENCES

American Psychiatric Association. (1994). *Diognostic and statistical manual of mental disorders (DSM-IV).* Washington, DC: Author.

Chen, D. (Ed.). (1999). *Essential elements in early intervention: Visual impairment and multiple disabilities.* New York: AFB Press.

Chen, D., & Dote-Kwan, J. (1995). *Starting points: Instructional practices for young children whose multiple disabilities include visual impairments.* Los Angeles: Blind Children's Center.

Greenspan, S. I. & Weider, S. (1998). *The child with special needs: Encouraging intellectual and emotional growth.* Reading, MA: Addison Wesley.

Hunt, N., & Marshall, K. (1994). *Exceptional children and youth.* Boston: Houghton Mifflin.

Koegel, R. L., & Koegel, L. K. (1995). *Teaching children with autism: Strategies for initiating positve interactions and improving learning opportunities.* Baltimore, MD: Paul H. Brookes.

McEachin, J., Smith, T., & Lovaas, O. I. (1993). Long-term outcomes for children with autism who received early intensive behavioral treatment. *American Journal on Mental Retardation, 98,* 359–372.

Mesibov, G. B., Schopler, E. & Hearsey, K. A. (1994). Structured teaching. In E. Schopler and G. Mesibov (Eds.), *Behavioral Issues in autism* (pp. 195–210). New York: Plenum Press.

Roizen, N. (1997). Down syndrome. In M. Batshaw (Ed.), *Children with disabilities* (pp. 361–424). Baltimore, MD: Paul H. Brookes.

Ruskin, E. M., et al. (1994). Object mastery motivation of children with Down Syndrome. *Amercian Journal of Mental Retardation, 98*(4), 499–509.

Williamson, G. G., & Anzolone, M. E. (1997). Sensory integration: A key component of the evaluation and treatment of young children with severe difficulties in relating and communication. *Zero-to-Three, 17,* 29–36.

3

Arranging the Physical Environment to Support the Inclusion of Children with Special Needs

Chapter-at-a-Glance

How the physical environment is arranged can positively or negatively affect children's learning and behavior

Children with special needs need to feel physically and emotionally safe. This requires creating environments that are easily accessible and free of hazards (particularly for children who are visually impaired or who have significant motor disabilities). Daily schedules and environments should be predictable and allow as much independence as possible.

- **Arrangement of the physical environment can support independent access.** To accommodate adaptive or supportive equipment such as wheelchairs, the available physical space must be carefully arranged.
- **Floor plans require careful consideration.** For example, some children may need access to an enclosed space. Floor plans should minimize clutter and include clearly marked boundaries; they must accommodate adaptive equipment.
- **Activity areas must include materials appropriate for children with different types of disabilities.** For example, materials that appeal to children functioning at developmentally young levels and toys and tools that are interesting and motivating to children with motor and sensory disabilities.

INTRODUCTION

Even if you are working in a center or classroom where the environment has already been arranged, take time to study that environment to determine if it is appropriate to accommodate young children with special needs.

61

Remember that how an environment is arranged can determine how behavior within that environment is managed. Time spent thoughtfully arranging space and materials may prevent time lost and stress spent later on managing negative child behaviors.

CREATING A SAFE ENVIRONMENT

In creating the most positive environment possible, the arrangement of the elements within a learning environment should promote two features: *safety* and *independent access.*

Psychological Safety

Children must be and feel both physically and psychologically safe. Early childhood educators tend to be tuned into ensuring physical safety but may give less attention to psychological safety. Experienced educators observe that children who do not feel safe will test the limits until they understand the organization and limits of their environment. *Therefore, arrangement of space and materials must have order and stability.*

These elements contribute to the predictability children need to feel safe. For example, if objects are kept in the same place every day, children feel secure in knowing where to find and where to return materials. Just consider how anxious anyone feels when something is not in its expected place. Remember how you feel as you search for your keys?

Physical Safety

Creating physically safe environments for children with special needs may require specific considerations.

- Children who are unstable and fall easily need to be able to rely on sturdy and stable furniture. Thus, shelves and cabinets may need to be secured.
- Sharp corners can be adapted with rubber or foam edges.
- Some outdoor play areas may need rubber matting
- Handrails may need to be added for children with unsteady gaits and for children with low vision.
- Obstacles in main traffic ways need to be clearly marked for children with low vision. For example, you can place a black and white checkerboard pattern on a post that children must walk around.
- Curbs and steps must also be clearly marked for children with low vision.

Encouraging Independent Access

To accommodate adaptive or supportive equipment such as wheelchairs that may be necessary to facilitate inclusion, the available physical space must be carefully arranged. However, it is important not to *overadapt*. Making only necessary adaptations will minimize the focus on children's disabilities and encourage all children to learn to navigate around the normal barriers of a natural setting.

Spaces must be designed and materials selected that invite children to become *independently* and *actively involved* with their environment. Walkways must be wide enough for children who use wheelchairs or crutches to have access to each activity area provided.

Helpful Hint

Ideally for children with severe motor disabilities, a team that may include an educator, physical or occupational therapist, augmentative communication specialist, and parents should be involved in the design or adaptation of the space and selection or adaptation of the materials.

Architectural Considerations. Examples of some of the architectural considerations to ensure safety and independent access are doors, ramps, toilets, chairs, and tables.

Doors. Doors can be difficult for many young children to open. When children with physical disabilities are included, ease of opening, closing, and holding doors open may be a significant problem. Also, they may need to be wider than standard doors to accommodate wheelchairs.

Ramps. When more than one wheelchair is to be accommodated, ramps wide enough to allow two chairs to pass are ideal. The slope of any ramps will need to be somewhat less steep than those designed for adults.

Toilets. Toilet seats should be at variable heights. Toilet stalls need to be more than 36 inches wide to facilitate transfers from wheelchairs to toilets. It may be necessary to adapt a potty chair or toilet for a child with a disability.

Table height and seating. For many children with special needs adaptations may be needed in table height and seating to ensure proper positioning. Children may need smaller chairs so their feet can touch the floor; children with low tone may need arm rests and back support. While seating adaptations may require extra effort initially, the payoff will be increased participation and comfort for the child. Figures 3–1 and 3–2 demonstrate examples of effective seating adaptations.

Often adapting the physical environment in even small ways can increase independence for children who have special needs. This in turn reduces the burden on staff to provide individual assistance. An important goal for children with special needs is physical independence. This independence will also help prepare children to function successfully in future learning environments.

Figure 3–1   Seating and table adaptations.

Figure 3–2   "Low-tech" seating adaptation.

> **Helpful Hint**
>
> To learn more about how to design space for inclusion of young children with physical and sensory disabilities, readers may contact the U.S. Architectural and Transportation Barriers Compliance Board, 1331 F Street NW, Suite 1000, Washington, DC 20004.

FLOOR PLAN CONSIDERATIONS FOR CHILDREN WITH SPECIAL NEEDS

While it is not necessary to create totally unique or adapted environments to include children with special needs, certain challenges may be of more frequent concern with this population. The following issues may be important considerations for some children.

Need for Quiet Area

Many children with special needs have low thresholds of tolerance for noisy and/or crowded busy environments. Providing a quiet area where children can be somewhat isolated and where the noise is damped can offer brief respites. There should always be a safe, comfortable area that children may seek out when they need or want to be alone. Children can be taught to take themselves to this private corner when they begin to feel overwhelmed. A staff member should monitor a child's behavior at all times while she is in the quiet area and can assist the child in developing self-control by letting her decide when she is ready to rejoin the group.

Avoidance of Large Open Areas

Some children with special needs may be overwhelmed by environments that seem disorganized and confusing. Divide large rooms into specific areas for activities, and clearly mark the boundaries of those areas with dividers, shelves, and other furniture and equipment. See the section later in this chapter on *Planning Activity Areas* for additional ideas.

Consideration of Some Children's Preference for Enclosed Space. Some children prefer a more enclosed, small space in which to play. It is helpful to arrange at least one area that is enclosed on at least three sides. However, the enclosure should not be more than about two feet in height to allow easy viewing of the area.

Need for Acoustic Adaptations

Highly resonant, noisy environments may create significant stress for many children with special needs—and many adults as well! This can interfere with children's ability to pay attention, increase irritability, and increase behavior problems and aggression. Sound can be dampened by use of acoustic tile, rugs, materials hung from the ceiling, and fabrics and artwork on the walls.

Visually Simple Presentation of Materials to Reduce Clutter

Children who appear to be unable to choose activities or seem to be at loose ends may be reacting to too much clutter or to disorganized presentation of toys and materials. The following are examples of suggestions that may make it easier for children to select materials.

- Store items in a consistent place.
- Group similar items together on shelves.
- Allow empty space between items (children with visual processing difficulties or low vision may not recognize items that are jammed together).
- Use pictures to clearly label containers of **manipulatives,** or small toys and objects that aid in the development of fine motor skills.

Helpful Hint

In planning the environment, consideration should be given to inclusion of space to encourage parent involvement and parent activities as well as space for those providing supplemental services. Staff members need sufficient space to accomplish necessary tasks such as preparing activities and recording the progress of children. Parents appreciate a corner where relevant books, articles, and notices on bulletin boards can be found. However, given limited space, this chapter will focus primarily on environmental considerations for children with special needs.

PLANNING ACTIVITY AREAS FOR CHILDREN WITH SPECIAL NEEDS

Activity areas are spaces within the room designed to facilitate different types of activities ranging from a small group tabletop game to more robust activities such as block building and pretend play. Differential design will encourage children to learn that different behaviors are expected in various settings and that as activity demands change, so should behavior. Too much open space invites running and wandering around. Too much clutter is difficult for children who have trouble focusing.

Children tend to become more readily engaged in activities when the space is arranged into well-defined areas of activity. Well-defined activity areas have visible boundaries, surfaces to accommodate the activity, and adequate space for display of materials and storage. Instead of encircling all activity areas with bookcases and storage units, more creative boundaries can be used. For instance, fluid boundaries might include the use of canopies, streamers, mobiles, carpeting, or different colored surfaces. Whatever the cues that designate different areas, they must be clear and consistent, and they should be of sufficient contrast to attract the notice of a child with visual impairments. (See Figure 3–3.)

One goal should be to achieve an appropriate *balance* of activity areas suited to the developmental levels, skills, and interests of all children. Arrangement of the activity areas also will need to take into consideration the daily schedule. For example, if children are to participate in several small tabletop activities at once, then several areas with tables will be necessary.

Versatile materials such as paints, clay, musical instruments, blocks, or a combination of materials may offer a broad continuum of possible adaptations to meet the needs of children at different developmental levels. Materials should be displayed at a height accessible to children.

The following considerations are recommended in arranging each activity center: library corner, art and water play area, tabletop manipulatives center, buiding area, and dramatic play area.

Library Corner

This quiet, calm area might be carpeted, offer large pillows, and feature a variety of literacy materials. Some sturdy infant-toddler books must be included along with talking books, pop-up books, and copies of books used at group story time. The library corner also might include writing paper, magic markers, envelopes, stickers, a toy mailbox, and a blackboard.

Art and Water Play Area

A *messy* center for art activities and water play might include easels, a sand/water table, and storage for paper and art materials. Easily cleaned flooring is a must. Even children with severe disabilities often enjoy water play; they like feeling running water on their hands and the soothing activities of filling and pouring. In the sand table, hiding and finding objects and burying their hands can engage young children.

Tabletop Manipulatives Center

A manipulatives play center features a table and shelves to hold well-marked containers of puzzles, small toys, and manipulatives. Initially children with severe disabilities may prefer to *dump and fill* in this area; they may not be able to play appropriately with small manipulatives without specific training. Be sure to include a variety of empty containers for this purpose,

(A)

(B)

Figure 3–3 Examples of Clear Boundaries (A) Rugs create contrast to help define space. (B) Movable shelves create boundaries.

such as jars with lids, cylinders, dump trucks, and buckets. Because developmentally young children may put small items in their mouths, some children will need to be closely supervised when they play in this area.

Building Area

Children with special needs often enjoy stacking and knocking down block towers (or knocking down towers that others have stacked!). The instant effect of the falling blocks can be quite motivating. This activity can provide opportunities for motor development and development of social skills of turn taking and respecting other children's creations. Another engaging activity is building ramps and letting cars and balls roll down the ramp. The greater the effect at the bottom of the ramp, the more interesting it is.

Dramatic Play Area

A dramatic play center may offer dress-up items, especially skirts with elastic waists, adult shoes, hats, and purses. These items can provide opportunities for staff to help children with disabilities practice dressing skills. Clothing should be easy to put on, take off, and fasten. Dolls, doll beds, baby bottles, high chair, a small rocking chair, and housekeeping toys (stove, dishes, pots and pans, and brooms) are some of the easiest toys for developmentally very young children to use to begin pretend play scenarios.

ARRANGING MATERIALS WITHIN ACTIVITY AREAS

The level of child involvement in activities is influenced by the arrangement of materials and space within activity areas. Activity areas that are well defined, neat, and clean tend to invite use and cleanup at the end of an activity.

Visibility and Consistency

Visibility and consistency of materials help to stimulate children's interest. Toys and materials should be consistently available and placed in the same location to allow children repeated access to materials so they can practice emerging skills. However, periodic change of a few items can be planned to stimulate interest and promote new skills.

Large items can be stored on open shelves while small items such as cubes or crayons should be in containers on the open shelves. The teacher should seek to find out how a setting appears at the child's level. Are there interesting items for children to see and touch? Are some of the materials and toys accessible to a child even if she is minimally mobile?

Accessibility

Familiar items found in homes should be included along with commercially available educational materials. This is particularly important for children whose home culture differs from that of the center.

Accessible materials that are easy to take out and store are more likely to be used and returned than less accessible items. Arrange materials so that they can be easily viewed, taken from shelves and storage units, and returned to their proper place.

Helpful Hint

Some items should be difficult to access but visible. This will provide important motivation and opportunity for children with language delay to use communication skills to request these items.

Labeling

Picture labels on shelves facilitate proper placement of items and prereading skills. Photographs of what happens in each area assist children with hearing loss to function more independently in that area.

Traffic Management

Traffic should be minimized and must flow freely. **Traffic management** includes nearby storage of materials, space for adaptive equipment, absence of cross traffic, and recommended routes for travel that can be identified with footsteps or colored lines, for example. When planning a center, efforts should be made to ensure that a child in a wheelchair can navigate in and out of the spaces provided. It is helpful to specify the number of children allowed in each center at any one time.

Noise Control

It is crucial to control the noise level, especially when children who are easily distracted or children with hearing loss are included. Children who wear hearing aids and children who have information processing problems often have difficulty discriminating sounds and blocking out background noise. Some quiet space should be available for children to work with minimal noise distraction. Obviously, the quiet, calm area should not be placed next to the large muscle or dramatic play areas. Sound-absorbing material, such as cork or carpeting, can be used in high noise areas.

Lighting

Consider lighting when arranging an area that requires close, visually demanding activities. Even young children with normal vision are naturally somewhat farsighted, and activities requiring attention to visual details can be tiring. Adding incandescent lighting and natural light from windows and skylights can counteract the stress sometimes caused by fluorescent lighting. For children with low vision, it is helpful to use lamps that can be attached to tables and moved from place to place as needed.

DESIGNING SPECIFIC ACTIVITY CENTERS

Reading/Preliteracy Areas

A quiet, calm area should be created to provide opportunities for children to relax and be exposed to books and other materials designed to develop preliteracy skills.

Organizing the Reading Area

- To reduce distractibility and facilitate attention and concentration, this center should be located in the quieter area of the room.
- The area must be well lighted to assist children with low vision (as well as aging staff members!).
- Large-print books and books with textures to allow tactile exploration are important for children with low vision. Pictures with bold clear lines and "scratch-and-sniff" books are also recommended.
- Furnishings should be inviting and encourage relaxation. Carpeting, bean bags, and comfortable chairs lend themselves to quiet involvement. A rocking chair can be invaluable in calming children who have difficulty with overarousal, such as children with autism.
- Physical therapists can assist in the selection of appropriate furnishings to provide optimal positioning for children with physical disabilities.
- Books should be displayed on an open rack with covers clearly visible in the line of children's sight.
- Other materials that might be available in this area include a flannelboard with story pictures, magazines, puppets, felt or magnetic letters, lotto games or picture word cards, and writing materials.
- Adaptive equipment to hold a book, turn pages, or activate tape recorders may be needed for children with physical disabilities.
- Accompanying storybooks with flannelboards or puppets may help maintain interest for developmentally young children who are not motivated by picture representations alone.

> **Helpful Hint**
>
> Be sure to include books that portray children with disabilities along with those depicting a wide variety of cultural groups.

Sensory Experiences, Art, and Water Play Centers

All young children and especially those with sensory impairments need a wide variety of multi-sensory experiences. Developmentally young children will enjoy the simple activities of sensory motor exploration. For children with low vision, art and water play provide important information through the alternate sensory channel of touch.

Art and water play centers are most appropriately placed outside or in a noncarpeted area near a sink to facilitate cleanup. Plastic aprons will help children with fine motor challenges avoid worrying about getting clothes wet or stained.

Materials to be included depend on the developmental levels of the children included. Some children with special needs do not know how to use materials such as crayons and scissors and may not learn through simply observing others.

Adaptive equipment such as the those illustrated in Figure 3–4 allow children with special needs to function independently. While some adaptations allow children to be better positioned to engage in fine motor activities, others directly modify the art utensils. Teachers can make simple adaptations. For example:

- Paintbrush handles can be built up with tape or other material to ease handling for children with motor impairments.
- Crayons can be stuck through tennis balls to make a larger gripping area.
- Children with visual impairments can enjoy the sweeping motions involved in moving paint brushes, especially across large areas such as on wide pieces of paper or on real-life objects such as fences or big cardboard boxes.
- Water play tubs can be moved outdoors in good weather so spilling isn't a concern. Or water can be replaced with other sensory materials such as leaves, styrofoam packing materials, sand, noodles, or water with soap suds. Some children with special needs may need to be carefully supervised to prevent them from putting the materials in their mouths.

Small Manipulative Activity Centers

Use of manipulatives can create special challenges for children with special needs.

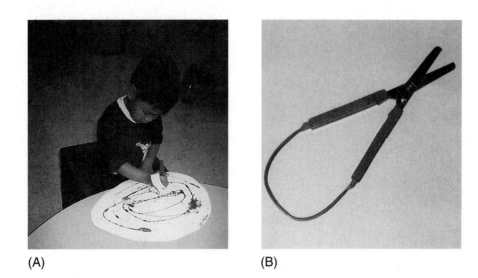

(A)   (B)

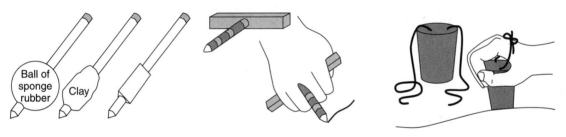

(C)

Figure 3–4   Specially designed equipment for accessing art activities (A) Paint brush attached to child's hand with velcro (B) Adapted scissors (C) Simple ways of adapting crayons and markers.

- Children with special needs may need to be closely supervised to prevent choking on small items.
- Any centers featuring manipulative activities on a table must have child-sized tables sturdy enough to hold the weight of a minimally mobile child who may need support.
- Often it is easier for everyone if the manipulatives are placed on a carpeted floor.
- If working on the carpet, it may be helpful to use tape to create borders to define work areas.

To assist children with physical disabilities, the following adaptations can be made:

- Consult with physical and occupational therapists to determine positioning and adaptive equipment needs.

- Use kidney-shaped tables or tables with cut semicircles to allow children in wheelchairs or adapted seating to get closer to materials.
- Adapt battery-operated toys, radios, tape players, and other equipment using simple assistive technology devices such as pressure switches.
- Put a rim around the table edge to prevent small objects from being knocked off easily.
- Use larger versions of manipulative toys.
- Tape paper to table edges so paper doesn't move around.
- Add wooden or plastic knobs to puzzle pieces.
- Place stiff plastic around shoe laces or use pipe cleaners for bead stringing.
- Glue magnets to manipulatives and use on cookie sheets.
- Put knobs on puzzle pieces for easier grasping.

To assist children with visual impairments, consider the following:

- Consult a vision specialist to determine individual needs and appropriate adaptations.
- Give children wide markers so lines are easier to see.
- Put puzzles in a tray so children can keep track of the pieces.
- Provide knobbed puzzles and fit-in puzzles.
- Use glue to mark a line to be cut or traced.
- Put textured boundaries to define work areas. Placemats define work areas well for all children.
- Paste different textured fabrics on toys to help differentiate their parts and make them more interesting.

Outdoor Play Areas

Outside play is essential for children with special needs. Outdoor activities offer unique opportunities that may not be easily replicated indoors. It is important to maximize these opportunities through careful planning and use.

Helpful Hint

Be sure to check with parents about special concerns or restrictions for children in outside environments. Seizures, sun sensitivity due to medication or medical condition, and perceptual and balance difficulties are potential concerns.

The outdoor environment provides a significant change in sensory-motor environment that is often very desirable.

1. Noise is less resonant and more diffuse so the outdoors may be less stressful for children who have auditory sensitivity.

2. Natural light is an advantage, though sunlight may pose problems for certain visual conditions.
3. Outdoor spaces offer access to certain gross motor and mobility activities that are not possible indoors, such as riding tricycles, pulling wagons, and swinging.

Certain considerations involving outdoor play environments may be particularly important for children with special needs:

- Swings need to be adapted with safety harnesses.
- The ground surface needs to be soft and resilient.
- To accommodate children with low vision, ground surfaces from one area to the next—such as the swing area to the sandbox to climbing structures and slides—need to be marked in some way, perhaps with bumps between areas or astroturf in certain areas.
- Climbing structures need to be low, with easily grasped rails.
- Some pedal and wheel toys may need to be adapted with foot blocks and velcro to accommodate smaller stature and poor motor control of legs.
- Bike tracks and "traffic" patterns need to be clearly marked and enforced.
- Sand tables, sand boxes, and water tables or small wading pools should be included and made easily accessible.

SUMMARY

Careful planning and arrangement of the physical environment can make a significant difference in how young children with disabilities adapt and enjoy inclusive environments. These modifications can benefit all children and help ensure that the physical environment supports rather than interferes with learning.

CASE STUDY

Boundaries for Sung and Rafik

Mr. Ramirez is the teacher in a community preschool program. His classroom is in a small converted room in an old house. He has been frustrated about the fact that he really does not have enough room to design a good classroom environment. Two new children have joined the classroom, both of whom have some specific challenges. Sung has very limited vision, though her glasses enable her to be mobile and she can move around the room fairly safely. However, with the crowded space and clutter she is unable to identify specific play areas or favorite toys. To solve the space problem, Mr. Ramirez has placed several bins of toys and

(continued)

materials on movable carts, which tend to be placed wherever is convenient at the moment to get them out of the way.

Rafik is a boisterous child in constant motion. According to his mother he is currently being evaluated for ADHD (attention deficit hyperactivity disorder). He wanders around the classroom and is rarely able to focus on one activity. He may pick up an object, but then he throws it down and moves completely away from the area to another part of the room. Rafik particularly has trouble with circle time. It seems impossible for him to sit more than two minutes, after which he gets up and begins moving around the room as usual. Because there is not enough room for a separate area for circle time, Mr. Ramirez conducts his circle time in different areas: sometime in the block area, sometimes outside, sometimes at the snack table. With the addition of the two new children, the classroom space now seemed intolerably small.

Mr. Ramirez is very concerned about meeting the special needs of Sung and Rafik. He asks Ms. Thomas, the inclusion support provider, if she has any suggestions for managing the two children. After observing the children on several occasions and talking at length with Mr. Ramirez and the assistant teacher, Ms. Thomas suggests several strategies. First, the movable carts need to be housed in one place until they are needed. Moving the carts into the appropriate area as they are needed has been incorporated into the daily schedule as a predictable, separate task with which children are assigned to help. Rafik especially enjoys pushing the cart from one place to another. This keeps the carts from just being part of the clutter.

Another strategy is to use colorful reflecting tape to mark off specific areas of the room (each with a different color and one with a contrasting broken line pattern): the block area, the library corner, and the dress-up area. Also, Mr. Ramirez has actually reduced the toys and materials available by a third, eliminating the less preferred or broken toys. This makes it easier to arrange materials on shelves with more space between them and to label the shelves so the materials can be consistently stored in the same place.

Finally, Mr. Ramirez has decided that his class will have circle time each day in the library corner, since he often includes reading as a circle time activity. He has also noted that this is the area where Rafik seems to be the calmest, perhaps because it is a fairly enclosed space.

With some assistance Sung has learned to use her residual sight to move quite confidently around the room and to find her favorite toys, which are now stored in a consistent place. Rafik seems calmer and has begun to prefer the block area and the library corner, where he spends at least a few minutes focusing on a single activity.

Case Study Questions

1. *Which accommodations were most helpful for Rafik? Why?*
2. *Which accommodations were most helpful for Sung? Why?*
3. *If Mr. Ramirez were given $5,000 to improve his classroom environment, how would you recommend he spend it?*

KEY TERMS

activity area   traffic management
manipulatives

HELPFUL RESOURCES

Organizations and Reports

American Society of Landscape Architects, 636 Eye Street NW, Washington, DC 20001-3736, (202) 898-2444, Web site: <www.asla.org>

Assistive Technology Education Network, Web site: <www.webable.com>

Handbook for public playground safety, U.S. Consumer Product Safety Commission, Washington, DC 20207, (800) 638-2772, Web site: <www.cpsc.gov>

International Play Equipment Manufacturers Association, 8300 Colesville R., Suite 250, Silver Spring, MD 20910, (301) 495-0240, (800) 395-5550, Web site: <www.ipema.org>

Report and model law on public play equipment and areas, Consumer Federation of America, 1424 16th St. NW, Suite 604, Washington, DC 20005-0999, (202) 387-1621, Web site: <www.consumerfed.org>

Standard consumer safety performance specification for playground equipment for public use #F1487-98) and *Standard specification for determination of accessibility of surface systems under and around playground equipment* (#F1951-99), American Society For Testing And Materials, 100 Barr Harbor Drive, West Conschocken, PA 19428, (610) 832-9585, Web site: <www.astm.org>

U.S. Architectural and Transportation Barriers Compliance Board, 1331 F Street NW, Suite 1000, Washington, DC 20004-1111, (202) 272-5434, or (800) USA-ABLE, Web site: <www.access-board.gov>

Playground Equipment Companies

ABC School Supply, Inc., 3312 N. Berkeley Lake Rd, Box 100019, Duluth, GA 30096-9419, (800) 669-4222, Web site: <www.abcschoolsupply.com>

KOMPAN Inc., 7717 New Market St., Olympia, WA 98501, (360) 943-6374, Web site: <www.kompan.com>

PlayDesigns, 1000 Buffalo Road, Lewisburg, PA 17837-9795, (800) 327-7571, Web site: <www.playdesigns.com>

Catalogs for Adaptive Equipment

AbleNet Inc., 1081 Tenth Ave. S.E., Minneapolis, MN 55414, (800) 322-0956.

Crestwood Company, Communication Aids, 6625 N. Sydney Place, Milwaukee,WI 53209, Web site: <www.communicationaids.com>

Guide to toys for children who are blind or visually impaired, American Toy Institute, Inc., Toy Manufacturers of America, Inc., 200 Fifth Ave., Suite 740, New York, NY 10010, (212) 675-1141.

Rifton, P.O. Box 901, Rifton, NY 12471-0901, (800) 777-4224.

Tumbleforms, J.A. Preston Corporation, (800) 631-7277.

Curricula

Dodge, D., & Cokler, L. (1992). *Creative curriculum for early childhood.* Washington, DC: Teaching Strategies Inc.

4

Preventing and Managing Challenging Behaviors

Chapter-at-a-Glance
Many behavior problems often displayed by children with special needs can be prevented using simple strategies.

A *behavior problem* is not an absolute. A behavior may be considered to be a problem in one situation and not a problem in another context or by other people. Behavior problems are socially and culturally determined. Teachers must be able to specifically define the behavior and state why the behavior is unacceptable.

- **Children who have special needs may be more likely to develop challenging behavior patterns.** This may be due to difficulties with impulse control, low frustration tolerance, hyperirritability, and lack of appropriate communication skills.
- **Inappropriate behaviors in young children with special needs may represent an attempt to communicate.** They may be signaling a need to escape an unpleasant situation or sensation, a desire to obtain a preferred object or activity, or a need for attention.
- **The assistance of a behavior specialist or inclusion consultant may be needed** for persistent and severe behavior problems. Specialists conduct a careful functional assessment of the antecedents and consequences of persistent and severe behavior problems, and design a behavioral intervention plan that will eventually modify the child's behavior.
- **Positive behavior support techniques consider many challenging behaviors as attempts to communicate.** In these cases the goal is to provide acceptable replacement behaviors that allow the child to communicate in more appropriate ways. This approach also focuses on identifying the trigger or antecedent of the behavior.

INTRODUCTION

One of the most common causes of failure of inclusive placements of children with special needs is the challenge of dealing with difficult behaviors. Young children with special needs often have behavior that is atypical or inappropriate. Sometimes this behavior is truly disruptive. Occasionally the behavior is dangerous. Early childhood educators must have some understanding of how such behaviors develop and which strategies and resources are available for preventing and managing them.

WHAT IS A CHALLENGING BEHAVIOR ANYWAY?

While some behaviors—particularly those that cause pain or injury to others—are clearly unacceptable, many behavior problems are defined by the individuals or community around the child. In these cases the behavior problem often consists of breaking a rule. For example, when you visit two elementary school classrooms, you notice that Mrs. Quincy's classroom is very quiet, while Mr. Nelson's class is very noisy. This reflects the rules and expectations set by the two teachers. Mrs. Quincy believes that a quiet classroom is essential to learning. Mr. Nelson, on the other hand, believes that children must be actively engaged in the learning process and that children cannot learn in silence. Thus, while children's noisy chatter in Mr. Nelson's classroom is considered evidence of active learning, the loud talkative child in Mrs. Quincy's room may be considered a behavior problem.

Another example: You visit two preschool classrooms. In the first classroom you notice a three-year-old boy aggressively push another child away who is trying to take his toy. His teacher says to him, "Don't push him. Tell him, "No, I'm playing with this now." Later you are observing another preschool classroom. A similar episode occurs. But in this classroom the teacher swiftly intervenes saying, "That's too rough. You may not push him. You can go to the time-out corner until you are ready to play nicely and learn to share." The teacher in the first class sees the boy's behavior as age appropriate, and not a problem. She believes with proper modeling the child will eventually learn more appropriate behavior. The teacher in the second classroom strongly believes any kind of physically aggressive behavior is unacceptable and wants children to learn this quickly.

In the first preschool class the behavior is seen as normal; in the second it is considered a behavior problem. Sometimes the easiest way to deal with such problems is simply to change the rules. The story of "Joey's Shoes" demonstrates this idea in practice.

Joey's Shoes

Joey had been in the center-based program for three months. On a hot day shortly after beginning the program, his teacher, Miss Puente, took all the children's shoes off so they could wade in the wading pool. Joey

---

enjoyed this activity. Unfortunately from that day on, Joey insisted on taking his shoes off every day as soon as he arrived at the center. Every day a major battle was waged over Joey's shoes. He was unhappy until his shoes were off. Then he seemed fine. The teacher spoke with his father about the problem. He insisted Joey should keep his shoes on. Joey's father bought him a new pair of shoes, just in case he had outgrown the old ones, which might make them uncomfortable. Joey still insisted on taking off his shoes at the center, and he would cry and kick when the teacher put them back on.

One day Miss Puente asked dad if Joey also insisted on taking off his shoes at home. Dad indicated that Joey did not do this at home, only at the center. In that case, Miss Puente suggested, it might be all right to let him take off his shoes at the center if he wanted. Joey's father reluctantly agreed.

Once this policy was implemented, Joey's tantrums subsided and he participated willingly in the daily activities. He continued to wear his shoes at home with no problem. Within three months Joey began to *forget* about taking his shoes off on some days at the center. By the end of the year the *problem* had disappeared.

In Joey's case, the so-called *problem behavior* was simply redefined to not be a problem. Teachers are often hesitant to change a rule or expectation because it may seem as if they are giving in. But sometimes, as happened with Joey, the behavior eventually disappears when it is no longer an issue.

BEHAVIOR CHALLENGES IN CHILDREN WITH SPECIAL NEEDS

Any child, regardless of whether he has special needs, can develop patterns of behavior that are disruptive or considered unacceptable. The characteristics of certain disability conditions, however, may increase the likelihood that a child will develop a behavior problem.

Neurological Disorders

One common cause of behavior problems in children with neurological disorders is difficulty with impulse control. These children often react quickly and aggressively to any situation that increases frustration. Young children who have suffered head trauma may be *emotionally labile,* resulting in frequent unexplained crying.

Autism

Children with autism often engage in disruptive behaviors such as tantrums or running away. They frequently have extreme sensitivity to certain sounds and to being touched (**tactile defensiveness**). As a result they may engage in inappropriate behaviors to escape certain unpleasant or overwhelming situations. Some children may engage in **self-stimulatory behavior,** such as twirling objects, hand flapping, and rocking, as a means of reducing anxiety and calming themselves. Self-stimulatory behavior often helps the child block out something stressful in the environment. As is the case with many children with special needs, children who have autism often have difficulty coping with unpredictable environments. Thus the less predictable and organized the environment is, the greater the likelihood that children will develop challenging behaviors.

Communication Disorders

Children who have limited communication skills may develop disruptive behavior patterns as a primitive means of controlling their environment and communicating wants and needs. Assisting these children in learning functional communication skills, including words, gestures, signs, or pictures, will often significantly reduce behavior problems.

Seizure Disorders

Occasionally, unusual or explosive behaviors can be the result of seizures. Teachers must be aware of seizure disorders in children and their medications. Teachers should also be aware that it is possible for a young child to have an undiagnosed seizure disorder.

CAUSES/FUNCTIONS OF INAPPROPRIATE BEHAVIOR

If you've determined that a behavior can't simply be defined away or ignored and that it is truly disruptive (e.g., screaming or throwing things) or potentially harmful (e.g., biting, hitting, or self-injurious behavior), the next step is to determine its cause and/or function. There are a limited number of possible reasons why a child might engage in unacceptable behavior, including the following:

- To escape something unpleasant
- To get attention
- To gain access to something the child wants

Escape

In some cases the child may be trying to escape an **internal state.** For example, the child may be in some kind of discomfort or may feel extremely stressed or anxious, related to physiological or biological factors rather than external conditions. Such internal states may be affected by medication, diet, illness, and emotional upset at home or in the classroom. Children who are extremely hyperactive due to Attention Deficit Hyperactivity Disorder (ADHD) may experience a strong neurologically based drive to move and act on the environment. If this is not properly directed, this hyperactivity can easily translate into behavior problems.

More often, the child is trying to escape environmental conditions that cause stress, anxiety, or discomfort. A child with sensitive hearing (often the case for a child with autism, for example) may experience discomfort in a noisy room. The most common environmental conditions that cause stress or discomfort include:

- Noisy and/or highly resonant acoustic environment
- Too many children
- Other children in close proximity
- Cluttered disorganized classroom
- Visually overstimulating environment such as one with colorful materials on every bit of wall space and collages hanging from the ceiling
- Large open spaces with no boundaries

The child may be trying to escape a specific task or activity he dislikes. For example the child may hate brushing his teeth, or he may not want to play with the cornstarch-and-water *goop.*

Examples of Escape Behaviors. Some escape behaviors are obvious, such as running away or refusing to stay seated. Just as often, however, the behaviors are less easily interpreted (see Figure 4–1). Consider the following list of behaviors that are frequently caused by a need to escape:

- Running away
- Refusing to stay seated

Figure 4–1   Child displaying escape emotions.

- Crawling into enclosed space or under table
- Having a tantrum
- Covering ears
- Screaming
- Throwing objects
- Hitting or biting
- Biting own hand or other self-injurious behavior
- Rocking, hand flapping, or other self-stimulatory behavior

Attention Seeking

Many children, with and without disabilities, need and enjoy adult attention. Frequently the primary motivation of unacceptable behavior is to gain attention and interaction from a caregiver or significant adult. An effective general strategy to significantly reduce behavior problems is to make sure you are giving children adequate individual attention. *Make sure you connect with each child on an intimate, one-on-one basis, frequently throughout the day.* This means being at children's eye level, patiently listening to both words and feelings, and validating them as individuals (see Figure 4–2). The following are common attention-getting behaviors.

- Running away
- Wandering in the classroom
- Leaving an activity

Figure 4–2 Teacher regarding child's needs.

- Picking on peers
- Having a tantrum
- Removing clothing
- Destroying property
- Turning water/lights on or off
- Crawling under table

Helpful Hint

As you may have noticed, many of the same behaviors are listed as escape and attention-getting behaviors. The *type* of behavior does not indicate its *function.* The same behavior by two children may serve completely different functions.

Gaining Access

In this case the child engages in unacceptable behavior to gain access to an object, sensation, or activity the child finds pleasurable. For example, the child may not be running away to escape or to gain attention, but because he loves being outside. The child may turn the lights on and off not because he wants the teacher's attention, but because he loves the visual effect of the flickering lights.

GENERAL STRATEGIES FOR PREVENTING AND REDUCING THE OCCURRENCE OF PROBLEM BEHAVIORS

Certain classroom organization strategies and ways of interacting with children can significantly reduce the frequency of unacceptable behaviors in the center-based setting. This section summarizes those strategies.

Keep the Number of Rules Small

The more rules there are, the more likely the child is to get into trouble. Keep rules to no more than three or four. Some children with special needs may not be able to handle more than one or two rules. Rules must be clearly defined and realistic for the range of developmental levels represented in the group.

Select Rules Carefully

Important rules for very young children are intended to prevent behaviors that are harmful to themselves or to other children. Thus, aggressive behavior—hitting, biting, throwing, or kicking—is always unacceptable, as is behavior that is dangerous to oneself, such as climbing up on a counter, head banging, or running inside. Teachers should clearly inform and remind children that such behavior will not be permitted. This is especially crucial for children who have impulse control problems. Learning self-control can be a major challenge, but it is critical to children's success.

Even though they are not as serious as aggressive behaviors, certain disruptive behaviors, such as loud screaming, knocking toys off shelves, or emptying storage containers, may also be unacceptable. These behaviors can be stressful and upsetting to other children.

Be Clear and Consistent about Enforcement

Children with special needs have difficulty learning rules if they are not clearly demonstrated and followed up with consistent consequences. Keep in mind that some children who have special needs cannot comprehend what you say through words alone. They will need clear demonstration. Simply saying to the child "One of our rules is that you may not climb on the tables" may have no effect on some children. Only through consistent consequences for climbing on the table do these children eventually learn that this is unacceptable. Your facial expression and intonation also help convey that the behavior is unacceptable. Saying "Let's not climb on the table" with a pleasant facial expression will not help the children understand that they are breaking a rule. Since they may not understand your words, if the intonation in your voice is pleasant and you're smiling, they may think they're doing a good thing!

Avoid Overstimulating, Disorganized Environments

Environments that have unclear traffic patterns and are noisy, visually *busy*, cluttered, and messy are more likely to produce behavior problems (see Chapter 3).

Maintain a Predictable Daily Schedule

ECSE teachers insist this is one of the most effective strategies for reducing behavior problems. When children are confident about what happens next and activities are scheduled in ways that maximize participation and minimize fatigue, they are less likely to engage in unacceptable behavior. See more detailed discussion of the daily schedule in Chapter 1.

Carefully Plan Transitions

Transitions from one activity to another can present challenges for children with special needs. Carefully planned transitions take into account signals, sequences, and consistency.

A Clear Signal. Develop a series of signals to signify the end of an activity and the beginning of a transition, such as turning lights on and off, playing or singing a certain song, or ringing a bell. Many children with special needs may respond well to objects or pictures as signals rather than to auditory signals.

A Specific Sequence. Follow a regular line-up of events within the transition, such as this example of progressing from an outside activity to snack:

1. Bell rings signaling end of outside activity.
2. Teacher says, "Okay, time to go in for snack."
3. Children put away trikes, cover sand and water tables, and collect other toys.
4. Children line up at the door.
5. Teacher says, "Okay, everyone is ready to go in for snack!"
6. Teacher leads children inside.

Consistency. Use the same cues and sequence each time the transition occurs.

Give Attention *Before* Inappropriate Behavior Occurs

For children whose disruptive behavior seems to be motivated by the need for adult attention, paying extra attention to them before they demand attention can significantly reduce inappropriate behaviors.

Use Touch to De-Escalate Behavior

Sometimes touching a child can help the child gain control of himself. This may be particularly true for a child who has problems with attention and hyperactivity or for a child with poor receptive language who cannot rely on verbal cues alone.

Helpful Hint

For children with autism or severe behavior disorders, providing trunk pressure by enfolding the child from the back with your arms across his chest can sometimes de-escalate severe tantrums (see Figure 4–3).

BEHAVIOR MODIFICATION AND THE USE OF REINFORCEMENT TECHNIQUES

One of the most commonly used strategies for dealing with difficult behavior is referred to as **behavior modification.** Space does not allow a detailed

Figure 4–3   Using firm trunk (chest and back) pressure to de-escalate a temper tantrum.

description of this procedure here. However, the basic principle of behavior modification is simple: *What happens immediately following a child's behavior can either strengthen or weaken that behavior, depending upon whether the child enjoys it or dislikes it.*

- What happens immediately *following* a behavior is called a **consequence.**
- If the child finds the consequence pleasant and the behavior increases or is strenthened, the consequence is called a **reinforcer.**
- If the consequence is unpleasant, it is called an **aversive stimulus.** If the behavior is weakened or decreases in frequency, the consequence is considered a **punishment.**

For example, if every time a child tries to pet a dog the dog growls and walks away, the child will soon quit trying to pet the dog (assuming that he finds the dog's growling unpleasant). On the other hand, if the dog comes closer and licks him, he will probably pet the dog even more (assuming that the child enjoys being licked!).

Identifying a Reinforcer

Of course the key to using positive reinforcement is figuring out what is positively reinforcing. If the child does not experience the consequence as *pleasurable*, it will have no effect.

For example, a teacher may intend to reinforce a child for sitting during circle time by using praise such as "I like the way you're sitting." However, if the child does not appreciate the praise, it will have no effect on increasing sitting. On the other hand if each time the child sits down, his favorite adult sits down next to him and puts his hand on his shoulder (which the child enjoys), he will continue to sit down willingly at circle time.

Decreasing Undesirable Behaviors

Several approaches can help decrease undesirable behaviors once they are already established.

1. Determine whether the behavior is being inadvertently reinforced and remove the reinforcing consequence (see example of Elena).
2. If possible, teach a new *replacement* behavior that is more acceptable. For example, teach a child who kicks when a toy is taken away to say "no" instead.
3. Positively reinforce the replacement behavior. This can be especially effective if the replacement behavior is incompatible with the problem behavior, such as when a child signs "Stop" rather than hitting.
4. Provide natural consequences that are unpleasant. For example, a child's playmate may get up and leave the offending child alone in the play area.

Elena's Favorite Adult

Elena had difficulty focusing on any appropriate activity during free play. She tended to simply wander around the room, occasionally stopping to kick or push another child. This behavior usually resulted in her favorite teacher, Miss Long, taking Elena by the hand and pulling her away from the other child. Miss Long would get Elena engaged in playing with a toy and then walk away. Thus, Elena was being reinforced for kicking and pushing because it resulted in interaction with her favorite adult. She was being punished for playing with a toy because as soon as she became interested in it, her favorite adult walked away!

Using the principles of behavior modification, Miss Long decided to try another approach. Each time she noticed Elena engaged in any appropriate activity, she approached her and played with her. When Elena behaved aggressively toward another child, Miss Long would have a classroom volunteer or other less familiar adult approach Elena and sternly say, "Elena, you may not kick!" Then the adult would swiftly move her to another part of the room. In this way Elena was being reinforced by the presence of Miss Long for appropriate behavior, and her aggressive behavior was not reinforced.

Use of Extinction

When the purpose of a behavior is primarily to gain attention, another effective way of decreasing the behavior is through **extinction.** Extinction results from ignoring a behavior. Obviously some behaviors are too serious to be ignored. However, for behaviors that are not extremely disruptive or dangerous, extinction can be an effective strategy. With this procedure the child learns that the behavior produces no effect. Eventually the rate of the behavior will diminish significantly. However, the behavior may intensify initially for a period of time. It is important for all staff to expect this result, or they will become discouraged with the procedure.

Extinction Procedure for Jill

Jill dumped out all the Legos™, scattering them on the floor, almost every day. Mr. Clay began to suspect that this was a way of getting his attention. His typical response was to express his frustration by saying, "Oh there she goes again!" He would promptly sit down beside her while he helped her put the Legos back in the box.

Mr. Clay implemented an extinction procedure by paying no attention to Jill at all when she dumped the Legos. He also had to ignore the children who were compelled to tattle on Jill when he failed to notice her. For about a week Jill dumped the Legos two or three times a day. But no adult responded to her behavior. By the end of the fourth week, Jill no longer dumped the Legos.

Problems with the Use of Punishment

While it is possible to decrease the rate of a problem behavior by punishing the behavior, in most cases, particularly with young children, use of punishment should be avoided.

A common type of punishment used in early childhood programs is the familiar **time out.** This procedure should be used cautiously and infrequently and never with children under the developmental age of two. A carefully implemented time-out procedure can provide an opportunity for some children to *reorganize* themselves after losing self-control. Some children actually learn to use a self-imposed time out, which can increase their self-confidence in their ability to manage themselves (Cook, Tessier, & Klein, 2000). If you choose to use a time out, the following considerations are important.

- Make sure the child understands exactly what behavior will result in a time out.
- Warn the child, calmly, only once.

- Be sure the child is within the teacher's view at all times.
- Keep the time out very short.
- Be positive at the end of the time out; praise the child for being in control of himself.
- Help the child choose and engage in another activity.

Another commonly used punishment is taking something away or not rewarding the child, such as not giving the child a sticker. For developmentally young children this is an ineffective and inappropriate practice. Young children, especially those with cognitive disabilities, will have a difficult time understanding the meaning of delayed reinforcers that are not given at the time of the behavior. They will not grasp the connection between the behavior and the punishment.

Finally, even if punishment can sometimes help control an undesirable behavior, it may produce unwanted and unnecessary emotional side effects. Thus, punishment should only be used for the most severe behavior disorders and should be used in collaboration with a behavior specialist.

ASSIGNING A ONE-TO-ONE AIDE

If the behavior is extremely difficult to bring under control, it may be necessary to assign a **one-to-one aide** (assistant) to shadow the child for a period of time. In most cases the role of this individual is to provide another pair of eyes and hands to intervene to prevent such behaviors as running away, hitting or biting other children, destroying property, or endangering himself. The assistant must learn to identify the behavioral cues and environmental factors that indicate that the child is about to engage in the behavior.

For example, when the noise level in the room increases, one child may briefly cover his face with his hands, then suddenly bolt for the door. The assistant would learn to recognize these cues and either use a prevention procedure, such as moving the child to a quieter area, or a control procedure, such as simply holding him so he cannot run. Obviously this is not a permanent solution to managing the child's behavior. A carefully planned behavioral program should be implemented with a goal of eliminating the need for a one-on-one assistant.

A Word of Caution on the Use of One-to-One Aides

Some potential problems associated with the use of a one-to-one aide may cause additional behavior problems.

- The child may become extremely attached and refuse to interact with any other staff or peers.
- The assistant may do too much for the child, making the child too dependent on her.

- The teacher may come to expect the assistant to do nearly all of the interacting with the child, thus isolating the child from the rest of the staff and from other children.

It is important to clarify precisely the role of a one-to-one aide and to use the assistant only to the degree necessary to manage the behavior. The early childhood educator should not assume that the one-to-one aide has received any training. It is very important to determine how (or whether) the assistant has been trained. Parents or the inclusion specialist should be able to provide this information and arrange for any necessary training of the assistant.

DESIGNING POSITIVE BEHAVIOR SUPPORT PLANS

Positive behavior support is an approach to managing behavior that focuses on understanding the function of the behavior and attempts to prevent the behavior rather than following through on consequences for the behavior after it occurs. (Koegle, 1996) This approach also determines what factors can be put in place that will support positive behavior rather than triggering or reinforcing negative behavior.

Understanding Problem Behaviors as Communication

Often problem behaviors occur in children who cannot express themselves verbally. Many children with special needs have limited language skills. They frequently express strongly felt needs in nonverbal ways. All too often these nonverbal communications are inappropriate and consequently identified as behavior problems (see Figure 4–4).

An important step in reducing problem behaviors is to determine the **communicative function** of the behavior. One effective way to determine the communicative function of a behavior is to do an **ABC analysis** (see Figure 4–5). In this analysis one carefully observes the *antecedent,* the *behavior,* and the *consequence* of the behavior over several days. By determining the antecedent and consequence of an undesirable behavior it is possible to speculate about the purpose of the behavior.

Once this is determined a more appropriate communicative behavior can be trained. This is referred to as a **replacement behavior.**

Understanding Frederika's Behavior as Communication

Frederika was a very tactually defensive child. She hated being touched and crowded by the other children. When another child got too close to her, especially if the child was noisy and moving fast, she would immediately throw whatever object was within her reach.

CAN'T YOU SEE I'M TRYING TO TELL YOU SOMETHING!!

Figure 4–4   Disruptive behavior may be a child's only or most effective way of communicating. A replacement behavior must be taught.

Throwing things was the only way (and a very effective way) she knew to communicate that children were getting too close to her. Her teacher selected a more acceptable communication behavior as a replacement. Frederika was taught to hold up the palm of her hand to signal "Stop!" The other children in the class were taught to respect this communication and to back away slightly. This gave Frederika a great feeling of control. Once she had generalized this communicative response to several play situations, she rarely threw things. She also gradually became more tolerant of children in close proximity.

Traditional applications of behavior modification have concentrated on eliminating the unacceptable behavior by applying consequences such as time out. However, in recent years there has been an increasing emphasis on preventing problem behaviors by analyzing the cause and/or purpose (function) of the unacceptable behavior. This approach emphasizes identifying the communicative function of the behavior and finding an acceptable replacement behavior whenever possible. This requires a systematic approach but can be extremely effective in a developmentally appropriate

Behavior Observation Chart
ABC Analysis

Student Name: _____   Observer Name: _____

Date	Activity (Where, when, who, what?)	Antecedents (What happened immediately before behavior?)	Behavior (What actually happened?)	Consequences (What happened immediately after behavior?)	Comments

Figure 4–5   ABC analysis form.

94

way. It also may require the assistance of an extra person. The elements of this technique follow.

Positive behavior support procedure

Step 1: Conduct an ABC analysis using the form in Figure 4–5 to carefully observe the behavior over a period of time (at least a week).

A is for antecedent:

What happens just *before* the behavior occurs?

B is for behavior:

What does the child actually do?

C is for consequence:

What happens immediately following the behavior?

Step 2: Carefully describe the unacceptable behavior.

What does the child actually do? Describe the sequence:

- Child looks at teacher.
- Child begins to scream.
- As teacher approaches, child runs toward door.

When does he do it?

Where does the behavior occur?

Who is usually present when the behavior occurs?

Step 3: Hypothesize about why this behavior occurs.

Is the cause internal (e.g., medication, illness, fatigue, low threshold)?

Is the child trying to escape?

Is the child trying to get attention?

Is the child trying to obtain a desirable object or activity?

Step 4: Determine possible communicative value of the behavior.

Is the child using this behavior to try to tell us something from Step 2?

- "I'm in pain."
- "Let me out of here!"
- "Please touch me (look at me, talk to me, come close to me)."
- "I would rather play with the Legos™ or be outside on the swing."

Step 5: Identify behavior triggers.

Use information from Step 1 regarding the antecedent.

What sets off the child's behavior?

Step 6: Plan environmental changes to reduce triggering the behavior. In other words, change the antecedent.

For example:

- Place certain items out of reach.
- Keep other children a certain distance away.
- Change acoustic characteristics of the room to dampen sound.

Step 7: Identify replacement behavior, if appropriate.

For example:

- Child will make sign for "stop" rather than hitting.
- Child will point to card that says "Quiet Zone" when he needs to escape to a less stimulating area.
- Child will sign "all done" when he is full rather than dumping food.

Step 8: Carefully plan with staff what the consequence will be if the behavior still occurs occasionally.

Remember, if you choose to use an extinction procedure, the behavior will probably occur more often for a while.

Step 9: Monitor frequency and intensity of behavior to make sure it is decreasing.

Teachers must realize the behavior is not going to just suddenly disappear overnight using this procedure. Thus it is important to periodically *measure* the behavior (in terms of how many times per day the behavior occurs or how long the behavior episode lasts) to determine if it is gradually decreasing. Often teachers think the procedure is not working and abandon it too quickly.

Julian's Towel

Julian is a four-year-old with Down syndrome who was recently placed in a Head Start program. Julian is an only child of older parents, and this was his first experience in group care. His teachers complained that whenever he was in the manipulatives area (a U-shaped configuration of shelves with containers of Legos™, small blocks, dominoes, and other toys), Julian would frequently throw manipulatives around and would sometimes bite other children. The teachers reported that he did not play appropriately with any of the toys there, though occasionally when the area was less crowded, he would entertain himself by dumping the Legos™ back and forth from one container to another.

Working together with the inclusion support specialist using an ABC analysis, the teachers quickly identified that Julian was most likely to be aggressive when other children got too close to him. Several simple interventions eliminated this behavior challenge.

1. The teacher limited the number of children who could play in the small manipulative area at any one time.
2. The teacher bought a beach towel with Disney characters on it (Julian's favorites) for Julian to sit on when he played in this area. The other children were taught that this was Julian's space; if they wished to share the towel space with Julian, they need to ask permission. (see Figure 4–6)
3. Julian was taught a replacement behavior to use instead of biting when a child did bump or crowd him. He learned to extend his arm to convey "you're too close!"
4. If Julian did bite someone or have an outburst of throwing things, he was immediately removed from the area and placed in a less preferred play center.

Within a month of consistently using these procedures.
- Several children requested their own towels to sit on!
- Julian learned to use the arm signal fairly quickly, though the other children did not always comply.
- By the end of the month biting had disappeared and the frequency of throwing things had diminished.
- A peer was able to engage Julian in dumping and filling a toy dump truck with Legos™.
- Julian's tolerance for other children crowding and touching him had signficantly decreased.

Figure 4–6   Example of a space buffer.

SUMMARY

Behavior problems present some of the greatest challenges to successful inclusion of children with disabilities. It is critical that teachers design classrooms in ways that decrease the likelihood that difficult behaviors will emerge. There are also effective strategies for preventing behavior problems before they occur. Despite use of these best practices, however, some children need carefully planned interventions. Early childhood educators must be realistic and understand that in these cases they may not have the time, resources, or staff necessary to adequately manage and accommodate for such a child. It is only with the teamwork of parents, specialists, and inclusion support personnel that an optimal solution can be implemented. This is a standard worth pursuing.

CASE STUDY

Roberto's Behavior Intervention Plan

Roberto is a four-year-old with severe communication delays. His speech is difficult to understand. He speaks infrequently, in one- and two-word utterances. Roberto frequently pushed other children or fell into them. Roberto's teacher believed this behavior was simply aggression that needed to be controlled. She had been using a time-out procedure, but it did not seem to be working. The pushing had actually increased. In consultation with the inclusion support facilitator and a behavior specialist, the teacher decided to do a careful ABC analysis.

Careful data collection by the behavior specialist over several days showed that at the beginning of the day Roberto would engage in solitary play for only a few minutes. He would then begin looking around the room. He consistently appeared to focus on the same two children, approach whichever child was closer, and say something in jargon. Then as the child looked at him, he would push the child, laugh, and run a couple of feet away. Then he turned to watch what happened. The pushed child usually fell down (Roberto's choices were the smallest children in the class) and began to cry. An adult would intervene by taking the assaulted child over to talk to Roberto, encouraging the child to say, "I don't like that." The adult would then explain to Roberto what he had done wrong and place him in a time-out corner.

The team discussed the results of these observations and decided that Roberto was receiving a great deal of attention for the pushing behavior both from the adult and from peers. This was rewarding! He was not being helped to approach children in more appropriate ways to get their attention and play appropriately with them. They decided to enact a behavior plan that incorporated positive support and a modified time out with redirection as a last resort.

The support plan requires an adult to watch Roberto when he is engaged in solitary play. As he begins to look around the room at peers, the adult moves physically closer and begins shadowing him. As he approaches a peer, the adult touches Roberto's arm and says, "Tell her, 'I want to play.'" As he comes closer to the child with arms outstretched to push her, the adult increases physical control and continues to prompt him to say, "I want to play." After doing this consistently for several days, Roberto begins to need less physical intervention by adults. When given the prompt, he says "Play," and he does not push. The child is encouraged to stay near Roberto (with the adult close by) and play.

There are still occasions, however, when an adult cannot shadow Roberto and he pushes a child. When this occurs, a time-out intervention is implemented. One adult immediately approaches and comforts the pushed child while another adult sits Roberto in the closest chair available. The adult uses no eye contact and says, "You need to stop. You may not push." Roberto sits in the chair for one minute while the adult stands nearby without looking at him. At the end of the minute, the adult looks at him and reiterates, "You may not push *child's name.* Choose another place to play." He is not allowed to return to that child and the adult stays next to him until he reengages in an appropriate activity in another area.

This time-out scenario has been used over three weeks. Eventually, the physical assistance is faded completely as Roberto begins to respond to the teacher's voice issuing a warning: "You need to use your words." After one month, Roberto often looks at the teacher as he approaches a child. If his arm is held forward (as if to push), the teacher says his name sternly. Often he drops his arm, says "Want play," and sits down next to the child.

Occasionally Roberto is observed beginning to approach a peer in an excited or agitated manner; then he slows down and looks for a chair! He sits down on his own for several seconds before standing up and approaching the peer in a more controlled and appropriate manner. Roberto is clearly learning self-regulation and impulse control. He learned this gradually by being taught that an appropriate replacement behavior was more likely to get him the peer attention he needs and that the aggressive pushing consistently results in loss of attention and interaction, a consequence that is not reinforcing.

Case Study Questions

1. *The use of time out as a strategy for managing difficult behavior must be planned and implemented carefully. What are the critical factors in use of time out to ensure safety and developmental appropriateness?*
2. *Do you think these factors were considered in Roberto's case?*
3. *Is there anything you would change in the behavior plan used for Roberto?*

KEY TERMS

ABC analysis
aversive stimulus
behavior modification
communicative function
consequence
extinction
internal state
one-to-one aide

positive behavior support
punishment
reinforcer
replacement behavior
self-stimulatory behavior
tactile defensiveness
time out

HELPFUL RESOURCES

Articles and Books

Cook, R., Tessier, A., & Klein, M. D. (2000). Promoting social and emotional development. *Adapting early childhood curricula for children in inclusive settings* (pp. 196–245). Columbus, OH: Merrill/Prentice Hall.

Division for Early Childhood. (1999). Practical ideas for addressing challenging behaviors. *Young Children Monograph Series.* Denver, CO: Sopris West.

Essa, A. (1998). *A practical guide to solving preschool behavior problems.* Albany, NY: Delmar.

Katz, L. G., & McClellan, D. E. (1997). *Fostering children's social competence.* Washington, DC: National Association for the Education of Young Children.

Koegel, L. K., Koegel, R. L., & Dunlap, G. (Eds.). (1996). *Positive behavior support: Including people with difficult behavior in the community.* Baltimore, MD: Paul H. Brookes.

Neilsen, S. L., Olive, M. L., Donovan, A., & McEvoy, M. (1998). Challenging behaviors in your classroom? Don't react—teach instead! *Exceptional Young Children, 1*(10), 2–8.

Porter, L. (1999). *Young children's behavior: Practical approaches for caregivers and teachers.* Baltimore, MD: Paul H. Brookes.

Strain, P., & Hemmeter, M. L. (1997). Keys to being successful when confronted with challenging behaviors. *Exceptional Young Children, 1*(1), 2–8.

Walker, J. E., & Shea, T. M. (1999). *Behavior management: A practical approach for educators.* Upper Saddle River, NJ: Prentice Hall.

Organizations

Council for Children with Behavior Disorders, Web site: <www.ccbd.net>

The Division for Treatment and Education of Autistic and Related Communication Handicapped Children (TEACCH), University of North Carolina, Chapel Hill, School of Medicine, 310 Medical School, Wing E, CB 7180, (919) 966-2174, Web site: <www.unc.edu/depts/teacch/teacch.htm>

Empowering People: Positive Discipline, Web site: <www.positivediscipline.com>

National Association for School Psychologists, 4340 East West Highway, Suite 402, Bethesda, MD 20814.

Videos

Understanding and managing behavior of young children, Learner Managed Designs, Inc., P.O. Box 747, Lawrence, KS 66044, (800) 467-1644.

REFERENCES

Cook, R., Tessier, A., & Klein, M. D. (2000). *Adapting early childhood curricula for children in inclusive settings* (5th ed.). Columbus, OH: Merrill/ Prentice Hall.

Koegle, L. K., Koegel, R. L., & Dunlap, G. (Eds.). (1996). *Positive behavior support: Including people with difficult behavior in the community.* Baltimore, MD: Paul H. Brookes.

5

Monitoring Individual Child Progress

Chapter-at-a-Glance

A key to successful inclusion of children with special needs is ongoing monitoring of their progress

Specific documents and procedures are used to outline educational goals and monitor the progress of children with special needs.

- **The Individualized Family Services Plan (IFSP) and Individualized Education Plan (IEP) are legal documents.** Each child with special needs placed in an inclusive setting will have either an IFSP or an IEP that spells out the specific goals, outcomes, and priorities for that child.
- **The teacher must have those documents.** If the parents and/or service coordinator don't provide a copy, the teacher should request one.
- **The teacher, parents and specialists must plan how the child's goals will be addressed in the ECE program.** The child's specific goals are included in the IEP or IFSP.
- **The child's progress must be monitored and documented.** The ECE teacher must work with the inclusion specialist to determine who is responsible for each aspect of progress monitoring.
- **Progress must be monitored on a regular basis.** The progress monitoring system must be designed so that it is easy to use and functional.

INTRODUCTION

Early educators need to realize that an Individualized Family Service Plan (IFSP) or an Individualized Education Plan (IEP) has been developed for

101

each child who is eligible for special education support or services. These are legal documents that result from a process involving individual child and family assessment and multidisciplinary planning.

If the child is under three years old, then the document is referred to as an **Individualized Family Services Plan (IFSP).** It contains a list of the services that must be provided to the family to meet the child's needs. It also contains specific outcome statements that teachers should use as guides when they plan adaptations or activities for the child.

For children over three years old, an **Individualized Education Plan (IEP)** is used. It contains specific goals and objectives that also should guide program planning. Teachers should request and carefully review these documents. They can be obtained from the parents, from the **service coordinator,** or from a special educator who provides **inclusion support.**

Early childhood programs that include young children with special needs must assist children in achieving the specific goals, objectives, or outcomes that are contained in these documents. This chapter will briefly discuss these individual plans and programs and will present ways of monitoring children's progress toward reaching the stated goals, objectives, or outcomes.

THE INDIVIDUALIZED FAMILY SERVICE PLAN (IFSP)

The IFSP is the written document specified in the law to guide the implementation of services for infants and toddlers from birth to age three. Formats for the IFSP document vary from state to state, but in all cases the outcomes described in the IFSP should be the result of a collaborative process between families and professionals involved in assessing and serving the child and family. Therefore, it is desirable for any agency serving the child to be a part of the IFSP process. Other participants include the parent or parents of the child, other family members as desired by the parent(s), an advocate if requested by the family, the child's service coordinator, a person or persons involved in the assessment process, and others who may be providing direct services to the child and family, such as a physical therapist or speech-language pathologist. The two parts of the IFSP that relate most closely to the goals for the child and family are the Family Concerns section and the Outcome Statements.

Family Concerns

These are often stated in the parents' words and reflect what concerns them in regard to their child's developmental progress or their ability to parent the child effectively. Families are encouraged to prioritize their concerns related to both family issues and concerns about the child.

Examples follow:

We are concerned about our ability to help our child learn. Cerebral palsy seems like such a serious disability.

Our greatest priority is that he have friends someday.

Outcome Statements

Each IFSP must include outcome statements that clearly state changes family members want to occur for their child or themselves. In other words, what do they hope will happen over the next six months. These outcome statements are expected to directly reflect the family concerns and are used to guide the choice of services to be delivered. These statements should refer to practical activities that fit into a family's daily life and represent skills that enhance the child's ability to cope with daily environmental demands. Early childhood educators should plan adaptations and involve the child in activities clearly designed to help promote the changes listed in the outcome statements. Examples of such outcome statements follow:

Mr. and Mrs. Gomez will attend the support group at Centro de Ninos y Padres in order to learn more about parenting a child with cerebral palsy.

Jose will make more attempts to communicate to let people know what he wants and to positively interact with others.

Early childhood educators can use the outcome statements as guides in assisting parents to obtain services, planning activities appropriate for all children, selecting strategies, adapting environments, and recording progress. In addressing the outcome statements for the Gomez family, information is provided to parents about how to become involved in an appropriate support group. Perhaps Mr. and Mrs. Gomez might be introduced to other parents who are available to answer questions and provide support and encouragement. Jose will be included in activities that encourage communication, and specific strategies will be planned to foster positive interaction with others. His attempts to communicate will be charted to note progress before his IFSP is reviewed after six months.

An IFSP must be developed for each child within 45 days of initial referral for special education services, and it must be reviewed and updated every six months. Early educators must be certain that the contents of the most recent version of each child's IFSP is available to be used in activity planning. They should realize that parents must give written permission to their service coordinator to make the contents known to anyone not directly involved in the IFSP process.

THE INDIVIDUALIZED EDUCATION PLAN (IEP)

The IEP is the legal document that directs services for a child over the age of three. It is the result of a multidisciplinary assessment and planning process conducted by the local public school district in which a child lives. Again, early educators who serve children with special needs should seek to be involved in this process if at all possible. Others who may be involved include:

- The child's parents or guardians
- At least one regular education teacher if the child is involved in a regular education program
- A member of the school staff who is qualified to provide supervision of any specially designed instruction
- An individual who can interpret assessment results
- A school administrator who can make commitments for the school district
- Other individuals whose expertise may be desired by the family or child

The IEP often differs from the IFSP in that it contains more specific statements related to goals and objectives, rather than the sometimes broadly stated outcomes found in the IFSP. Early educators should pay particular attention to the goals and objectives listed on the IEP.

Identifying Person(s) Responsible for Achievement of Goals

At the time of this publication, policies at both the state and federal levels do not clearly identify who is the individual responsible for monitoring the child's progress toward annual goals and for insuring that these goals are met. The ECE teacher should attempt to determine what individual or individuals are responsible for meeting the IEP or IFSP goals. Without this accountability the effectiveness of the document is undermined. The ECE teacher can begin with the school district or state agency responsible for generating the IFSP or IEP. Parents must also be part of the process of determining who will take responsibility for monitoring and achieving goals.

Goals and Objectives

IEPs are required to include year-long goals and short-term objectives that represent achievements on the way toward reaching the annual goal. With parent permission, early educators should review the IEP goals and objectives that are recorded for each child. These should be systematically incorporated into the child's daily activities. Daily activities and teaching strategies used should help the child make steady progress toward each objective. For example, note the following goal and objectives.

Long-Term Goal—*Marti will cooperatively play with her peers.*
Short-term Objectives—*While in the dramatic play area with one or two other children:*
    Marti will share the dress-up clothes.
    Marti will show some response to the verbal initiations of others.

Daily Instructional Objectives

When writing daily instructional objectives, educators should include behaviors and teaching activities that typically occur or can be easily incorporated into routine activities. (Examples of how to break down daily activities into small, teachable steps are included in Chapter 1.) These objectives should contain three components:

1. Under what conditions will the child be expected to demonstrate the behavior? What will the adult do? In what activity? Where? For example:
    "When playing in the block area with no more than three children . . ."
    "When given no more than two verbal prompts . . ."
    "After being assisted to move from the table to the sink . . ."
2. What will the child do? Describe the desired behavior in detail so all adults know exactly what to look for. For example:
    "Jeremy will play comfortably alongside other children without hitting or running away."
    "Sarah will sign 'Eat cookie' to request a snack."
    "Joshue will place his cup and plate in the sink and will place his napkin in the trash, without prompts."
3. How well or how often do you expect the child to perform the behavior? How do you know the child has achieved the objective? What are the criteria? When can you move on to the next step or the next level of performance? For example:
    ". . . for at least five minutes on four out of five days over a two-week period."
    ". . . on three of five occasions over a three-week period."
    ". . . without being restrained will kick no more than once each day over a one-month period."

The following objectives might guide daily activities designed to accomplish the long-range goal stated earlier for Marti.

1. Marti will tolerate two other children being in the dramatic play space and will not hit or cry when another child puts on a clothing article, in three out of four different occasions over a two-week period.
2. With no more than a single verbal prompt from an adult, Marti will initiate at least one interaction and will respond appropriately (nondisruptively) to another child's initiation at least once in each dramatic play episode over a one-month period.

PLANNING INCLUSION SUPPORT AND MONITORING PROGRESS

Developing an IEP requires careful consideration of the strategies likely to be most effective in supporting inclusion and monitoring progress.

Defining the Purpose of Inclusion Support

When planning specific interventions and strategies for inclusion support and considering ways of monitoring progress, an important question is *progress toward what?* Families and professionals must determine what constitutes successful inclusion. For example, successful inclusion could be defined as the child being able to "participate in some way in all activities in the daily schedule." Some might add to this definition, "with a minimum of disruption and interference in the smooth operation of the program." Another definition might add "demonstrating steady progress toward IEP goals and objectives." These represent different standards and thus may require different types or levels of support.

Types of Inclusion Support. Inclusion support is provided in a variety of ways, depending on the needs and desired outcomes for the child. The terms *adaptations* and *accommodations* generally refer to environmental changes that can be made to provide access to the early childhood setting and enable the child to participate in all activities. Though the terms *adaptation* and *accommodation* tend to be used interchangeably, **adaptation** is more likely to be used in reference to something children use to enable them to adapt to or fit into a setting or activity. Adaptations include using equipment like a wheelchair or walker for a child who is not ambulatory, attaching a specially designed paintbrush to the child's hand with Velcro, and using assistive technology to enable the child to communicate or turn on a battery-operated toy. The term **accommodation** is more likely to refer to a change in the larger environment (or program policies) that removes barriers and allows comfortable access to an environment. Such accommodations would include adding access ramps, rearranging the space in a classroom, providing a one-to-one aide to keep a child from running away, placing high-contrast markers to help a child identify certain materials, providing a developmentally simpler task for a child with a cognitive disability, or reducing the ambient noise in a classroom to accommodate the needs of a child wearing a hearing aid or a child who is sensitive to certain sounds.

Adaptations and accommodations need to be planned carefully and are obviously necessary for many children to remain in the inclusive setting. While access is a legal right and is necessary, many families and professionals insist that access alone is not sufficient. They advocate for the use of **specialized teaching techniques and strategies** to enable the child to learn specific skills and achieve IEP goals. Examples of these might include speech and language training techniques, physical therapy techniques to teach ambulation, step-by-step techniques to teach self-feeding or bladder control, sensory integration techniques to help a child with self-regulation, specific training to teach Braille or sign language, and use of task analysis to help a child master certain daily living skill sequences and achieve greater independence.

Rationale for Progress Monitoring

Many early childhood programs are not accustomed to systematically recording the developmental progress of children. However, when children with special needs are included, certain information must be recorded, updated regularly, and made available to parents and other members of the child's intervention team. That is, progress must be monitored on a regular basis. Progress monitoring is critical for children with special needs for several reasons.

1. The law requires that efforts to achieve outcomes and goals stated in the IFSP or the IEP be planned and carried out. Thus there must be some documentation that the plan is being implemented.
2. Progress for a child with special needs may occur slowly and in very small steps. Without careful data recording, it may be difficult to know for sure if the child is learning the desired skills and behaviors.
3. It is important to determine whether or not a particular intervention or teaching strategy is effective and whether steady progress is being made toward achieving the child's outcomes and goals. If not, a change must be made in the instructional plan and methods.

Ideally, the early childhood teacher would rely on the inclusion support provider to design and implement data recording systems. Realistically however, this level of support may not be available for every child.

Obviously, for children included in large group settings, the monitoring system must be simple or it will not be used. In addition, the system must be designed to be functional; notes and records must be able to used immediately to make adjustments in program adaptations whenever necessary. In short, records of each child's progress must be kept, and that the system must be simple enough to be used on a regular basis (see Figure 5–1).

Figure 5–1   Behavior specialist monitoring child.

Types of Data Recording

The kinds of data recording addressed here are informal records that will assist with evaluation and documentation of child progress on an ongoing basis. More formal evaluations will also be carried out at annual intervals by special educators and therapists to determine whether new goals need to be identified and to recommend appropriate program modifications or placement changes. The following discussion of data recording considers the purposes as well as the formats. Three purposes are described: (1) assessment, (2) planning, and (3) progress monitoring.

Informal Assessment. Some informal assessment is usually necessary to plan effectively for inclusion support. Two examples of informal assessment are an Activity/Standards Inventory (Beukelman & Mirenda, 1992), and systematic observation of child behaviors. Careful observations of the child in various activities can be made to determine her greatest needs for support. Here are examples of the kinds of systematic observations that may be helpful. Observe *each* of the following for at least three minutes:

- Observe the child playing alone and list what the child does.
- Observe the child playing with toys or objects and describe how the child uses the toys. Also describe the child's pace of activity.

ACTIVITY/STANDARDS INVENTORY

Child's name: <u>Frankie</u>   Date: <u>9-15-2001</u>

Situation/Activity	Peer Behavior How do peers participate?	Target Child Behavior	Barriers to Participation
Requesting song during circle time	Call out name of song	Waves hands; vocalizes	No way to make song selection audible and intelligible to teacher

Figure 5–2   Activity standards inventory.

- Observe how long the child plays with one toy. How often does the child switch activities?
- Observe the child playing with other children. What does the child do during that time? Does she initiate interactions with others? Does she respond to initiations of other children?
- Observe the child with an adult. How does the child interact with the adult?

An **activity/standards inventory** (see Figure 5–2) carefully observes how the children *without* disabilities participate in an activity (hence the *standard*) and compares this with the participation of the child who has special needs. The differences, or discrepancies, between the two are noted. Then the barriers that are responsible for the discrepancies are analyzed, and the necessary adaptations to enable the child to participate are identified and planned.

Finally, the IEP goals and objectives for each child should be obtained and summarized. They should be readily available for frequent review, and they should be incorporated into the planning documents described in the next section.

Planning Inclusion Support. Figure 5–3 is a checklist summarizing the kinds of adaptations that may be necessary for a child.

More specifically, the adaptations and teaching strategies to be used to support the child's successful participation in each activity of the day must be planned and written on an easily understood form. In addition, specific strategies that are necessary to help the child learn certain skills related to IEP objectives must also be written on a planning form. This should be done both for the routine activities in the daily schedule and for special activities. Figure 5–4 describes the support that will be used for a given child in each daily activity.

Child's Name:_____ Date:_____

Inclusion Adaptations Checklist
Check adaptations anticipated for this child.

PERSONNEL
_____ No extra support necessary
_____ Part-time extra support (specific parts of day)
_____ Full-time extra support (1:1 aide)

PHYSICAL ASSISTANCE
_____ No physical help necessary
_____ Physical help as needed
_____ Partial physical help
_____ Full physical help

CURRICULUM
_____ Adapt for lower cognitive level
_____ Adapt for vision impairments
_____ Adapt for hearing impairments
_____ Adapt for physical handicaps

PACING AND AMOUNT OF TIME PER ACTIVITIES
_____ Same pace and time as all other children
_____ Less time than other children (e.g., less attention)
_____ More time than other children (e.g., goes slower)
_____ Slower pacing necessary for understanding (e.g., more wait time for comprehension and/or action)

HIERARCHY OF PROMPTS
_____ Full physical help to complete activities
_____ Partial physical help to complete activities
_____ Direct verbal reminders to complete activities (e.g., "Sit down")
_____ Indirect verbal reminders to complete activities (e.g., "What do you need to do?")
_____ Gestures to complete activities (e.g., pointing)

ENVIRONMENT
_____ Seating adaptations (e.g., chairs too high, child does better sitting next to specific peers, etc.)
_____ Reduce/minimize distractions or stimulation
_____ Define limits (e.g., physical and/or behavioral)

BEHAVIOR
_____ Define limits (e.g., physical and/or behavioral)
_____ Use positive reinforcement
_____ Determine behavior plans through use of ABC (antecedent, behavior, consequences)

Figure 5–3 Inclusion adaptations checklist.

INDIVIDUAL SUPPORT SCHEDULE

CHILD'S NAME: J.T.   **DATE:** 9-15-2001

TEACHER NAME(S): Martha   **CENTER:** Kid's Place

INCLUSION CONSULTANT'S NAME: Anne

SCHEDULE	SPECIFIC SUPPORTS / ADAPTATIONS (what staff will do for child that will help child be part of activities)
ARRIVAL	Assign favorite adult to greet J.T. Help him find cubby; prompt him only if necessary Use consistent phrase: "Find your cubby"
MORNING ACTIVITIES (FREE PLAY)	Encourage JT to play next to peer, then face back If he begins self stimulatory behavior, try to re-engage him w/peer
CLEAN-UP	Give JT one simple direction at a time: "Put the block in the box" (Provide physical assistance if necessary) "Now, put the box on the shelf."
TOILET/HAND WASH	Etc.
SNACK	
CIRCLE TIME	
SMALL GROUP (WORK TIME)	
OUTSIDE PLAY	

Figure 5–4   Individual support schedule.

OBJECTIVE-BY-ACTIVITY MATRIX

Child's Name Rafik   Date: 10-30-2001

OBJECTIVE

ACTIVITY	Self feeding	Take off jacket	Requesting	Using marker	Attend to story
9:00 Arrival		X			
9:15 Free Play			X	X	
9:30 Circle			X		X
9:45 Centers			X	X	X
10:15 Outside		X			
10:45 Potty					
11:15 Snack	X		X		
11:30 Story/Music					X
11:45 Departure					

Figure 5–5   Objective-by-activity matrix.

An **objective-by-activity matrix** (see Figure 5–5) is a commonly used planning form that depicts where IEP objectives will be addressed across the activities of the daily schedule. Each activity in the daily schedule is placed on a grid. At the top each IEP goal is listed. Within the matrix, notes can be made related to whether and how that goal will be addressed during each of the daily activities. (This could also be used as a weekly recording form to comment on how the child performed during each of the daily activities.)

It is also important to plan specifically for a special, nonroutine event. Novel, unfamiliar, or unexpected activities can be stressful for many children who have special needs. For this reason, it is important to plan ahead and try to anticipate extra supports that may be necessary to enable the child to access and enjoy the activity (see Figure 5–6).

Data Recording to Monitor Progress. When keeping track of progress toward the accomplishment of IFSP outcomes or IEP goals or objectives, **anecdotal record keeping** can be a simple yet effective record-keeping strategy. Anecdotal records, diaries, or logs may be kept on a daily, weekly or biweekly basis. One simple strategy for recording observations is to make a single page for each child, listing the outcomes or objectives in each domain along one side of the page and leaving ample space to write comments next to each outcome or objective. Each week the progress for each outcome or

SPECIAL ACTIVITY PLAN

Child's name J.T. | **Date: Sept 30, 2001**

ACTIVITY	STRATEGIES
Description: Trip to library. Students will walk 1 block to library for preschool story time	**Peers:** Assign "best friend" to walk with JT, holding his hand
Purpose & Objective(s): For Group: To learn about the library: Goal for JT: To handle unfamiliar situation without trying to escape	
Materials: None	**Adults: 1.** Begin to prepare JT the day before by showing him photo of library and use the phrase "Go for a walk to the library" **2.** Will keep close proximity to JT, and will keep him away from street, will take his other hand if he becomes upset

• EVALUATION •

Outcomes:

Suggestions for Future Activities:

Figure 5–6   Special activity plan.

ANECDOTAL RECORD OF DEVELOPMENTAL PROGRESS	
Name: Marti	**Date: 10-20-2001**
SUMMARY OF OBJECTIVES	**COMMENTS**
Social Skills 1. Increase # of children Marti will tolerate 2. Increase appropriate social initiations 3.	1. Has played with Sharon and Fabio several times this week 2. Offered Sun Yee one of her Barbies
Communication 1. Will use signs to request play materials 2. Will use sign to request choice of snack 3. Will sign "stop" when children try to take away toy	1. Still only does this if prompted 2. Will use either "juice" or "milk" sign at snack—now does this consistently. 3. Still hitting children. Procedure doesn't seem to be working
Motor Skills 1. 2. N.A. 3.	
Self-Help 1. Will clean up after lunch w/o prompts 2. 3.	Has met this goal—has done this appropriately for the past two weeks. Will begin working on putting his jacket and getting backpack at end of day.

Figure 5–7   Anecdotal recording form for monitoring student progress.

objective is summarized, providing a running narrative of progress across all targeted outcomes or objectives. This information is then readily available to review during parent conferences and during team planning meetings. A sample of such a record sheet is shown in Figure 5–7.

More precise **data recording** procedures may sometimes be necessary to monitor progress toward specific goals where change has been slow or inconsistent. For example, it may be important to determine whether a specific behavior plan is working or whether progress is being made in toilet training. When change occurs slowly it may be impossible to objectively determine whether there is improvement through informal observation and

PROGRESS DATA

NAME: Jon

OBJECTIVE: Jon will urinate when placed on potty

KEY: D = dry   W = wet   V = vocalized
P = placed on potty
+ = urinated in potty   — did not urinate in potty

Time	MONDAY	TUESDAY	WEDNESDAY	THURSDAY	FRIDAY
8:00	D	D	D	D	D
8:30	W	W	P—	VP+	P+
9:00	D	D	W	D	D
9:30	D	D	D	D	D
10:00	D	VP—	D	D	D
10:30	VP—	D	D	VW	VP+
11:00	W	W	VP+	D	D
11:30	D	W	D	D	D

Figure 5–8   Monitoring progress in toilet training.

anecdotal records alone. In these situations it may be necessary to keep more precise records. Figures 5–8 and 5–9 are examples of data recording to monitor two different objectives: toileting and self-feeding.

It can also be helpful to simply monitor the child's participation in each activity of the day. It is useful to record whether the child performed the task independently or with assistance, as shown in Figure 5–10.

Another example of the need for precise data recording is to monitor changes in disruptive behavior, such as the use of an ABC analysis. Refer to Chapter 4 for a review of this topic.

Blank forms and additional examples of planning and data recording forms are included in Appendix A. (Also, see Bricker, 1998)

Issues Related to Resources for Progress Monitoring

Careful progress monitoring can be time consuming and sometimes labor intensive. This can be a challenge in typical early childhood settings. These strategies may be helpful.

- Assign a portion of the progress monitoring responsibility to the inclusion support provider.
- Use trainees or volunteers as data recorders.

115

PROGRESS SUMMARY

Name: Sung Lee   **Week: Jan 7–11**

OBJECTIVE: Drink from cup independently at lunch

KEY: + = bring cup to mouth independently, holding cup with both hands
$\oplus$ = support at elbow only
A = total assistance required

Trials	MONDAY	TUESDAY	WEDNESDAY	THURSDAY	FRIDAY
1.	A	A	$\oplus$	A	A
2.	A	A	A	A	$\oplus$
3.	A	$\oplus$	A	$\oplus$	+
4.	A	$\oplus$	$\oplus$	+	+
5.	A	A	+	+	+
6.	A	A	A	$\oplus$	$\oplus$
7.	A	A	A	$\oplus$	+

Figure 5–9   Monitoring progress in self-feeding.

Child's Name Sheree   **Week of Oct 7–11**

LEVEL OF PARTICIPATION IN DAILY ACTIVITIES

ACTIVITY	Monday	Tuesday	Wednesday	Thursday	Friday
Free play	wandered	X-A	X-A	Wandered	X-I
Circle	X-A	X-A	X-I	X-I	X-I
Outside play	wandered	wandered	X-A	X-A	wandered
Snack	X-I	X-I	X-I	X-I	Refused snack
Toileting	Refused	X-A	X-A	X-A	X-A
Centers	wandered	wandered	X-A	wandered	wandered
Computers	X-I	X-I	X-I	X-I	X-I
Good-bye circle	X-A	X-A	X-I	wandered	X-A

X = Participation
A = Participated with assistance
I = Participated Independently

Figure 5–10   Level of participation in daily activities.

116

- Keep Post-Its® handy and collect them at the end of the day and simply paste them into a record book.
- Keep duplicates of forms around the room in each activity center.

SUMMARY

While the importance and social advantages of inclusion in a high-quality early childhood program cannot be overstated, it is equally important to ensure that the specific goals identified for children with special needs are met. To help children achieve their potential, educators must take care to address and carefully monitor progress toward specific outcomes. Just as important, when this monitoring indicates that progress is not being made, changes in curriculum and teaching strategies can be made in a timely fashion.

CASE STUDY

Lazaro's Potty Training

Lazaro's mother expressed a great deal of frustration that, even though he was potty trained at home, she still had to send him to school in diapers. The teachers commented that they had tried putting him in training pants a few times, but he was still having accidents and they just didn't think he was ready. Lazaro is nearly five years old and would be transitioning into a regular kindergarten. However, his mother knew that if he was not toilet trained, he would present a major challenge to the kindergarten teacher.

Lazaro's teacher, Sarah, agreed to work with the early childhood special educator to prioritize this important goal. The first step was to take careful data to determine whether Lazaro's bowel habits were regular and also to determine if Lazaro was currently using any communicative cues indicating that he needed to go to the bathroom.

A simple recording system was devised. A student from a local community college volunteered to take data. Every hour the volunteer checked Lazaro to see if he had had a bowel movement. The teacher also recorded what Lazaro's activity had been during the time period prior to the bowel movement. After three weeks, they could detect no regular pattern related to time. However they noted that he was most likely to go following vigorous exercise of some kind. They also noted that he frequently stopped in the middle of whatever he was doing and put his hand briefly on his stomach.

After evaluating this data, a plan was devised in which they would watch him carefully following any energetic activity. As soon as he touched his stomach the teacher would say in a very positive way, "Lazaro, let's go to the bathroom!" Fairly quickly, Lazaro started looking for the teacher and trying to make eye contact when he felt the need to void. All the staff were particularly vigilant and sensitive to his cues, until he was consistently indicating his need to go and he could delay voiding until he was placed on the potty.

(continued)

Case Study Questions

1. *Careful data collection and record keeping are often labor intensive. What are some ways of dealing with this problem in programs that are already short staffed?*
2. *How might greater involvement of the parent have been helpful in Lazaro's toilet training at school?*
3. *Can you think of ways of structuring the daily schedule of a child care program that would build in support for toilet training for all the children who need it?*

KEY TERMS

accommodations
activity/standards inventory
adaptations
anecdotal record keeping
data recording
inclusion support

Individualized Education Plan (IEP)
Individualized Family Services Plan (IFSP)
objectives-by-activity matrix
service coordinator
specialized teaching techniques and
  strategies

HELPFUL RESOURCES

Allen, K. E., & Marotz, L. (1999). *Developmental profiles: Pre-birth through eight* (3rd ed.). Albany, NY: Delmar.

Arena, J. (1996). *How to write an I.E.P.* Novato, CA: Academic Therapy Publications.

Beaty, J. J. (1997). *Observing development of the young child.* Englewood Cliffs, NJ: Merrill/Prentice Hall.

Benjamin, A. C. (1994). Observations in early childhood classrooms: Advice from the field. *Young Children, 49*(6), 14–20.

Beukelman, D. R., & Mirenda, P. (1998). *Augmentative and alternative communication: Management of severe communication disorders in Children and Adults.* Baltimore, MD: Paul H. Brookes.

Boehm, A. E., & Weinberg, R. A. (1997). *The classroom observer: Developing observation skills in early childhood settings.* New York: Teachers College Press.

Bricker, D. (1998). *An activity based approach to early intervention* (pp. 149–169). Baltimore, MD: Paul H. Brookes.

Cohen, D. H., Stern, V., & Bataban, N. (1997). *Observing and recording the behavior of young children* (4th ed.). New York: Teachers College Press.

Cook, R. E., Tessier, A., & Klein, M. D. (1999). *Adapting early childhood curricula for children in inclusive settings* (5th ed.). Englewood Cliffs, NJ: Merrill/Prentice Hall.

Johnson-Martin, N. M., Jens, K. G., Attermeier, S. M., & Hacker, B. J. (1991). *The Carolina curriculum for infants and toddlers with special needs.* Baltimore, MD: Paul H. Brookes.

McGonigel, M. M., Kaufmann, R. K., & Johnson, B. H. (Eds.). (1991). *Guidelines and recommended practices for the individualized family service plan* (2nd ed.). Bethesda, MD: Association for the Care of Children's Health.

Niolson, S., & Shipstead, S. G. (1998). *Through the looking glass: Observations in the early childhood classroom.* Upper Saddle River, NJ: Merrill/Prentice Hall.

REFERENCES

Beukelman, D. R., & Mirenda, P. (1998). *Augmentative and alternative communication: Management of severe communication disorders in Children and Adults.* Baltimore, MD: Paul H. Brookes.

Bricker, D. (1998). Monitoring and evaluating child progress. In D. Bricker, *An activity based approach to early intervention* (pp 149–169). Baltimore, MD: Paul H. Brookes

Cook, R. E, Tessier, A., & Klein, M. D. (1999). *Adapting early childhood curricula for children in inclusive settings.* (5th ed.). Englewood Cliffs, NJ: Merrill/Prentice Hall.

Part II

Adapting Daily Activities in Inclusive Early Childhood Settings

6

Managing Arrival, Departure, and Other Transitions

Chapter-at-a-Glance

Well-managed transitions can create important teaching and learning opportunities.

Arrival and departure mark important transitions of a child's day. Children with special needs often require assistance with transitions. However, transitions, if planned carefully, can provide important learning opportunities.

- **Arrival, even though it is a routine event, still creates for children a *new experience*.** It may take children with special needs longer to adjust to the hustle and bustle of a typical child care center. This settling-in period each day may need to continue for long as children attend the center.
- **Arrival provides an opportunity to touch base with parents each day.** Some kind of consistent contact with parents is extremely important to successful inclusion of children with special needs.
- **Arrival provides an important opportunity to help children work on separation.** If parents do not stay at the center with their children, separation can be particularly challenging for children with special needs.
- **Arrival and departure can provide occasions to work on many functional skills.** These include taking off and putting on jackets, recognizing one's own name, and mastering the independence of placing and identifying one's belongings in the proper cubby.
- **All transitions need to be carefully planned and viewed as important learning opportunities.** In addition to the major transitions of arrival and departure, transitions occur throughout the day.

INTRODUCTION

Arrival and departure mark the beginning and the end of the center-based day. Thus they represent major **transitions** of the day. For children with special needs these two transitions may pose significant challenges. In addition, transitions from one activity to another that occur within the daily routine of the center-based program can also present difficulties for young children with special needs. Depending upon the nature of the disability, children may find transitions physically or emotionally overwhelming. They may be unsure of what is happening; the increased noise and activity level may feel threatening; and ending a comfortable, familiar activity may be difficult. This chapter suggests strategies for dealing with these challenges and ideas for maximizing the learning potential of these daily events.

ARRIVAL

A child's arrival at an early childhood education center presents both challenges and learning opportunities. In this section we will consider strategies to deal with both.

Arrival Challenges

The Challenge of a New Experience. For many children the early childhood center is a new experience. Even those children who have been attending center-based early intervention programs may find the hustle and bustle—the rapid pace, the noise level, and the large numbers of children—of a typical child care center or preschool program very different, at times even overwhelming.

They will need extra time to *warm up*, both in the long run and in the immediate situation. In other words, the transition into the center may be difficult for several weeks or longer. In addition, children may take an unusually long time each morning to settle in to the routine.

Change in Environment. Even when a child is familiar with the center-based environment, traveling to the center and entering a room containing a number of active children can create a challenging transition, even though it occurs every day.

Separation from Caregiver. **Separation** can be a major hurdle for young children with special needs.

This may be their first experience with separation in a strange environment. Perhaps more often than is the case for typical children, a child with special needs may have had very little or no experience with babysitters and unfamiliar adults. Depending upon the nature of the disability, parents may have difficulty finding competent care providers for their child.

Many parents are simply reluctant to leave their children with anyone other than a familiar family member.

Developmentally, young children may not be ready for separation. A four-year-old who is functioning at the two-year level will have the same difficulty as a two-year-old separating from his primary caregiver.

Caregivers may send ambivalent messages. The parent may be somewhat fearful about how the child will manage in an environment with peers of different functional levels. Young children with special needs seem to be particularly sensitive to the emotional state of their primary caregivers, and their behavior may reflect this anxiety.

Learning Opportunities During Arrival

Depending on how arrival time is managed, educators are presented with many important opportunities for supporting the development of children with special needs (see Figure 6–1).

- Regular opportunity to touch base with a child's parents
- Opportunity to make one-on-one contact in welcoming the child
- Support for transition from home to center

Figure 6–1   Teacher welcoming child and parent.

- Opportunity for development of self-help skills and emergent literacy.
- Consistent arrival routine to create confidence and security in children

Useful Strategies During Arrival Time

Keep Arrival Routine Fairly Consistent. Try to maintain a regular pattern for arrival. For example:

Parent brings the child to the center.
Teacher greets the parent.
Teacher greets the child.
Teacher guides the child to place things in the cubby.
Teacher helps the child transition to the free play area.

Welcome Children at Eye Level. Whenever possible, it is best to speak to young children at eye level. This approach is even more crucial when communicating with children with special needs. It is easier for children to focus on your face and process what you are saying. For children with vision or hearing loss, eye-level communication increases the intensity of the signal by moving closer (see Figure 6–2).

Speak with Parents. Taking this natural opportunity to communicate and build rapport with parents can enhance your understanding of a child's special needs.

Touching base with parents is important. Children with special needs may have health-related concerns, financial issues, and requirements for multiple services that significantly impact the family's daily life. In addition children may have sleep and feeding disorders and behavior problems that further complicate family and child functioning. Parents may find it helpful to explain some of these issues, though they may not necessarily bring up concerns and questions unless they are asked. Also, this information can be helpful to teachers in that it increases their overall understanding of the children.

Ask specific questions to elicit information. Simply asking "How are you?" or "How are things going?" may not be sufficient. You may want to pose questions that invite more detailed information: *"How is Andrew doing this morning?" "Did he have a good night?" "Have there been any problems?"*

Accentuate the positive. Be sure to routinely mention positive things about the child. "He ate a really good lunch yesterday." "Those are great looking new shoes." Also, reinforce the parent: "Thanks so much for your note yesterday; I like that you keep me informed."

Work on establishing true rapport. This type of communication helps establish a rapport with parents that will eventually make it easier for parents to share more difficult information and feelings. Keep in mind:

- The more you know about the child, the easier it will be to support him.
- No one has more information about the child than the parent.
- The better your communication is with the parent, the easier your job will be!

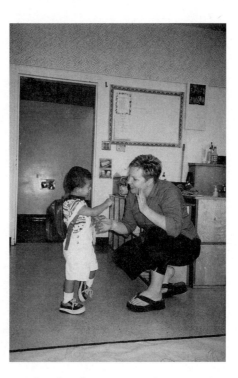

Figure 6–2   An eye-level welcome.

Support Self-Help Skills. Arrival is an easy time to work on independence. Taking off one's jacket, finding the correct cubby, hanging the jacket, and placing a backpack in the proper place are self-help skills that children can usually learn readily with consistent practice and support (see Figure 6–3).

Support Emergent Literacy. Arrival is an easy time to reinforce name recognition. Cubbies should be clearly marked with the children's names. Photos may also be attached. Each day, encourage children to find their own cubby. Point out their printed name. It is also helpful to point out other children's names and to notice the differences: "Oh look, here's Robert's name. His name starts with R just like yours. And here is Ann's. Her name starts with A. Her name is very short."

Children's belongings should also have names on them in clear large print so these names can be compared to the name on the cubby. These simple strategies do not represent a major investment of time, but they can make a significant contribution to children's awareness of print.

Help Children Enter the Free Play Area. Without brief assistance it may be difficult for children with special needs to direct their attention to this activity and successfully engage with a peer or focus on a specific play activity.

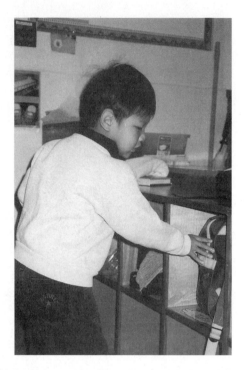

Figure 6–3   Child independently retrieves backpack for departure.

Linking children with a peer or interacting briefly with children with a favorite toy will make this transition easier.

Assist Children with Separation. When parents leave, include good-bye ritual such as, "Daddy's leaving now. Give Daddy a kiss. He'll be back after lunch. Tell Daddy good-bye." Parents of children who cry when they leave are often tempted to sneak away to avoid having to deal with a scene. Teachers should encourage parents not to do this. This practice leads children to believe that their parents may disappear at any time without warning, and that fear can increase children's insecurity. Children can learn to be confident that they know when their parents are leaving and returning. A clear good-bye routine helps the child anticipate the separation. Despite the emotional protests, this ritual actually increases children's ability to cope.

PLANNING EFFECTIVE DEPARTURES

Departure marks another significant transition in the center-based day. For most children departure is not as stressful as arrival, since it usually involves reunification rather than separation. However, it is still a good idea to plan the departure routine carefully.

Establishing a Consistent Departure Routine

Obviously a child care setting does not necessarily have a consistent end of the day because parents pick children up at different times. As a result, there may not be a group routine related to departure such as a good-bye circle. However, it is still possible to have a brief individual routine.

Example of an individual departure routine
1. Alert the child that it is almost time for the parent to arrive.
2. When the parent arrives, help the child gather artwork and other projects to take home.
3. Communicate with the parent, and draw attention to any written communication, such as teacher notes and newsletters.
4. Say good-bye to the center's pet rabbit.
5. Encourage the child to find his own cubby.
6. Assist with putting on the child's jacket as necessary.
7. Make specific reference to the next day.
   "Tomorrow is Thursday. I'll see you then. Remember it's pudding day." Or, "Tomorrow is Saturday, then Sunday. I'll see you again on Monday."

Example of group departure routine
1. If your center day ends at the same time for all children, you may want to include a short good-bye circle.
2. Finish snack; potty children as needed.
3. Clean up; signal circle time by playing or singing the good-bye song.
4. When children are convened in the circle, sing the good-bye song again.
5. Briefly recall events of the day.
6. Discuss events that will occur the next day.
7. Call children's names to line up at the bus, or, if most children are picked up by parents, have the children stay in circle until their parents arrive. (In the latter case, have the assistant lead the circle so the teacher can touch base with parents.)
8. Help children gather any artwork to take home; then go to cubby. Provide assistance as necessary, helping children recognize names on belongings, put on boots, and button jackets (see Figure 6–3).

Don't Rush

One of the most difficult situations for children with special needs is being rushed to leave. Because departure is the final event of the center's day, if the teacher is behind schedule, the departure may feel harried and disorganized. It is important for teachers to be aware of time so that the departure routine need not be rushed.

Support Development of Time Concepts

Departure is an ideal opportunity to support the development of time concepts and memory skills. For example, you can:

- Help children anticipate that it is almost time to go home.
- Emphasize the concepts of today and tomorrow. In circle time, ask children, "What did we do today?" "What day is tomorrow?"
- Teach past and future tense: "Who can remember what we did today?" "What will we do tomorrow?"

PLANNING OTHER TRANSITIONS

As we have noted, arrival and departure present major transition challenges for many children with special needs. Though smaller in magnitude, other transition challenges continue to occur throughout the day. Simply moving from one activity to another can be difficult and stressful for some children. Here are some of the reasons:

Challenges Posed By Transitions

Even moving from one minor routine to another can upset some children.

- Transitions require ending an activity in which the children may have just *settled in* and become fully engaged.
- Transitions require refocusing, which may be difficult for some children.
- Transitions introduce ambiguity and often reduce predictability.
- During transitions, events and other children's behaviors are less predictable. Some children may become fearful if they are not sure exactly what is going to happen.
- Transitions are often characterized by an increase in noise level and many children bustling about, going in different directions. Children who are hypersensitive to noise and touch may feel out of control.

Successful Transition Strategies

Careful planning of transitions can significantly reduce problems that may arise for children with special needs. The following are suggestions for successful **transition strategies.**

Use a Clear Signal. Initiate the end of one activity and the beginning of a transition with a recognizable sound, gesture, or routine. Ideally a different signal would be used for each major transition. The most effective signal varies with the special needs of children. For example:

- For children who have limited vision, auditory cues such as a bell with a verbal announcement may be most effective.
- For children who have auditory processing difficulties or hearing loss, visual cues such as turning the lights off and on and signing may be helpful.
- For children with multiple disabilities, some kind of touch cue may be necessary, such as allowing child to feel an object representing the next activity, say a spoon if it is time for the transition to lunch.

Use a Specific Sequence of Events. The accompanying boxed text presents an example of a specific sequence within a transition from a free play activity to snack.

Example of transition sequence: Transition from outside activity to snack

1. Teacher gives child with special needs a two-minute warning of end of play time.
2. Teacher blinks lights and begins singing clean-up song.
3. Children clean up toys with teacher help and pick up other toys.
4. Teacher sends children to sink to wash hands as each area is cleaned up.
5. Teacher puts snack on table and waits for children to sit down.
6. Teacher shows children snack ingredients and distributes snack.

Use Multiple Cues and Redundancy. A single verbal announcement, such as "Okay, it's time to clean up," may be the least effective signal for children with special needs. However, consistently pairing other more meaningful cues with verbal signals can help children begin to understand the spoken instructions. For example, sound a chime before giving the verbal cue.

Be Consistent. Using the same cues and sequence each time will increase the ease of the transition. If possible, try to use a different cue for each major transition so that the cue itself conveys to the child what is coming next.

Examples of Effective Transition Cues.
The following are just a few examples of transition cues that have been effective in programs including children with a wide range of disabilities.

- Playing the song "Hi ho, hi ho. It's off to work we go!" to signal a transition to activity centers
- Use of a chime or bell to signal the start or end of an activity
- Chants such as "Clean up, clean up, let's all clean up" to signal the end of free play
- Switching lights off and on to signal the end of rest time

- Pointing to large pictures posted on the wall that represent the sequence of the day's major activities to point out what comes next
- Touching the hand of a child who has hearing or visual impairments with a spoon to signal the transition to lunch

SUMMARY

Transitions provide important opportunities for learning. However, they can present special challenges for many children with special needs. The key is careful planning. Arrival may require consideration of the difficulty separating from the caregiver and the need for support in adjusting each day to entry into the group setting. Throughout the day, any transition, however seemingly insignificant, has the potential to be stressful. Departure, though generally less stressful, should also be carefully planned to maximize its value as an opportunity for learning.

CASE STUDY

Marta's Dessert

Marta is a shy, quiet four-year-old. She is blind. With the help of her orientation and mobility specialist, she is learning to move around the room independently. One of her favorite activities is eating. She especially likes desserts! The staff notices, however, that almost every day as Marta eats her dessert, she appears upset and sometimes starts to cry. She remains upset as the other children clear the table and throw away their trash, and she often does not calm down until she is safely settled in the good-bye circle before departure for home. The teacher Mr. Jamal carefully observes lunchtime to try to discover why Marta gets upset. At first Mr. Jamal theorizes that something might be wrong with the taste of the dessert or with Marta's utensil. As he observes more carefully, however, Mr. Jamal realizes that the end of lunch is quite chaotic. As the children finish, they leave the table in a haphazard, noisy way and crowd around the trash can to throw away their trash.

Marta has not yet learned to accomplish this task. She remains seated until an adult notices that she is finished. Then she is led by the hand to circle time. Mrs. Jamal wonders if perhaps Marta finds this time confusing, maybe even scary. There is a great deal of activity, but she seems to be left alone. Maybe as soon as she receives her dessert, she realizes chaos will immediately follow. Mr. Jamal believes Marta reacts negatively in anticipation of this time of the day when she feels vulnerable.

As a solution, Mr. Jamal and the assistant teacher design a transition plan in which he clearly announces, "It's time to clean up and throw away our trash." Who's already finished? Jason, would you like to clear your table and throw away your trash?" Rather than having a free-for-all after lunch, children take care of their trash one at a time, with the teacher describing who is doing what, so Marta understands what is happening. Also, Mr. Jamal asks the orientation and mobility specialist to begin working with Marta so she can participate independently in clearing her own dishes. Within a few days, Marta becomes much more comfortable with this transition.

Case Study Questions

1. *While this strategy worked well for Marta, can you see any disadvantages or problems with the solution?*
2. *Think about a child who is just learning to use crutches. How might such a child react in the same situation as Marta?*
3. *What kinds of adaptations might be helpful for a child using crutches during the transition described in this case study?*

KEY TERMS

separation
transition

transition strategy

HELPFUL RESOURCES

Dombro, A. L., Colker, L. J., & Trister-Dodge, D. (1997). *Creative curriculum for infants and toddlers* (pp 169–178). Washington, DC: Teaching Strategies Inc.

7

Engaging Children with Special Needs in Free Play

Chapter-at-a-Glance

Unstructured play presents significant challenges for many children with disabilities.

Some children who have disabilities may need special assistance in free play activities. While free play provides important opportunities for child initiation, choice, and exploration, it can be challenging because of its lack of structure and its unpredictability.

- **Free play provides many opportunities to assist the development of young children with special needs.** These include opportunities for one-on-one scaffolding and following the child's lead, teaching language through labeling and repetition, and supporting peer interaction.
- **Many strategies are designed to support children's engagement during free play.** Examples include teaching children to engage in trial and error exploration, arranging the physical environment in certain ways, teaching children how to activate a toy or play a game with peers, training peers, and requesting help from the disability specialist to adapt toys.
- **Careful consideration of the types of toys available can increase children's participation in free play.** Some toys are more easily adapted to a wide range of abilities and interests than other toys. Teachers may need to include toys appropriate for developmentally younger children, and some toys may need to be specially adapted.

INTRODUCTION

Free play or *unstructured* play is a major component of all early childhood programs, though the proportion of time devoted to unstructured play varies considerably among early childhood programs. This can be a difficult time for young children with special needs. Some children may find free play chaotic and react with increased behavior problems. Other children may find the lack of structure disorganizing and may simply withdraw. Still others may need assistance engaging in meaningful play with others. A variety of strategies may be helpful in engaging children with special needs in free play.

POSSIBLE CHALLENGES OF FREE PLAY FOR CHILDREN WITH SPECIAL NEEDS

Some children with special needs have particular difficulty with unstructured child-directed play. Children with special needs often require support during free play, at least initially, for the following reasons:

- They may be unfamiliar with the toys and materials and have no idea what to do with them.
- They may be overwhelmed with the number of choices.
- They may have difficulty selecting and getting started with a toy or activity.
- They may have poor task persistence.
- They may be easily distracted and have difficulty focusing.
- Increased noise levels during free play may be stressful.
- They may not find the available materials interesting because they are not developmentally appropriate.
- They may not have achieved the ability to engage in trial-and-error exploration.
- They may feel threatened by the number and proximity of other children in the room, all doing different, unpredictable things.

SPECIAL OPPORTUNITIES TO ASSIST LEARNING IN FREE PLAY

Free play provides several important opportunities for adults and peers to assist children's learning, particularly by incorporating many of the generic facilitating techniques described in Chapter 1.

An Opportunity for Self-Initiated Exploration

It is critical that the child realizes that he can discover interesting things and solve problems by himself. The child, who has learned self-initiated

trial-and–error exploration and has developed some **task persistence,** will be greatly rewarded. Many children with special needs, however, need to be assisted in these important cognitive processes. You may need to teach the child to use trial-and-error exploration and task persistence as in Jason's example.

Teaching Trial-and-Error Exploration

Jason often appeared to be in a daze during free play. He would briefly examine a toy, but then throw it down and stare off into space. Miss Monson sat down next to him and showed him a small radio. She said, "I wonder how this works." She shook it and encouraged him to do the same. Then she started pushing anything that looked like a button and again encouraged Jason to do it. Then she turned the On-Off knob until the radio came on. She said, "Oh, that's how it works!" She turned it off and handed it to Jason, who promptly turned it on and then off. She then left Jason alone. He spent several minutes turning the radio on and off and eventually learned how to turn the volume way up. Not everyone was pleased with his discovery!

Teaching the Child How to Play with Toys

Often children are limited in their ability to play successfully with others because they don't know how to play with certain toys. During free play the teacher can directly teach certain skills, thus increasing the likelihood that the child can play on his own or join in the play of others. It is especially helpful to use this opportunity to directly teach children how to play with blocks and manipulatives.

Opportunities for One-on-One Interaction

Free play allows the teacher to use strategies such as following the child's lead, which takes advantage of the child's existing motivation and interest, and scaffolding (see Chapter 1) to push the child to the next skill level. Children with special needs sometimes are not easily motivated. Thus, when a child is engaged in an activity and you want to assist the child's processing and learning from the activity, it is important to follow the child's lead and build on this interest, rather than attempting to redirect the child's attention.

As you observe the child, you can determine what kind of support he needs to perform the task at a slightly higher level. This is called *scaffolding*. The following example demonstrates these one-on-one strategies.

Following the Child's Lead and Scaffolding

Miriam's teacher notices her trying to pull off the dolly's dress. She is repeatedly just pulling at the hem of the dress. She is beginning to get frustrated. The teacher joins Miriam and says, "You're trying to take her dress off, aren't you? Can I help you?" She then points to the doll's arms and says, "We have to take the arms out first." She demonstrates by pulling the doll's arm out of the sleeve. She then pulls the other arm half way out and encourages Miriam to pull it the rest of the way. The teacher then pulls the dress half way over the doll's head and shows Miriam how to pull it the rest of the way.

The next time she notices Miriam trying to get the dress off, she points to the doll's arm and says, "Remember? Arms first." Miriam pulls each arm out, but still can't get the dress over the doll's head. The teacher again pulls the dress halfway and lets Miriam pull it the rest of the way off.

Within the next couple of days, Miriam has learned how to take off the doll's dress. She now busies herself taking off all the dolls' clothes. Her teacher makes a mental note to use the same technique to show Miriam how to put the clothes back on!

Building Language Skills During Free Play

Specific language input strategies to teach vocabulary, concepts, and sentence structure can greatly enhance children's development of communication. One-on-one or small group interaction during free play provides an ideal opportunity to offer careful language input. Using key words and phrases that match what the child is focusing on, repeating those key words, and expanding on the child's own words are important strategies.

Language Mediation with Roger

Roger is stacking blocks, then knocking them down. Mrs. Chen joins him, saying, "I see you're stacking the blocks, Roger." She starts counting as he places each block: "One block, two blocks, three blocks" Roger enjoys her participation and starts to wait for her to count before placing the next block. Soon he starts to imitate her counting, repeating the number. When the stack gets quite high, Roger knocks it over. Each time he knocks over the stack, Mrs. Chen says "Oh oh. The blocks fell down!" Roger does not imitate her. However, later in the day a stack of empty boxes fell over. Roger noticed this, looked at Mrs. Chen, and said "Oh oh. Fell down!"

Helpful Hint

For children who have *visual disabilities,* remember to add tactile and auditory—even olfactory—cues to language input. In Roger's example, the teacher could help the child by placing his hand on the top block, then helping him feel as they add a block together. The teacher could scaffold to help Roger take his turn until he learns to judge how to place the next block. The noisier the blocks are as they stack them, the better. For the blind child it is better to do this activity on a hard surface rather than a rug so there is more sound when the blocks crash. After the blocks crash, help the child feel that they are now scattered all over the floor.

Helpful Hint

For the child who has a *hearing loss* and who uses manual sign, be sure to sign the key words. Also emphasize speech by speaking close to the child. (This is an advantage of a one-on-one situation over a group activity.) You can provide a more optimal acoustic signal by speaking close to the child's hearing aid. Also, be sure to direct the child's attention to the noise the blocks make when they fall; otherwise, he will not be aware of this sound.

Demonstrating Interaction and Teaching Strategies to Parents

If parents are visiting the center or stay with their child, free play can be an opportunity to demonstrate how to use scaffolding, how to follow the child's lead, and how to use language in ways that enhance the child's opportunity to learn.

Encouraging Children to Play with Peers

Often children who have special needs prefer interacting with adults instead of with other children. One of the challenges for children with special needs in a typical child care center is that they may feel overwhelmed and threatened by the number and proximity of other children. Because they have difficulty processing the many children and activities going on around them, free play may be a particularly stressful situation for children with special needs. It may be helpful to find ways to enable the child to feel *safe* from these other children.

Strategies for encouraging peer interaction

- **Begin with one peer rather than several.** If the child has expressed some preference for a particular peer, encourage that peer to be a play partner. Keep the same partner until a successful pattern has been established, then gradually introduce new playmates. Also, gradually increase the number of children.

- **Begin with parallel play.** If the child with special needs resists the proximity of a peer, begin by having the peer engage in **parallel play,** rather than interactive play, and keep the peer out of reach of the child.
- **Have the peer participate in something in which the child is already engaged.** Rather than trying to engage the child with special needs in the peer's activity, invite an interested peer to join in something in which the child is already involved. This may need to be done very carefully at first.

  A simple way to encourage peer interaction is to create a turn-taking game out of the child's activity. Let's say, for example, that the child is engaged in pounding a drum. The peer might interrupt the pounding by taking his own turn. The child with special needs often finds this type of interaction fun because:
  - He is obviously interested in it because he was already doing it.
  - He understands the activity.
  - The activity is predictable; he knows what to expect.
  - He can make sense of it, and the activity is nonthreatening.

Helpful Hint

This strategy is particularly useful with children who have *low cognitive ability.* Finding activities that appeal to the child who is functioning at a significantly younger developmental level can be frustrating for both teachers and peers. Making a turn-taking game of a simple activity in which the child is already engaged can help establish an interaction.

- **Select simple activities that *require* interaction or cooperation.** The best example is playing catch or batting the ball. Also good are activities that require cooperation to be successful, carrying something very heavy, or riding in a wagon.

Helpful Hint

For the child who has a *motor disability,* ask the therapist or disability specialist for assistance in adapting activities. Try to figure out what kind of simple adaptation might enable the child to participate in some way. For example, a child who is unable to use his hands and arms may be able to use his leg or head to bat a small beach ball. A basket could be attached to the front of the wheelchair tray in which to *catch* the ball.

Helping to Develop Crowd Tolerance

Children with special needs may have more difficulty tolerating large numbers of other children than do most typical children. They may also feel

Figure 7–1   Example of a space buffer.

threatened by the proximity of other children. The following strategies may
be helpful.

- **Provide a *quiet zone*.** This should be a somewhat enclosed space, such
  as a library corner, which is relatively quiet and where there are only
  two or three children at a time. Children should be allowed to *retreat*
  here whenever the environment becomes overwhelming because of
  noise level, too many children, or too many different activities. It provides a calm environment whenever the child feels stressed, even if
  there is no external reason.
- **Introduce number and proximity of play partners gradually.** It may
  be helpful to allow only one play partner at a time to be within the
  child's physical space. By gradually increasing the number of children
  playing in this space, the child with special needs can gradually
  increase his tolerance.
- **Avoid large open spaces.** Some children with special needs have difficulty in large open spaces and feel particularly threatened by numbers
  of peers roaming around in such a space. During free play these children may be more comfortable playing within an area that has at least
  a partial boundary or enclosure of some kind, such as shelves placed at
  right angles. (See Chapter 3.)
- **Create a space buffer.** For example, a child can sit on a favorite towel
  or blanket (see Figure 7–1). Other children learn that they may not cross
  the boundary of the blanket edge unless the child invites them to do so.

SELECTING TOYS AND MATERIALS FOR FREE PLAY

As with any child, it is impossible to predict exactly what toys will be the most interesting and engaging for the child who has special needs. Experienced teachers in the field of ECSE, however, find certain types of toys to be more captivating and accessible.

It is important to identify those toys that appeal to a wide range of developmental levels. Examples of appealing and accessible toys are listed later in this chapter.

Typical early childhood programs often rotate toys to maintain children's interest. For children who have special needs, some toys should stay constant and always in the same location. Children with special needs often need many more repetitions—more practice and exposure—to master a toy, activity, or skill. In addition, once they are very familiar with the toy (or book, or song), they do not usually get bored with it. Rather, they often love the sense of mastery and competence that comes with something highly practiced. Indeed, don't most of us prefer doing things we're really good at rather than struggling to master new things?

We absolutely do not wish to suggest that children with special needs should never be encouraged to experience new things! Rather, the point is that it is important that certain things be predictable, familiar, and comfortable. Only within that context of a secure base will the child feel confident enough to try the difficult and unfamiliar.

Toys That Appeal to Different Developmental Levels

Some toys are easier than others to adapt to any skill level. For example, even the simplest computer game requires certain minimal motor, perceptual, and cognitive skills. However, a chalk board or easel with large markers can be challenging to both the child who is just beginning to get the hang of making marks on a surface and to the precocious artist who is drawing cities and landscapes.

These materials are also open ended in the sense that there is no one right way to play with them. For example, there are very few variations for playing with a jack-in-the-box. To experience the toy successfully, the child must turn the crank a certain number of revolutions in a certain direction. A toy like Bristle Blocks™, on the other hand, allows for an infinite number of creations, while being simple enough to provide enjoyment to the child who just wants to stack them, pull them apart, or match the colors. Play Doh™ is another toy that has wide appeal to all ages and lends itself to adaptations that allow engagement with the material regardless of the disability.

Two toys that have wide appeal—though they are more appropriate as outside or circle time activities rather than free play—are beanbags and parachutes. Beanbags are a simple toy with multiple possibilities for all children. They are easy to grasp and hold. They provide a low-risk opportunity for aggressive throwing and *mock injuries* when someone is hit. They enhance gross motor abilities of throwing and catching that can support development of valuable ball-playing skills. They provide an easily accessible opportunity for competitive games of throwing the bags into a large basket or through a small hole.

Another universally appealing toy is the parachute. It allows for participation in a group as everyone raises and lowers it. It has the same appeal as tents and blankets for hiding or crawling under and out of it. And it can provide an appealing motor kinesthetic experience when children are swung in it.

An example of a common commercial toy that has wide appeal is the Fisher-Price Garage™. Typical peers will make up pretend scenarios and sequences related to getting gas, parking, and getting auto repairs, and they may increase complexity by incorporating Fisher-Price™ *people*. At the same time children with limited cognitive ability can enjoy the cause-effect feature of cranking the car up the lift, watching it roll down the ramp, and stopping at the traffic arm if it is down. Children who are just understanding the cognitive achievement of object permanence will enjoy putting the car inside the garage and closing the doors, then being delighted to discover it is still there when the doors are opened again!

Finally, bubbles are universally appealing, particularly to children with special needs. Bubbles are interesting to look at, they move slowly so they are easy to track and to reach for, and they appear and disappear. Bubbles lend themselves to teaching communicative requests ("more bubbles!") to describing events by saying "Pop!", to understanding cause and effect, and to developing fine motor skills of opening the container, dipping the wand, and blowing.

Considerations for Developmentally Young Children

Often what is fun for children are those activities and tasks that activate the specific cognitive skills the child has just mastered. Thus, developmentally young children (for example, a child who has a cognitive delay associated with Down syndrome) who are just mastering object permanence find looking for hidden objects particularly intriguing. A child at an even lower level might prefer the simple sensations offered by sensory experiences such as water and sand play.

On the other hand, a child at a slightly higher level may just be beginning to enjoy the symbolic representation of *autosymbolic play*, such as pretending to have a tea party, wash the dishes, take a nap, or be the mommy putting the baby to bed. When a child with special needs seems unable to engage in a particular activity, try to adapt the activity for the child or select an activity that is a better match for the child's developmental level.

Common Toy and Activity Categories

This section considers the most common types of early childhood toys and activities and makes suggestions regarding their use with children with special needs.

Dramatic Play Materials. Children who have special needs often have difficulty engaging in pretend play. This is particularly true for children with low cognitive ability, children with limited vision, and children with difficulties in self-regulation. Children with motor problems who do not have cognitive delays can enjoy pretend play as long as appropriate adaptations are made for their physical limitations.

These pretend play materials often have high interest value for children with special needs because of their familiarity and opportunities for repeated exposure in daily life:

Telephone	Doll bed and bedding	Shirts and jackets (good
Dishes (tea set)	Baby bottles	for self-dressing
Plastic utensils	High chair	practice)
Pots and pans	Purse	Shopping cart
Broom and mop	Hats	Food cartons with
Sink and stove	Shoes	recognizable brand
Doll		logos

Children may need initial assistance in participating in dramatic play activities. With a little bit of coaching from the teacher, peers can effectively involve children in ways that are appropriate to their developmental level.

Helpful Hint

The traditional *tea party* and feeding a doll are two of the most engaging ways of introducing children with special needs to pretend play.

Also helpful can be the development of **mini-scripts.** This involves creating routines, such as putting the doll to bed or having a tea party, which the teacher models in pretty much the same way each time until the child learns the sequence. Once the child has mastered such a script, she has a way of participating with peers, even if the peers don't *stick to the script* exactly. (See the Case Study at the end of this chapter.)

Blocks. Children with special needs may have difficulty creating three-dimensional structures and including additional objects, like cars, trucks, and animal and people figures, in their block play. When attempting to involve children with special needs in block play, it is helpful to be aware of what younger children do with blocks. Figure 7–2 reviews the developmental stages of block play.

DEVELOPMENTAL STAGES OF BLOCK PLAY

1 to 1½ years	Child mouths, bangs, bangs together, drops, and watches block fall.
1½ to 2 years	Carries blocks around or puts/drops into container.
2 to 2½ years	Stacks blocks or lines them up on floor (single line).
2½ to 3 years	Uses blocks to make "road"; pushes car along road.
3 to 3½ years	Makes enclosure (fence); places animals inside.
3½ to 4 years	Makes three-dimensional structures, such as bridge, garage, or abstract design.
4 to 6 years	Increasingly complex structures; groups of structures. Incorporates play themes into structures. Often provides setting for dramatic play.

Figure 7–2   Developmental stages of block play.

Even though the child may not be able to play at the same conceptual level as peers, blocks can still be very motivating. The following are examples of the kinds of block play activities that may be appealing.

- Stacking blocks and knocking them down.
- Lining them up. (You can help the child elaborate this activity by incorporating cars and trucks and making *block highways*.)
- Using blocks to make fenced in enclosures. (Help the child elaborate by placing animals in the enclosures.)
- Assisting child in setting blocks up like dominoes, then knocking them down.
- Building a ramp and letting cars race down the ramp.
- Sorting blocks by color or shape; placing in proper bin or shelf at cleanup time.

The type of blocks selected may be a consideration for some children. For example:

Traditional wooden blocks can be dangerous for children who throw them or enjoy knocking down stacked blocks.

Soft foam blocks have many advantages: they are lighter and easier to manipulate, they're not dangerous, and they can be used in water because they float. One disadvantage is that younger children may bite or chew them.

Oversized cardboard blocks are cheap and easy to stack. Larger structures and taller stacks can be made, and they are safe. You can make your own cardboard blocks by placing milk cartons inside one another (see Figure 7–3).

Play-Doh™. With some adult or peer help and repetition, Play-Doh can be a motivating medium for young children with special needs. If your class includes children with cerebral palsy or children who have low muscle tone, it is important that the modeling clay not be too stiff. Children may have difficulty manipulating the dough with just their hands, so a variety of *utensils* are helpful.

Rolling pins. Children may need help at first rolling the rolling pin. Once they get the hang of this, however, it will be easier for them to roll

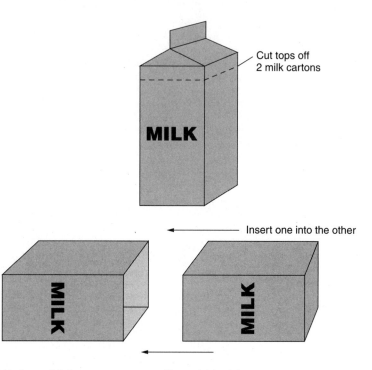

Cut tops off
2 milk cartons

Insert one into the other

Figure 7–3   Make your own cardboard blocks.

snakes, which is often difficult for children with low tone or muscle control problems.

Cookie cutters. Cookie cutters can be used to help children learn sequences.

1. Roll the dough flat.
2. Push the cookie cutter down and pick it up.
3. Examine the resulting imprint.
4. Pick up the play dough cookie.

Helpful Hint

For the child with *severe motor disability,* rolling the dough and picking up the cookie may be impossible without help from an adult. However, a disability specialist should be able to help you adapt the cookie cutter so that it can be attached to the child's hand (so she doesn't have to grip it). For example, it might be attached by wrapping a piece of Velcro around the child's hand or wrist. This way the child only has to press her arm down and lift it up to see the imprint of the cutter. If the child has some ability to grip, another *prosthetic* adaptation might include attaching a large wooden knob to the cookie cutter.

Figure 7–4   Child with car toy activated by a switch.

Plastic knives and scissors. Children love cutting sections from snakes. This provides an opportunity to practice using scissors and knives on something easier to cut than paper or food.

Mini-muffin or cupcake tins. Children may enjoy pushing the Play-Doh™ into small muffin tins or other small containers.

Candles. Making birthday Play-Doh™ cupcakes and putting in the candles is a fun *pretend* activity. Be sure to sing the Happy Birthday song!

Cause-and-Effect Toys. Many cause-effect toys are uninteresting or lose their appeal quickly. However, the following cause-effect toys tend to maintain some degree of interest.

- Baby pop-up toys and busy boxes may be engaging for children with significant cognitive delay.
- Jack-in-the-boxes are enticing, but many children with special needs will require special help learning to turn the crank through several rotations. They may also need to develop learning persistence.
- Specially adapted or commercially available **switch-activated** toys interest many children. Examples are a car or tape player that can be turned on by pressing a large button, toy computers, and music boxes (see Figure 7–4).

Helpful Hint

Toys like marble mazes can be interesting for children with special needs. These toys result in an interesting effect that lasts a few seconds, and they allow children to anticipate where the object will wind up. Unfortunately, these toys usually only have one outcome and one way of activating them. Nevertheless, they can be good cause-effect toys because the *effect* is slow and allows children some additional processing time.

Water Play. Many children with special needs love water play. They also may often enjoy washing things like tabletops and dirty bicycles. The trick is to help them *explore* different ways of playing with water. Otherwise, for some children, the activity can become highly repetitive and somewhat mesmerizing, as when a child constantly pours water out of a container, fills it, and pours again.

Suggestions for High-Interest Water Play Activities

- Counting the number of cups of water required to fill a large container
- Making paper boats; sinking boats when you make waves
- Filling squirt bottles; making designs on dry concrete or wall
- Painting wall or fence with water
- Filling bucket with soap and water, making suds, and then washing dirty things like outside play equipment (bikes, etc.) tables, windows, and slide
- Giving the doll a bath, including undressing and dressing the doll
- Wiping off tables following snack or art activity
- Washing dishes
- Playing in a plastic wading pool

Helpful Hint

For the child with a *cognitive disability* who is functioning at a very early developmental level, some water activities can be used to help demonstrate cause and effect. You can reinforce these concepts with language:
  "If we make waves, the boat will sink."
  "We washed the bike; now the bike is *clean!*"

Helpful Hint

For children with *motor delays*, water play can be a fun opportunity to practice pouring from one container to another, which is often a difficult self-help skill. An advantage of this context is that there are no negative consequences of spilling!

Other Sensory Activities. Several other sensory activities may be available during free play, such as a sand or rice table or a wading pool filled with lightweight plastic multicolored balls. These materials often provide pleasurable sensations. For some children these activities may be very calming. See Figure 7–5 for a creative example.

For developmentally young children, hiding objects in sand or rice or under plastic balls may have substantial appeal. Helping children sustain a search for a hidden object can assist them with grasping the concepts of object permanence, trial-and-error exploration, and task persistence.

Books. Children with special needs have specific challenges related to enjoying books. Developmentally young children may not relate to pictures. Children with impulse control problems and high activity levels may have great difficulty concentrating on the auditory and visual properties of a book or story. Children with visual impairments and perceptual difficulties may not be able to make sense of the pictures in many books.

Books likely to appeal to young children with special needs have the following properties:

- Repetitive phrases and pictures
- Sturdy design and pages that are easy to turn
- Interactive components, inviting action through opening doors and pulling tabs
- Simple and clearly drawn pictures, with maximum contrast between foreground and background
- Illustrations that represent common objects and activities of daily life
- Depictions of appealing absurdities, such as someone wearing a shoe on her head (*Wacky Wednesday* by Theodore Lesieg is an excellent example of such absurdities.)
- Duplicates of a book read frequently by the teacher during circle time
- Rhyme and rhythm
- Story structure that invites *call and response* participation

Helpful Hint

For children with *visual impairments*, books can be adapted by adding meaningful textures or small representative objects to the pictures. For children who are blind and who have good cognitive skills, a VI specialist may want to start working on Braille versions of favorite books.

Figure 7–5   Creative use of a water table.

The following are examples of books that often appeal to children who have special needs. (See list at the end of the Chapter 13 for more ideas.)

Brown Bear (Bill Martin)
Rhythmic, clear simple drawing, repetitive, lends itself to other activities, such as finger puppets.
Where's Spot? (Eric Hill)

Supports memory object permanence (hiding theme is appealing), hands-on participation with opening doors, lifting flaps, and simple labels of familiar animals.

The Very Hungry Caterpillar (Eric Carle)

Bright pictures, simple concept (eating), repetition. (This book is a little too long for some children.)

Five Little Monkeys (Eileen Christelow)

Chanted rhyme and rhythm, finger puppets, simple number concepts, familiar interesting animal, simple pictures.

Bubbles. Bubbles are universally appealing, particularly to children with disabilities.

- They are visually interesting.
- They move slowly so they are easy to track and to reach out to touch.
- Bubbles demonstrate cause and effect as they appear and disappear.
- Bubbles lend themselves to teaching communicative requests ("more bubbles!") and to describing events by saying "Pop!"
- Blowing bubbles can be used to develop fine motor skills of opening the container, dipping the wand, and blowing.

Manipulatives. Manipulatives present many challenges. Most manipulatives, like small Legos®, can be a significant challenge for children who have special needs because they are physically difficult to manipulate and because they may be too complex to hold interest.

Large bins of small manipulatives may be overwhelming and often entice the child to dump and throw. In addition, choking is a potential hazard for developmentally young children who mouth objects.

Generally, manipulatives are not an ideal toy for children with significant challenges. The following suggestions may increase children's success with this type of toy.

- Manipulatives that are larger and easier to grasp and stick together easily will be more engaging. In the authors' experience the best manipulatives are Bristle Blocks™ and large Duplos®.
- Sometimes more appealing are less abstract manipulatives, such as separate containers with such items as small cars, small wind-up toys, Fisher-Price® people, or commercial souvenirs from fast-food restaurants and Disney™ movies. Such a combination of small items may offer more familiarity and interest than more abstract manipulatives.
- One strategy for storing manipulatives is to place picture labels that can be clearly understood on difficult-to-open containers. For example, keeping several toy cars in a large lunch box or tackle box offers the extra challenge of figuring out how to open the box.
- Collections of visually and tactually interesting items in such boxes may also be appealing. An example might be a collection of shells or rocks of varying colors, some that are prickly and rough and others that are shiny and smooth.

Balls. Balls offer a number of challenges for children with special needs.

- Children with special needs often require a great deal of help learning to throw (including both grasp and release) and catch.
- Catching is much more difficult to learn than throwing.
- Children may not be able to hold on to balls of stiffer material.
- They may have difficulty controlling the intensity and direction of their throw.
- When they first learn to throw, they may enjoy throwing the ball wildly and aggressively.

The following recommendations may enable children to play successfully with balls.

- Maintain a supply of several different types of balls.
- Keep beach balls on hand. They may be easier to hang on to and because these large, light balls move slowly, they are easier to catch.
- Offer Nerf™ balls, beanbags, and ping-pong balls. They are easier to grasp and cause less damage if thrown wildly!

SUMMARY

Free play can provide many opportunities for supporting the learning of young children with special needs that other activities cannot. If free play is to achieve its potential as a great learning activity, teachers must develop some skills in how to engage children with various disabilities in different types of play. They must learn how to adapt typical early childhood materials and activities.

CASE STUDY

Shopping Mini-Script for Raul

Raul has diplegia. He has learned to use a walker. He has fairly good use of his arms and hands, though fine motor movements are slow and inaccurate. He is good at recognizing logos, like the golden arches of McDonalds™, and he loves going to the grocery store with his mom. He enjoys being with other children and gravitates to the dramatic play corner, even though there is little he can do there. He cannot put on dress-up clothes or dress and feed the dolls, and the little plastic tea cups are too small for him to manipulate.

Miss Julia, his teacher, decides that Raul might enjoy a pretend game of shopping. With the assistance of the physical therapist, weights are placed in the toy shopping cart so Raul can use the shopping cart like a walker in the dramatic play area. The children help design a store that is stocked with empty containers of familiar grocery items, a counter, a cash register, and oversized play money. Miss Julia asks the physical therapist to show her how to help Raul grasp the bills and coins and place them in a small waist pack. This is excellent fine motor practice for Raul, and he seems to love practicing putting in and taking out the play money. He pushes his shopping cart a short distance, requests items, place them in his cart, takes out his money and gives it to the cashier, and pushes his cart away. Sometimes he gets stuck turning the cart, but one of the other children is there to help him. He thoroughly enjoys mastering this play routine.

Miss Julia decides to write a mini-script and tells the children they are writing a play. The script goes like this:

Cashier: *Good morning. Can I help you?*
Shopper: *Good morning. I'd like some orange juice, Cheerios, and a box of soap.*
Cashier (places items on counter): *That will be 5 dollars and 50 cents.*
Shopper: *Okay.* (He takes out some bills and coins and places them on the counter.) *There you are.*
Cashier (places money in cash register): *Thank you. Have a nice day!*
Shopper: *Thanks. You have a nice day, too. Bye.*

The children enjoy learning the script and repeat it for several days. By the time the children begin to tire of the script and start making up their own, Raul has learned the lines as a result of the many repetitions. He uses many key words appropriately and continues to participate even after the children start changing the routine. In the process Raul also greatly improves his fine motor skills, starts counting bills to five, and becomes much more mobile.

Case Study Questions

1. *Make a list of all the adaptations made for Raul. What skills did each of the adaptations support?*
2. *What might be another play scenario that would be motivating for Raul given his interests and his challenges?*
3. *Do you think the mini-script described in the case study would be fun for Raul's peers? Why or why not?*

KEY TERMS

mini-scripts   switch-activated
parallel play   trial-and-error exploration
task persistence

HELPFUL RESOURCES

Dodge, D. T., & Colker, L. J. (1992). *Creative curriculum for early childhood* (3rd ed.). Washington, DC: Teaching Strategies.

Morris, L. R., & Shulz, L. (1989). *Creative play activities for children with disabilities.* Champaign, IL: Human Kinetics Books.

8

Circle Time

Chapter-at-a-Glance

Careful planning of circle time will insure successful inclusion of children with disabilities.

Circle time can provide important learning opportunities for children who have special needs. It provides structure to the beginning or ending of the day, helps children learn to focus in group activities, and can assist children in learning names of other children.

- **Certain strategies can be used on a regular basis to increase the success of circle time.** For example, use a consistent format, plan seating carefully, avoid having to wait for a turn, and signal transitions clearly.
- **One challenge may be dealing with children who wander during circle time.** Specific strategies may be helpful, such as allowing the child to sit on the periphery of the circle, gradually increasing the length of time the child sits in circle, and allowing the child to bring a *security object* to circle time.
- **Some activities lend themselves to circle time better than others.** Examples include, Follow the Leader, parachute, and What's in the Box?

INTRODUCTION

For children with special needs, predictability, structure, and routine can significantly enhance their ability to make sense of the world and to learn concepts and specific patterns of behavior. Equally important, this structure creates feelings of mastery and security, which support the child's emotional development.

OPPORTUNITIES AND STRATEGIES IN CIRCLE TIME

Circle time presents children with special needs many opportunities for learning. However, there is also the potential for development of some problem behaviors. We will discuss how to make the most of learning and prevent behavioral challenges at circle time.

Learning Opportunities during Circle Time

Circle time, a brief period when children gather as a group with their teacher to listen & share with each other, can provide an important marker as the beginning or ending of the day. Rituals included in opening circle can provide excellent opportunities for concept development, especially the concepts of time during calendar time (e.g., *yesterday* and *today*), and for social development in self-identification and identification of others ("Who is here today?"). For preschool-age children circle time is also an ideal opportunity for development of number concepts ("How many children are here today?") and emergent literacy (recognition of name cards).

Opportunities for Development of Group Identity and Sense of Self. A group circle time that includes music and social routines of welcome and belonging can help create a positive sense of both self and group identity for the child with a special needs. Learning other children's and adults' names, as well as the process of coming together on a daily basis, can create a great sense of esprit de corps. While this may not be an important value for members of the white, dominant culture (who tend to focus more on child-directed and creative activity), such group activity may be highly valued by members of minority cultures. In addition, parents who attend the center may enjoy this activity as well (especially if the music is appealing!).

Opportunities to Support and Reinforce Emergent Literacy. Children with special needs often require many repetitions to master the prerequisites for the development of literacy. Circle time can offer specific opportunities for emergent literacy support and practice, such as:

- Choice of picture cards representing songs
- Name/photo recognition (of self and others)
- Reading snack/lunch menu
- Short story/flannel board stories told at circle time must be repeated frequently for this age range, include props and audience participation, and have multiple copies of same book available in book area.

Strategies to Make the Most of Circle Time

While circle time can be an important activity for children with special needs, it can also be particularly challenging. Many children with behavior difficulties will find participating in large group activities particularly difficult. (See Chapter 4 for suggestions.)

Use of the following general strategies can increase the likelihood that circle time will be an enjoyable learning activity for children with special needs.

- Ritualize certain aspects of circle time, such as:

  Greeting
  Name recognition
  Welcome song
  Some opportunity for choice
  Transition out of circle to next activity
  Consistent use of key words and phrases.

- Avoid the tendency to make circle time too long.
- Plan seating carefully for both children and adults, in terms of teacher proximity to children and the need to close gaps (see Figure 8–1).
- Avoid unnecessary waiting for turns in large groups.
- Plan careful transitions in and out of circle time. (For example, if a tabletop activity follows circle time, you may wish to demonstrate briefly while still in the circle.)

Figure 8–1   Assistant teacher in close proximity to children at circle time.

For children who wander or resist circle time, try the following:
- Allow the child to sit on the periphery.
- Encourage participation for only a brief time initially, then gradually increase time.
- *Enfold* the child on an adult's lap.
- Allow child to have a **security object,** (a familiar attachment object such as a piece of material or a favorite toy)
- Close up the circle.

Variable Features

In planning circle time, the following considerations should be made depending on children's characteristics and preferences.

- Whether to include an activity in addition to the circle time ritual (e.g., parachute, bubbles, what's in the box)
- Whether to have children sit on chairs or carpet squares
- Whether and how to include movement and dance

Best Circle Time Activities

Certain large group activities are more likely than others to maintain the attention and participation of children with special needs.

Hidden Objects. Any activity where things are *found* is appealing to children who are just mastering object permanence or children who like the challenge of discovery but need practice learning how to search systematically for something. Developmentally young children enjoy the simple activity of finding something inside a box or sack. While problem-solving and discovery strategies may be difficult for a child with a visual impairment or a severe attention deficit, it can be rewarding to master the art of systematic search.

Bubbles. Bubbles seem to be universally appealing to young children who have special needs. (See Chapter 7 for discussion.)

Imitation Games. Imitation games like Simon Says and Follow the Leader can be motivating learning opportunities for many children. Imitation games can teach attention and observation skills and can provide opportunities to practice certain motor movements and vocal production skills.

Small Parachute. While use of a large parachute usually requires a great deal of space and a large number of people, a small parachute can be used in many interesting and creative ways during circle time (see Figure 8–2).

Figure 8–2   Parachute activity.

Dance and Movement Games. One of the best ways to make circle time motivating and fun is to include music and rhythm, such as the **Freeze game,** rhythm or marching band, rock-and-roll or salsa dancing. An activity that is virtually ageless in its appeal from infancy to geriatrics is the Freeze game where participants keep time to a good beat but must stop when the music stops and wait for it to resume. *Freezing* awkward postures during wild uninhibited dancing can meet the needs of even the most active child!

Helpful Hint

For some children with *autism* and for children who are *hyperactive,* extended periods of aerobic exercise can be beneficial.

CIRCLE TIME PROTOTYPE

Using a consistent procedure at circle time will make it easier for children to maintain attention and participation. The following format is one that works well for an opening circle.

1. Transition Signal

Use a bell, lights on and off, or greeting song paired with the verbal cue, "It's circle time."

2. Arrange Seating

Students pick up carpet squares (which may be personalized with their name plus a picture of their favorite animal, for example), place them in a circle, and sit on them. Configuration of the circle is critical for children with special needs. Some children need to be close to the teacher. The traditional semicircle works well for small groups. However if groups are large, some children end up being too far away from the focal point; a *cluster* or two semicircle rows may work better in those cases.

Closing in the circle may reduce distractibility. However, sitting close may be difficult for children who resist the proximity of other children. Teachers must strategically assign positions of staff and other adults in the classroom to maximize the participation of each child. Some children will do better seated in an adult's lap, while others need to have an adult seated next to them or behind them. See Figure 8–3 for examples.

Closed-in small group circle
(T= teacher, A= assistant)

Large group circle
(T= teacher, A= assistant)

Not recommended

Random seating with nonstrategic
placement of adults

Figure 8–3   Examples of circle time seating arrangements.

Helpful Hint

Sitting on a carpet square may not be appropriate for some children with *severe physical disabilities.* Sitting in an adult's lap may be a solution. If the child must sit in an adapted seat or wheelchair, equalize the height difference between the child with a physical disability and other children by having everyone sit in a chair rather than on the floor.

For children with *low cognitive ability* the task of getting a carpet square and bringing it to the circle may need to be analyzed. Work toward increasing independence in motor skills and task sequence.

To assist children with *visual impairment* mark carpet squares with contrasting black and white design or put the name in large block letters. Place easily identifiable texture on the back of the square, such as sand paper or rubber.

3. Opening Welcome

Once children are all seated, the teacher says, "Good morning, boys and girls. Let's see who's here today." It is helpful also to include a **call and response routine,** in which children respond as a group. Children who may have difficulty responding alone may eventually participate with the group as it becomes more more familiar (For example teacher says: "How are you today?" children say: "Fine, Thank you!")

4. Roll Call

Roll can be taken in a variety of ways.
- A greeting song names and acknowledges each child.
- The teacher shakes hands with each child or says "Give me five" while all children count to five (Variation: "Give me two," or "Give me four.")
- The teacher selects a name card and each child responds. For variation other children can identify the owner of the name card.

Helpful Hint

For a child with *blindness,* write his name in large Braille on the card, help the child feel his name, and let him feel other cards without Braille. For a child with low vision, use large, black, block letters on white or yellow background.

- Each child comes up and selects his own name card, which is then hung on the *Here Today* board.
- Instead of a group choral response, each child can practice a formal greeting. The teacher says to each child, "Good morning, _____, and how are you today?" The child responds "Fine, thank you."

Helpful Hint

Children who have a *hearing loss* can sign their greeting. Children with *severe motor disabilities* can activate a tape loop or augmentative communication device with recorded speech output saying "Fine, thank you."

5. Songs

One or two favorite songs should always be sung as part of the opening circle routine. See Chapter 12 for considerations in selecting music and rhymes for children with special needs.

6. Calendar

Opening circle time for preschool children often includes a calendar ritual; for toddlers, however, calendar time is usually not appropriate. Calendars can be particularly problematic for most children with special needs because of their difficulty with time concepts. Cook, Tessier, and Klein (1996) describe a useful procedure of the calendar activity for children with cognitive disabilities. An adaptation of this procedure is presented in Figure 8–4.

7. Group Activity

Opening circle time may or may not include an activity. Novel activities during circle time can present particular challenges for many children with special needs. Attending to unfamiliar activities while in a large group can be difficult for children who have problems focusing attention or who cannot sit for more than a few minutes.

An advantage of including an activity during circle time is that it adds variety and interest. It also provides an opportunity to help build children's tolerance for novelty and unfamiliar experiences. In some cases keeping the beginning and ending of circle time the same may help children with special needs recognize and discriminate the new and interesting activity from the predictable and familiar routine.

Helpful Hint

Children with *autism* often present a *Catch 22* situation for the ECE teacher. They may have an obsessive characteristic called **insistence on sameness,** which renders them extremely agitated when environments are unpredictable and chaotic. For some children with autism even slight changes in routine or physical arrangement of their environment causes extreme stress.

Children with autism generally attend better and are calmer in a highly structured environment. At the same time, it is important for children with autism to develop strategies for coping with changes and unexpected or unfamiliar events and settings. Varying the activity within the structured framework of circle time can be a way of gradually increasing their tolerance for change.

Adapting Calendar Time

The calendar time procedure described here can assist many children with special needs in handling the relatively abstract concepts of time that are inherent in this activity.

Features of the adaptation include:
- Reducing the time frame to one week.
- Associating each day of the week with a special activity and a particular color.
- Using visual devices to help represent the passage of days and to depict *yesterday, today,* and *tomorrow.*

1. Create a large board with each day of the week represented by a different color.

Sunday	Monday	Tuesday	Wednesday	Thursday	Friday	Saturday

2. Make Velcro-attachable laminated pictures (either photos or drawings) of different activities done only on a certain day of the week. In the example below Monday is *Library Day*; Tuesday is *Discovery Walk Day;* Wednesday is *Popcorn Day,* and so on.

Monday	Tuesday	Wednesday	Thursday	Friday
Library Day	Discovery Walk	Popcorn Day	Garden Day	Clean-up Day

3. At the beginning of the week, ask children if they know what special activity is on that day. Select a child to place the picture on the board. Reinforce with the phrase "Today is Monday" (For children with severe cognitive disabilities, present the picture during the actual activity until child associates the picture with its reference.)

Sunday	Monday (Library Day)	Tuesday	Wednesday	Thursday	Friday	Saturday

4. Toward the end of the day, refer again to the calendar and ask, "Who knows what day it will be *tomorrow?* Tomorrow is Tuesday. What do we do on Tuesday?" The teacher can show the Tuesday card but does not place it on the calendar until the actual day.

Figure 8–4   Adapting calendar time.

5. On Tuesday, repeat the routine described previously. Have a child select the Tuesday card and place it on the calendar. Now ask the children, "What day was *yesterday?* Yesterday was Monday. What did we do yesterday? We went to the library."

Sunday	Monday	Tuesday	Wednesday	Thursday	Friday	Saturday
	Monday — Library Day	Tuesday — Discovery Walk				

6. Proceed each day in this way, always reviewing the concepts *yesterday, today,* and *tomorrow* as well as the days of the week. Eventually children will began to master the temporal concepts required along with the vocabulary. (As appropriate, the teacher can begin to place the weeks into a month-long calendar.)

Sunday	Monday	Tuesday	Wednesday	Thursday	Friday	Saturday
	Monday — Library Day	Tuesday — Discovery Walk	Wednesday — Popcorn Day	Thursday — Garden Day	Friday — Clean-up Day	

Figure 8–4   Continued

Examples of circle time activities for both preschool and toddler age children are included at the end of this chapter: What's in the Box?, Parachute Play, and Follow the Leader. These examples demonstrate the detail with which activities must be planned to ensure successful inclusion. These activities have been well tested and have a high probability of success with children with a wide range of special needs. They can be easily enhanced to challenge typically developing children

8. Introduction of Next Activity

The close of circle time should be used as a transition to the next activity. The next task may be centers or an art activity. It is helpful to demonstrate what children will be doing at the centers or art table. This provides an opportunity for children with special needs to establish an expectation or mental set for what will be happening next. It also provides an opportunity for the teacher to introduce and repeat key vocabulary and concepts. In an integrated setting *helping partners* can be assigned to children who can benefit from peer modeling and assistance.

Following is an example of how to introduce an art activity during circle time.

Introducing contact paper autumn collage activity at circle time

1. Children will have gone on a discovery walk the day before to collect leaves, sticks, and flowers. These have been placed in bags with their names on them.
2. During calendar time the teacher reminds the children they went for a walk the day before and collected many wonderful things.
3. At the end of circle time the teacher presents a tray with his bag of collected samples (with his name prominently written on the bag) and a square of contact paper.
4. The teacher labels and repeats the names of all the materials.

"Here is my bag from our walk yesterday. See, here is my name written on my bag," Mr. Gibbs. "I have some *sticks,* some *leaves,* and one blue *flower* in my *bag.* This is a type of *paper.* This is called *contact paper.* Can you say 'contact paper?' It's very sticky!"

Children can be encouraged to participate in feeling the sticky paper and naming items or describing items to whatever extent is developmentally appropriate for the children in the group.

5. The teacher then briefly demonstrates placing some of the items from the bag onto the contact paper.

9. End of Circle Time Song or Action

For children who have special needs, it is helpful to have a regular song, chant, or phrase that always marks the end of circle time. For example, if centers are the next activity, teacher and children can all sign and say, "And now it's time for work." Because this is a short phrase, it can also be easily translated into another language that everyone can learn.

10. Transition

The children put away their carpet squares and move to the area of next activity, such as the art table, selected center, or outside.

EXAMPLES OF DETAILED ACTIVITY PLANS

As we have noted, detailed planning is necessary to ensure that activities are designed to accommodate participants' special needs. The following examples offer appropriate activities for circle time and demonstrate the necessary level of planning.

Toddler Circle Time Activity: What's in the Box?

Toddlers love uncovering hidden things! One item that can be used over and over is a large box with *something* inside. Toddlers know something is in the box; they can remember what was in the box on a previous day and are constantly surprised when something new is inside the same box. The following plan can be used to introduce all types of circle time activities. When the box is used dramatically, it can increase toddlers' interest and attention to large group activities. Suggestions for objects that can be placed in the box follow.

Detailed activity plan

Step 1: Introduce the box.

1. Seat toddlers in a circle with the teacher as a participant. Children should be seated so that the teacher can reach each child with as little movement as possible.
2. Bring the box into the circle in front of the teacher. The box should contain props (objects) for game or activity. It can also be *hidden* in some part of the room after children become familiar with it. You can say, *"Where's my box? "Where is that box?"* Let children tell where it is or *find* it. Then exclaim, *"Oh! Here it is! Here's my box!"*
3. Begin to pat on the top of the box to get toddlers' attention. Keep patting until all attention is on you and the box. (You can also begin by shaking the box above the children's heads while saying, *"Listen,* what do you *hear?"*).
4. Say (very slowly), "Knock, knock, knock, *what's* in the *box?"*
5. Repeat the rhyme two or three times.
6. Stop patting and saying the rhyme, and ask the children, *"What's* in the *box?"*

   - Wait for children to give some type of response.
   - Toddlers may approach the box. Let them pat the top or push the box toward them so that they can stay in their assigned places but still touch it.
   - Hold the box lid down so that no one can lift it up until you are ready.

7. Lift up one corner of the lid and look inside, "I *see* it!" Be dramatic and build suspense.
8. Choose one child to open the box or do so yourself. Hold the box so that all children can see inside.
9. Take hidden object(s) out (with a flourish) and continue with related activity.

Step 2: Begin activity related to contents of the box (e.g., pull parachute out of box and demonstrate its use).

Step 3: End the activity.

1. Bring box out again.
2. Place in center of circle.

3. Return object(s) to box or have children return objects.
4. Close the lid saying, "We're *all done* with this activity (describe specifically)."
5. Foreshadow or introduce next activity or lesson.

Examples of objects that can be used with the box
- **Parachute**—children can feel the parachute inside the box, and then all can help to pull it out.
- **Musical instruments**—fun to shake in the box first and have children identify the instruments by sound. Continue with music activity after opening the box and distributing the instruments.
- **Beanbags or balls**—use for a variety of circle time activities.
- **Puppets**—use a special puppet for a specific song or several puppets for all children.
- **Wrapped** *presents*—one item for each child wrapped in tissue paper or placed in individual small bags so that children get a second hidden *something,* such as sunglasses if the class plan includes going for a walk that day, or cookies or another treat.
- **Small containers** that require different types of fine motor hand movement: ziplock baggies; zippered mini-bags; and screw-top containers, such as plastic spice or cake decoration jars. Place small treat inside containers so that toddlers are rewarded for opening them.
- **Song props,** such as plastic animals to accompany "Old MacDonald Had a Farm."

Specific Suggestions for Children with Special Needs. To make the box activity a success for children with specific disabilities, incorporate these strategies into your activity planning.

For children with visual impairments
- Keep the child seated close to the circle leader.
- Allow the child to touch all objects as they are presented to the group.
- Give the child a smaller replica of the large box with one object inside so he can take his time to explore the box and become aware of the *boxiness* of the object and then open the box to explore what's inside.
- Keep in mind that objects inside the box may be a bit scary because the only way a child will know what the objects are is to *touch* them, whereas the other children have all been able to *see* the objects and can then choose to touch!
- Use a hand-under-hand approach to help the child explore a new object by reaching his fingers through the safety of an adult hand first, then gradually feel more of the object when ready.

Children with behavior problems or inability to focus attention
- Seat the child with another adult if possible.
- Place the child off to one side of the lead teacher so the child is close enough to see objects.
- For some children, offering them the choice of a chair or sitting next to the leader of the group (or another preferred adult) will help them decide where they want to sit. If they cannot maintain control, then the consequence is sitting in a less desirable place.
- Allow the child to tap on the box or peek first so he does not have to wait for what might seem an excruciatingly long period. (Do not allow child to do this if he is misbehaving right at the moment—catch the child being good.)
- Allow the child to leave circle time early if he requests appropriately by saying "all done" or "go," for example. Gradually help the child increase the amount of time spent in the circle.
- Give the child a concrete action that will signal the end of circle time, such as, "When we sing the 'Wheels on the Bus' song, you can leave the circle."

Children with physical disabilities
- Position the child so he is seated at the same height as peers (in a teacher's lap, in a ground level adapted seat, etc.) as much as possible. If the child needs to be in a wheelchair, consider having peers sit in chairs for circle time rather than on the floor.
- Assign volunteer friends (or an adult) to help the child manipulate objects from the box if he needs assistance. Peers can share musical instruments and puppets, for example.
- Encourage peers to help the child unwrap *gifts* by asking the child if he needs help and waiting for an answer. If the child answers "yes," provide assistance; if the child indicates "no," return after a few minutes to ask again. (The child may want to watch other children first.)
- If containers are too difficult for the child to open, put objects in a container that is easier for him.
- Place musical instruments in the box and play a Freeze game. Provide a switch for a CD player so the child can start and stop the music when children are dancing or marching with instruments. Peers must freeze when music stops and wait for the child to reactivate the switch to turn the music on.

Children with cognitive delays
- Use this activity frequently and follow a similar sequence and script each time.
- Include familiar and favorite objects, toys, and snacks in the box.
- For unfamiliar items, provide later opportunities for the child to explore box and objects from the circle time, such as during a free play or outside time, so he becomes familiar with the various objects and has opportunities to use them successfully.

What's in the Box? for Ben

Tom is a toddler teacher at a child development center in Los Angeles. There are 12 two- to three-year-olds in his room and he has one aide. One of the children, Ben, has severe visual impairments. He can perceive bright light and with his left eye can perceive dark objects against a light background but otherwise relies on his other senses to *tell* him about the world. Ben wears glasses to help him focus more on the objects and to remind him not to poke at his eyes (a common self-stimulating activity) but he does not really like to wear them and will often toss the glasses if not reminded to wear them.

Today, Tom is going to introduce hats and sunglasses to the children by using the What's in the Box? lesson plan. After the children have found their glasses and hats, they'll go on a discovery walk together. Tom brings the children into the large group and sits Ben next to him as his aide is busy helping the other toddlers. He introduces the box, which contains 12 paper bags, each one with a pair of children's plastic sunglasses and a little baseball cap inside. He has used the box before in circle time, and Ben has had many opportunities to feel and climb around and into the box (during times other than circle time). However, this is the first time that bags with something inside are being introduced.

Tom proceeds through the lesson and helps guide Ben's hand onto the box as he lifts up the lid. As Tom takes out the bags (per the lesson format), he passes one to Ben so he can touch it. He places it between Ben and himself, tells Ben where the bag is and helps guide his hand to it. Ben touches the bag carefully while Tom distributes the rest of the bags and the children begin to open them. He has rolled the bags tightly closed so the children spend some time opening them, with help as needed from peers and adults.

Meanwhile Tom turns back to Ben and asks Ben to help him open the bag. He places Ben's hand on top of his and lets Ben feel as much as he wants to through Tom's fingers. When the bag is open, Tom asks Ben to feel what's in the bag. Ben slowly inches his hand in and feels a pair of glasses just like his! Ben smiles and pulls them out of the bag. Tom draws attention to Ben telling the toddlers that "they have glasses just like Ben." Ben smiles again. Later, Tom asks some of Ben's friends to let Ben feel the glasses on their faces. Tom pulls Ben's hat out of his bag, lets Ben feel it, then asks him if he wants it on his head. Ben taps his head and says "hat on head." Circle time ends with the children putting on their glasses and hats and going for the walk.

Toddler Circle Time Activity: Parachute Play

The parachute is an exciting activity for toddlers. The parachute can be used with or without music and with or without props. It can be introduced into a circle time or large group activity by using the box as described above or simply by removing it from its bag in front of the children. It is a good teaching opportunity to have children begin to follow simple directions. Occasionally, even a small parachute can frighten young children. Watch their expressions closely when first introduced. If a child is fearful, allow him or her to move away from the group and observe from a distance.

Detailed activity plan

This activity is most successful if at least three adults participate, each person monitoring one third of the parachute area.

Step 1: Introduce the parachute.
1. Use the What's in the Box? plan for introducing the parachute or bring the parachute to the circle in its bag.
2. Pass the bag around the circle and ask each child, *"What's in the bag? What can you feel?"* Encourage each child to squeeze the bag. Encourage children to verbalize when possible.
3. Slowly begin to pull parachute out of the bag with children's help. Say, "Who knows what this is? It's a *parachute!"* A *PARACHUTE.* Let's *pull* the parachute *out."*

Step 2: Begin the activity.
1. When the parachute is completely pulled out of bag or box, direct other adults to help toddlers sit in a circle around the perimeter and hold onto the parachute's edges. Some toddlers may do better sitting on adults' laps to help them stay seated or to obtain adult assistance to hold the parachute edge.
2. Begin to slowly shake the parachute saying, "Shake, shake, shake the parachute." Be sure to shake it slowly and low enough so that all toddlers can see over the top.
3. Speed up the motion, then say, *"Stop!"*
4. Pause long enough for all to stop, then slowly count, "One, two, three, and *GO!"*
5. Repeat this sequence several times using the same format. Some toddlers may begin to initiate the stop, go responses; follow their lead!
6. After about one minute, invite the adults (still sitting down) to lift the parachute up high and tell the children: "You can go *under* the *parachute."* You or another adult should plan to go under the parachute for the following reasons: to model this action, to assist any child who needs help, or to supervise the children for safety, such as kicking each other by mistake or grabbing the center opening. A song such as "Everybody Move and Let's Go Under" can facilitate this shift more smoothly.

7. Once the children are underneath, songs or chants can be used to move the parachute over their bodies ("Up, up, up it goes, to the very top / Down, down, down it comes / On your head it stops").
8. After one or two minutes of this activity, warn the children: "This is the last time, then we're *all done.*"

Step 3: End the activity.

1. Following the last turn, instruct adults to release the parachute on the count of three. Some toddlers will continue to hold on, so have aides help them to release. This release usually takes some practice but can be dramatic if all but the teacher release at the same time, in which case the parachute flows quickly and smoothly to the person left holding it.
2. Quickly roll the parachute into a small bundle and put it away saying, "We are all done with the parachute. It is all gone."
3. Foreshadow or introduce the next activity or lesson.

Variations on parachute

1. After children have become used to the parachute, they can crawl or walk on top of the material as the adults gently bubble it over the floor. This works best if one or two toddlers do it at a time.
2. Letting toddlers take turns swinging *inside* the parachute is a fun toddler activity, but it may be difficult for many children to wait for their turn.
   - Put the parachute on the floor and have the toddler climb on top and sit or lie down.
   - At least two adults should hold parachute tightly while standing on either side of the toddler.
   - The adults gently lift the toddler off the ground (no more than two or three inches is necessary).
   - It is helpful to sing a song such as "Rock-A-Bye Baby" to mark the beginning and end of each child's turn.
   - At the end, slowly lower child back to the floor telling him that he is "all done."
   - Help the child off or give a second turn depending on what language has been initiated and how many children are waiting.
3. Using balloons or light balls placed on top of the parachute as the children are holding and shaking it can be a fun activity.

Specific Suggestions for Children with Special Needs. Use these strategies to adapt the parachute activity for children with specific disabilities.

Children with visual impairments

- Keep the child seated close to the circle leader or a trusted adult. Allow the child to touch the bag or box and feel what's inside. Allow the child to help with pulling the parachute out but implement the hand-under-hand technique if the child is hesitant to touch the material.
- Introduce the parachute to the child before circle time so the child has some familiarity with what will happen.

- Be aware that the child may be frightened by the sounds the parachute makes and the shifting air.
- Verbally predict what will happen: "When we shake the parachute, you will feel cool air in your face."
- Remember the child who is blind knows only what he can feel in his hands. Trying to conceptualize the entire parachute may be too difficult until the child has an opportunity to explore it when other children are gone. Try to make time for this.
- Allow the child to choose whether or not he wishes to lie under or on top of the chute. The child may not want to until he has become more familiar with this activity.

Children with behavior problems or difficulty focusing attention

- Seat the child with another adult. Activities like this may either cause a child to escalate and begin running around, crawling on top of parachute or kicking at peers, or to become extremely fearful.
- If the child is afraid, allow him to retreat as far from the parachute as he chooses. Then help him observe the activity from that place.
- Use key words but don't overtalk. Allow time for the child to listen to what's happening.
- If the child begins to escalate and attempts to climb on or under the chute, remove the child's shoes before going under the parachute so if he does kick, it won't hurt the other children.
- Do not let the child participate in this activity unless another adult is available to be with the child throughout.
- Swinging the child in the parachute may be calming if he has become overstimulated. Be prepared for the child to have difficulty leaving the parachute when his turn is finished. Let him be the last child to be swung so other children don't have to wait.
- Allow the child to leave circle time early if he requests appropriately by saying "all done" or "go." Gradually help the child increase amount of time spent in the circle.

Children with physical disabilities

- Position the child so he is seated at the same height as peers (in a teacher's lap or in a ground level adapted seat) as much as possible. If the child needs to be in a wheelchair, consider having peers sit in chairs for circle time rather than on the floor.
- Try to have an adult available to help the child hold onto the parachute and participate in shaking it.
- Have an adult hold the child as he goes under the parachute. If the child is simply placed under the chute, he may become scared and feel extremely vulnerable with other peers who can move freely. Have an adult hold the child in a flexed and supported position and be aware of whether the child is fearful or enjoying the activity.

Shelly and the Scary Parachute

Miss Laura runs a toddler class of older two-year-olds. One of her students, Shelly, has been diagnosed with autism. Shelly finds it difficult to stay in any type of group setting. When she wants to leave the group she will begin repeating "all done, all done" but sometimes the words are embedded in jargon and the adults do not always hear her and respond. Shelly will often begin to cry and have a tantrum if she is kept in the group. Shelly may also have a tantrum when she is frightened of something that is not a regular part of her world. Miss Laura has one aide and Shelly has a one-to-one assistant to help her during the more structured parts of the morning, which include circle time.

Today, Miss Laura is going to use a parachute during circle time for the first time in several months. Shelly has not seen a parachute before. Prior to circle time, Miss Laura gives the parachute in its bag to Shelly's aide, Sam. She asks Sam to let Shelly see and feel the parachute before circle time. Shelly turns away but Sam holds the chute, places it on the floor near Shelly, and helps her touch it with her hand. At circle time, Miss Laura follows the parachute lesson plan. Sam has Shelly sit on his lap opposite Miss Laura. When she begins to pull the parachute out of the bag, the other toddlers surge forward to help her. Shelly pulls back and Sam lets her sit and watch. When the parachute is spread out, Sam holds the edge and Shelly reaches a tentative hand to it from where she is sitting in his lap. She watches as Miss Laura and the others shake the chute and stop it.

When the children go under, Sam scoots forward keeping Shelly on his lap so she is just underneath. She turns her head away from the parachute and as the chute goes up and down, she begins to say "all done" but Sam doesn't hear her above the other children. Shelly rapidly escalates and begins to kick and scream. At this point Sam, holding her, moves away from the parachute but Shelly has reached a point where it is difficult to calm her down. Sam ends up taking her outside until circle time is over and she is quiet.

Miss Laura and Sam discuss what went wrong and agree that he needs to allow Shelly to take the lead on how far she wants to pursue exploring an activity. He also needs to be aware of signs that she is beginning to escalate (turning her head away and saying "all done"). They agree that she was fine until the parachute began going up and down and she was moved underneath. They also agree that Miss Laura will do more parachute activities outside during the next week for any child who wants to participate. Sam will help Shelly look at what is happening but will not take her to the activity. He'll let her choose. They will try the parachute during circle time after several days have gone by but Sam will remove Shelly when the parachute is being pulled out of the bag so they can watch from the other end of the room. He will follow her lead on this activity.

Preschool Circle Time Activity: Follow the Leader

Preschoolers enjoy playing Follow the Leader in many situations. They will follow other children's leads during outside play, in the housekeeping area, and during block play. During large group or circle time, this activity can be used to attract and maintain children's attention. The game should end before losing preschoolers' attention—no more than 5 to 10 minutes. Use the game (with variations as needed) over several days. Children will become familiar with the idea and may begin to initiate their own suggestions during circle time. The following is an example of one way to use Follow the Leader. Suggestions for variations will follow.

Detailed activity plan

Step 1: Introduce Follow the Leader.
1. Get students' attention by putting your hands on your head.
2. Say "Look at me. Can you do the same thing?" Begin very slowly and give children verbal and visual cues such as, "Put your *hands* on your *head*."
3. Wait for all or most children to follow your lead.
   - Use teacher aides, parents, or other helpers to assist those children needing physical cues.
   - Tell classroom helpers to limit verbal cues. Have only one person (the teacher) tell children what to do; too much noise may result if everyone repeats the teacher's words.
   - Reinforce children's actions: "You did it, Luis! You put your hands on your head!"
4. Move hands slowly to another place, such as your legs or stomach or a chair, and say, "Can you put your *hands* on your *feet*?" Exaggerate motions and words to maintain children's attention. Always wait for most of the group to follow your lead and give verbal praise/acknowledgment to individual children.

Step 2: Continue the activity.
1. Repeat as described above.
   - Stress key words for objects and actions.
   - Pace movements to group response.
   - Physically model the verbal direction if children are not following through with verbal command only; gradually fade physical cues (i.e., begin but don't finish movement) as children become more familiar with game.
   - Be sure that classroom assistants are helping children who need extra support to stay with activity.
2. Introduce variety as children become more used to the activity.
   - Use other body parts instead of hands: "Stomp your feet." "Put your nose on your chair."
   - Use directions that require more movement: "Put your hand on the door." "Put your stomach on the floor." "Shhh, follow me quietly."
   - Use *humorous* commands to maintain attention and interest: "Put your head on your nose!"

3. Continue the activity for as long as most children are engaged (no more than 7 to 10 minutes).

Step 3: End the activity.
1. Give warning of the end of the game: "This is the last time—one more, then we're all done."
2. Finish the game with a final direction.
3. Say and sign, "We're all done."
4. Comment/summarize: "You guys did a great job. You really paid attention! We did some silly things, didn't we!"
5. Foreshadow or introduce the next activity or lesson.

Variations on Follow the Leader

Use verbalizations and facial expressions rather than body movement. Emphasize consonant/vowel combinations and *silly* sounds. This group activity is excellent for development of phoneme awareness for all children and for speech production practice for children with speech and language difficulties.

Use only visual cues with no verbal directions. Reinforce silence by putting finger on lips if children begin to make noise. Use exaggerated movements to maintain interest.

Play different types of music and do a silent Follow the Leader to various tempos.

Encourage children to take turns being the leader after you have modeled the activity several times.
- Ask for a volunteer: "Who wants to be the leader?"
- Model any action (verbal or physical) the leader makes to reinforce the idea of following that child.
- Reinforce the child's silent actions verbally to provide labels: "James is shaking his foot."

Use props (puppets, bells, streamers, scarves, etc.) to maintain continued interest over time.
- A puppet can "lead" the activity.
- Quiet props can be used for a silent Follow the Leader, such as draping scarves and waving flags.
- Noisy props, such as bells and maracas, can be used with music.

Specific Suggestions for Children with Special Needs. Use these strategies to get children with specific disabilities involved in Follow the Leader.

Children with visual impairments
- This activity needs to be verbally directed for the child with visual impairments. Have an assistant whisper directions to the child if doing the activity silently.
- Some children might also need physical cues from an adult or friend. For "Put your hands on your head," for example, a friend taps child's head.
- Allow time after each verbal direction for the child to think about what to do. Pause before giving physical cues as well.
- Use silly sounds and syllables rather than motor movements.

Children with hearing loss

- This is a wonderful opportunity for children with hearing loss because they can easily be successful since Follow the Leader often does not require auditory processing.
- To reinforce learning key words, use signs or have an assistant sign to the child.
- Don't avoid the *silly sound* version described earlier. This will encourage the child to really listen.

Children with behavior problems who cannot focus on the activity

- Seat the child next to the leader or with another adult.
- Provide touch cues to get the child's attention.
- Help the child respond, then reinforce him for imitating the leader.
- Use the silent variation described earlier. The reduced noise may help the child focus.
- Allow the child to ask to leave circle before he escalates inappropriate behavior.

Children with physical disabilities

- Position the child so he is seated at the same height as peers (in a teacher's lap or ground level adapted seat, for example) as much as possible. If child needs to be in a wheelchair, consider having peers sit in chairs for circle time rather than on the floor, so children are all at same level.
- Let this child be the leader after children understand the rules of the game. The child will model those movements he is capable of making, such as eye blinking, moving head, and making sounds. (See Case Study at the end of this chapter.)
- Teach the child to use an AAC device to activate a tape recorder or voice output device giving verbal directions. For example, the child could use a head switch to activate the device to say, "Put your hand on your tummy" or "Jump up and down and turn around."

SUMMARY

Circle time can offer important opportunities for children with special needs. It provides a pleasurable, salient contribution to the structure of the daily schedule. It offers opportunities for self and group identity. It provides an enjoyable context in which children can develop attention and self-regulation. If selected carefully, group activities during circle time can be designed to enhance many skills.

CASE STUDY

Amy and Bartholomew

Ms. Diaz turns on the dancing song that signals the start of circle time. As the children come to the rug, Ms. Diaz brings out a corner chair for Amy, who has a diagnosis of cerebral palsy. The corner chair is designed to provide support for Amy's back but the seat is on the ground. Amy sits independently in the corner chair, tailor style.

After welcoming the children and singing their regular morning song, Ms. Diaz tells the children they are going to play a new game today called Follow the Leader. She explains the lesson briefly and begins. The children are noisy at first but Ms. Diaz continues with simple directions and calls attention to children who are following. She notices that Amy is smiling as she watches her peers but is lagging behind on some of the commands. For instance, it is difficult for Amy to quickly move her hands up to touch her head. Ms. Diaz knows that Amy can move her feet back and forth on the rug while supported in the corner chair so she introduces that movement and is then able to compliment Amy. Ms. Diaz inserts directions throughout the lesson that she knows would be easier for Amy. Occasionally she reaches over and helps Amy with a physical movement that is more difficult.

The class participates in this lesson for several days in a row as Ms. Diaz introduces variations to keep it interesting. By the third day, she asks for a volunteer to lead the group. Bartholomew, who is frequently a behavior problem, volunteers. At first Bartholomew acts silly when he realizes everyone is looking at him but Ms. Diaz reminds him of the "rules," and he begins to lead the class. As the children practice taking turns being the leader, they begin to introduce variations of their own. Ms. Diaz asks Amy to choose a friend each day to help her with parts of the game that she can't do alone. Amy's favorite helper is Bartholomew, who loves this special status! Ms. Diaz coaches peers when and when not to help Amy so that she has opportunities to move on her own.

Amy volunteers on the fifth day of the lesson and the children imitate the movements she makes. Amy has difficulty saying words but this game doesn't need verbal directions so Amy can be the leader with no help from anyone. This makes her feel really good because she usually needs help for just about everything!

This activity has many positive outcomes:

- Amy begins to feel like a true member of the group.
- She can be truly independent during part of the activity and "call the shots."
- The group begins to understand and accept Amy.
- Amy and Bartholomew develop a special friendship.
- Bartholomew feels *in charge* when he is the leader, and it provides an appropriate outlet for his activity level.
- The activity itself encourages children to pay close attention and develop their observations skills.

A very successful circle time indeed!

(continued)

Case Study Questions

1. *What would be some of the challenges for the teacher in implementing the adaptations described in this case study?*
2. *If you were the teacher and had only one assistant in your center, how would you use the procedures described in the case study? Who would do what? What would you change?*
3. *What ideas come to mind from this case study that might be helpful in managing a child with a severe behavior problem?*

KEY TERMS

call and response routine
circle time
Freeze game

insistence on sameness
security object

HELPFUL RESOURCES

See Chapter 12 (Music and Rhythm) for music suggestions.

Hehr, J. & Libby-Larson, Y. (2000). *Creative resources for the early childhood classroom* (3rd ed.). Albany, NY: Delmar.

Hëhr, J., & Swim, T. (1999). *Creative resources, for infants and toddlers.* Albany, NY: Delmar.

Trister-Dodge, D., & Colker L. J. (1992). *The creative curriculum for early childhood* (3rd ed.). Washington DC: Teaching Strategies, Inc.

Dombro, A. L., Colker, L. J., & Trister Dodge, D. (1997). *Creative Curriculum for infants and toddlers.* Washington DC: Teaching Strategies Inc.

REFERENCES

Cook, Tessier, & Klein (2000).

9

Tabletop and Art Activities

Chapter-at-a-Glance
Often children with disabilities that affect the development of fine motor skills will need special support or adaptations for tabletop activities.

Tabletop activities can support the development of many skills for children with special needs. For example, fine motor skills, task sequencing, understanding cause and effect, language skills, concepts and representational skills are examples of the kinds of goals that can be addressed.

- **Specific strategies can be used to adapt tabletop activities to make them meaningful and accessible to children with disabilities.** For example, adjust the activity so it interests children, use physical adaptations of materials and equipment where necessary, analyze the task sequence, and plan concepts and vocabulary.
- **Certain types of art activity will be more appealing than others.** Most likely to engage children with special needs are simple activities in which they can see cause and effect. Art projects should provide interesting sensory experiences and be easy to repeat.
- **Tabletop and art activities can be important contexts for achieving IEP objectives.** With these projects, children with special needs can accomplish educational goals across developmental domains. In addition to fine motor and school readiness skills, communication, cognitive, self-help, and social skills can also be addressed.

179

INTRODUCTION

Tabletop and art activities can offer wonderful opportunities for children with special needs to not only develop important fine motor and school readiness skills, but to engage in activities that are creative, expressive, and enjoyable. However, these activities present certain challenges and may be complicated and difficult for some children. This chapter suggests specific adaptations of these activities to maximize enjoyment and educational value for children with special needs.

VALUE OF TABLETOP AND ART ACTIVITIES

In addition to being fun and creative, art activities have many potential benefits for children with special needs. The following briefly lists some of the most important aspects. More detailed examples will follow.

Fine Motor Skills for School Readiness

Children with special needs often require extra assistance learning fine motor skills that will be necessary for success in school. These include using paintbrushes and writing utensils, gluing and folding, and cutting with scissors. These are particularly challenging for children with physical disabilities, such as cerebral palsy, and for children with low muscle tone, a common characteristic of children who have Down syndrome. The ECE teacher must observe how the child currently manages these activities and assist her in gradually mastering these often challenging tasks.

Task Sequencing

Children with cognitive and information processing disabilities often have difficulty learning and understanding **task sequencing,** the sequence of behaviors and events that make up an activity. Explaining, demonstrating, and reviewing the steps of an activity can provide important support for the development of cognitive processes in these children.

Demonstrating Cause and Effect

Activities that dramatically demonstrate **transformations** are particularly helpful for assisting children with cognitive delays in understanding **cause and effect.**

Learning Key Vocabulary and Concepts

For a child who has special needs this is an important opportunity to develop vocabulary and concepts. If the child is truly engaged in the activity, hearing the teacher use key words several times as she observes the matching events provides a major boost to her vocabulary and concept development.

Development of Representational Skills

Art activities provide focused opportunities to assist children with special needs in the development of **representational skills.** Typically developing children will have already developed an appreciation for two-dimensional representation of the world via pictures and will have experience drawing simple figures; however, a child with special needs may not have achieved these skills even at a basic level. Problems with visual attention, cognitive delays, and reduced visual acuity may interfere with the child's understanding that pictures can represent objects and activities. This is clearly a critical prerequisite to the development of symbolic skills and literacy. It is also a potential source of shared enjoyment between child and caregiver and provides opportunity to enhance language development.

Planning Art Activities for Children with Special Needs

Art activities (and cooking projects) require more careful preparation than other activities. Particularly when children with special needs are included in the classroom, teachers must think through not just all the materials that need to be prepared, but the adaptations that may be necessary.

Helpful Hint

Children who have difficulty focusing and sustaining attention and children with *behavior disorders* may have extreme difficulty sitting and waiting for materials to be placed on the table. Teachers should either set up materials on the work table prior to having the child sit down or should have prepared materials an arm's reach away.

Providing a Clear Transition

Providing a clear transition into the art activity is extremely helpful. Showing the materials to be used, major steps in the sequence of the activity, and possible outcomes of the activity can help the child understand what is coming up and focus more easily.

Keeping the procedural logistics consistent will keep the stress level low and assist the child in moving easily to the activity table or center. The following is an example:

Step 1: An assistant has completed preparation by placing all materials near art tables.

Step 2: The teacher gives a clear cue that it is time for centers (which includes an art activity as one choice) or tabletop activity in which all children will participate. In this case the teacher puts on the song, "Hi ho, Hi ho, it's off to work we go" and the children automatically move to find their chairs at the art tables.

Step 3: Children put on smocks or shirts to protect clothing.

Step 4: Teacher shows children the materials that will be used in the activity and labels them. She demonstrates examples of how the materials can be used and shows examples of possible outcomes.

Helpful Hint

If circle time directly precedes the art activity, the teacher can demonstrate while the children are still in the circle.

SUPPORTING LEARNING OBJECTIVES THROUGH ART ACTIVITIES

Carefully planned art and tabletop activities can help children with special needs accomplish IEP and developmental objectives. This section offers strategies to support their learning.

Fine and Gross Motor Skills

Difficulty with fine motor skills is often the greatest challenge to full participation in art and other tabletop activities. ECE teachers need to systematically encourage and support the movements and coordination for such skills as cutting, painting, folding, gluing, stirring, and pouring. These skills involve both fine motor movement (manipulation of arms and hands, and eye-hand coordination) and gross motor skills (sitting, balance, and control of trunk, head, and neck.) The following simple steps should enable ECE teachers to provide important assistance to many children with these challenges.

Obtain Pertinent Information from Fellow Professionals. An occupational therapist (OT) or physical therapist (PT) can discuss the nature of the child's motor difficulty and suggest specific strategies to enhance her experiences with art and tabletop activities. Keep in mind that for children with severe physical disabilities such as cerebral palsy, *positioning* will be critical, as discussed in Chapter 2. If the child is not properly seated:

- She may not be able to concentrate on the difficult fine motor tasks presented because her energies will be directed toward maintaining balance.
- She may be uncomfortable when placed in an inappropriate position, thus decreasing motivation to participate.
- The position may interfere with head control, making it difficult for her to maintain her visual focus on the materials.

A simple general rule that can be used as a guideline for placing children in a seated position is the **90-degree angle rule** (Rainforth & York, 1987). As Figure 9–1 shows, the angle of alignment at the child's elbows, hips, and knees should approximate a 90-degree angle. However, this positioning should always be confirmed through consultation with a physical or occupational therapist for any specific child.

Perform a Task Analysis. Watch children who do not have special needs performing the skill and analyze the sequence of their actions. For example, what sequence of movements is required to use a paintbrush? Determine the activity/standards discrepancy as described in Chapter 5.

- The child grips the handle (certain grips work better than others).
- She dips the end of her brush into paint.

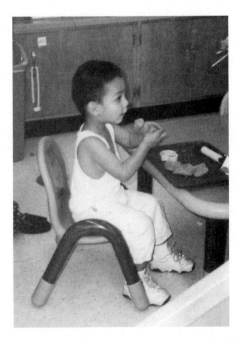

Figure 9–1   Child comfortably seated for tabletop activity.

- She wipes off extra paint on the side of the paint container.
- She swipes or dabs paint onto paper until there is little paint left on the brush.
- She repeats the sequence.

Carefully Observe How the Child with Special Needs Performs the Task. What parts of this task can she approximate? Which steps are most difficult? For example:

- JT can grip the brush handle.
- JT dips the end of the brush into paint.
- JT cannot wipe off excess paint; paint drips all over as she moves the brush to paper.
- JT has difficulty keeping the brush within the boundaries of the paper.

Provide Just Enough Assistance to Allow the Child to Do the Task. In JT's example, two types of assistance were needed. First she needed direct instruction on how to wipe off the excess paint. The teacher first demonstrated the movements for wiping off the excess and then used hand-over-hand techniques to help JT do it. An adaptation was also necessary to help JT stay within the paper boundary. The easiest solution was to place the paper inside a food tray.

Helpful Hint

For some children, particularly children with *severe motor disabilities,* it will be necessary to provide adapted equipment, such as specially designed scissors and paintbrushes with extra large handles that can be attached to the child's' hands. Also helpful is securing the paper to the table with tape so that it can't move around, or placing the paper in a shallow tray (see Figure 9–2).

Figure 9–2   Paper placed in shallow tray to stabilize the paper and create a boundary.

To the extent possible, gradually reduce the amount of assistance provided until the child can perform the task independently.

Developing Cognitive Skills

Children with special needs often require assistance developing certain cognitive skills. Two examples are understanding cause and effect for children with low cognitive abilities and task sequencing for children who have difficulty sustaining attention and processing information.

Cause and Effect. Activities that dramatically demonstrate transformations are particularly helpful for assisting children with cognitive delays in understanding cause and effect, especially when the teacher carefully uses language to map these events onto the child's experience.

For example, combining vinegar and baking soda results in a dramatic bubbling effect. The teacher repeatedly says things like "Now watch, when we pour in the vinegar, it will cause the baking powder to bubble." The teacher pours the vinegar, and adds, "See. We poured the vinegar, *then* it bubbled." The child with cognitive delay has the opportunity to observe the effect of a specific event and can see the task sequence.

For the child who does not have a language delay, this type of exchange can be an opportunity for development of more complex sentence structure. The teacher can model and repeat complex sentence structures that reflect the cause-and-effect relationships being demonstrated in the activity. For example, encourage the child to say:

"When we pour the vinegar in, the baking powder will bubble."

Also for the child who is cognitively more advanced, emphasizing cause and effect can be an opportunity for hypothesis testing and experimentation. For example, the teacher can ask, "What do you think will happen if we pour water on the baking soda?" Several different substances can be mixed and the results observed and described. *NOTE: The authors do not take responsibility for any explosions that may result from children generalizing this activity!*

Task Sequencing. Task sequencing is often a challenge for children with special needs. Children who otherwise seem quite capable may not be able to carry out a task that has multiple steps.

Explaining the steps of an activity before beginning a task can serve as an important opportunity for the child with cognitive challenges and information processing difficulties to learn and understand the sequence of behaviors and events that make up the activity. For example, the teacher can help the child anticipate an event by explaining the steps in the activity and demonstrating using a **picture sequence board,** shown in Figure 9–3.

1. First, we will lay out all the leaves we collected on our walk.
2. Next, we will put a little spot of glue on our sheet of paper.
3. Then we will put one of our leaves on the glue.

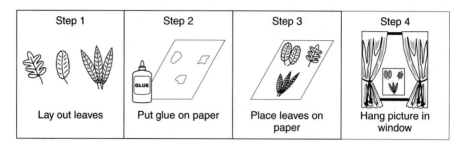

Figure 9–3   Picture sequence board for leaf collage.

4. Next, we put another spot of glue on the paper and put on another leaf.
5. We will do this until our paper is covered with leaves.
6. Finally, when the glue dries, we can hang it up on the window.

Helpful Hint

ECE teachers often resist this degree of direction and structure because it may inhibit more creative and experimental processes. The idea presented here is not that all children must do it this way. But for the child whose organizational difficulties interfere with her ability to participate and result in either frustration or disengagement, this kind of assistance with cognitive processing of the task can make an important difference because the child can better understand the task.

Learning Key Vocabulary and Concepts

For children with special needs, tabletop and art activities are an important opportunity to develop vocabulary and concepts. If children are truly engaged in the activity, hearing the teacher use key words several times *as the event occurs* provides a major boost to vocabulary and concept development.

In the earlier example involving vinegar and baking soda, depending on the child's level, the key vocabulary might be *pour* and *bubbles,* or it might be *vinegar* and *baking soda.* Key concepts might be the fairly abstract words *cause* and *effect.*

To ensure that these activities are effective in supporting vocabulary development for the child with a language delay or disability, keep the following points in mind:

1. *Plan* the vocabulary ahead of time. If necessary write out key words as a reminder to assistants so everyone is consistent in what things are called.
2. *Repeat* the key words several times. Encourage children to say the words.

Helpful Hint

For the child who does not produce speech or has a significant *hearing loss*, be sure to introduce a sign for the key words and assist the child in making the sign, or allow the child to point to pictures representing the key vocabulary.

For the child who is *blind* use a touch cue of some kind as you say the word. A child with *blindness* will not immediately understand the act of pouring. She will need to:

a. Feel the container.
b. Feel the liquid in the container.
c. Feel the movement of tipping the container to pour.
d. Feel the edge of the container.
e. Feel the liquid coming out of the container.
f. Feel the transformation of the mixture as the vinegar mixes with the baking soda.

Once this has been demonstrated, a potential touch cue to accompany the word *pour* might be moving the child's hand in a pouring motion or simply letting her touch the container as the teacher says, "Okay, now we're going to pour the vinegar."

3. *Repeat* the activity several times. Most children with special needs will have difficulty learning from a single event, unless the event is traumatic! Thus, once you have identified an engaging and interesting activity, it is important to repeat that activity often.

Helpful Hint

A potential conflict may arise from the ECE teacher's concern about typical children becoming bored. A simple solution here is to vary the activity in some way, starting with a basic, familiar activity and expanding on it in interesting ways. Thus, repetition is maintained for children with special needs while adding interest and challenge for other children.

Development of Representational Skills

Art activities provide focused opportunities to assist children with special needs in the development of representational skills. Unlike typically developing children, a child with special needs may not have already developed an appreciation for two-dimensional representation of the world via pictures or have experience drawing simple figures. Problems with visual attention, cognitive delays, and reduced visual acuity may interfere with the child's understanding that pictures can represent objects and activities.

This understanding is clearly a critical prerequisite for the development of symbolic skills and literacy. It is also a potential source of shared enjoyment between child and caregiver and provides opportunity to enhance language development. The ECE teacher can play a critical role in helping the child with special needs develop representational skills.

Obviously storybook reading is the most significant activity related to the understanding of pictures as representation. However, some children with special needs will not be ready to understand the meaning of pictures and storybooks. The ECE teacher can support the development of representational skills for these children within art and tabletop activities, such as:

- Learning to draw simple shapes and objects (circles, faces, houses, flowers).
- Outlining body parts (hand, foot, whole body).
- Looking for pictures in magazines to cut out and making collages or booklets around certain themes or categories of pictures.
- Taking Polaroid snapshots and making photo albums.

Strategies for Children with Tactile Defensiveness

Any fine motor task that requires coming into contact with a variety of unfamiliar textures and materials can be stressful for some children with special needs. Avoiding tactile contact, or *tactile defensiveness*, is particularly common in children who have autism. Also, children with severe visual impairments often appear to be tactile defensive. However, sometimes the issue for children who are blind is simply the lack of careful cueing to help them anticipate what is happening next. Thus, avoidance may be based more on fear and insecurity than on increased tactile sensitivity.

The following strategies can be helpful with children who demonstrate tactile defensiveness.

Use Hand-Under-Hand Guidance. Rather than trying to use a hand-over-hand method where you guide the child's hands through the required movements, place the child's hands on top of your hands while you engage in the activity. Hand-under-hand guidance allows the child to experience the activity initially through you, which allows her to feel more in control. Once she has become familiar with the activity you may try to guide her hands. (These techniques were discussed in more detail in Chapter 2. See Figure 2–10.)

Use the Premack Principle. The **Premack Principle** (Zirpoli & Melloy 1993) simply states that an unpleasant task or activity should be followed by a pleasant or highly desired one. You can encourage partial participation in an unpleasant activity, then allow the child to engage in a preferred activity. For example, encourage the child to finger paint briefly even though she resists somewhat, then allow her to go to the sink to wash her hands (an activity she loves). Or, after you help a child to glue two or three flowers on a collage, then allow her to return to the block area.

Incorporate the Child's Security Object. Particularly in the case of children who have autism, you may be able to use a favorite object within the activity.

For example, one child loves a set of tiny plastic bears that she carries around obsessively. She consistently refuses to play with Play-Doh™ or any such substance. One day her teacher buries the bears in the Play-Doh™. Though briefly upset, the child becomes intrigued with finding the bears in the Play-Doh™, and her tactile defensiveness is significantly reduced. As long as she can have her bears in the vicinity of the art activity, she is fairly willing to participate.

SUMMARY

Tabletop and art activities can be motivating for young children with special needs, particularly if they are carefully selected and planned and if they are repeated often enough to give the child a sense of mastery. These activities also provide important opportunities to work on specific skills that are part of the child's IEP. Again, planning is the key.

Tabletop activities can also present significant challenges to many children, particularly if they do not understand the activity or if the activity presents too many physical challenges. Several strategies can be used to increase children's successful participation in these activities.

CASE STUDY

Marciana's Resistance

Marciana joined Mr. Podvosky's classroom two months ago. Initially she was extremely agitated at the beginning of the morning and engaged in rocking and hand flapping. She was also obsessed with the plastic letters M and A, which she insisted on carrying with her at all times. By making sure that her arrival routine is consistent, she finally seems to be settling into the classroom routine. However, the one activity Marciana will have nothing to do with is any kind of tabletop activity.

After consulting with the early childhood special educator who observed Marciana carefully for several days, Mr. Podvosky determines that she is extremely uncomfortable and resistant to touching unfamiliar substances, though she enjoys water play. She has apparently come to associate all tabletop activities with materials like finger paint, glue, and glitter. The consultant describes her reaction as *tactile defensiveness.* She explains this is not something the child will simply grow out of, and it will be helpful to Marciana to increase her tolerance for tactile stimulation. The consultant also notes that Marciana does not enjoy situations where she feels crowded by other children.

The consultant and Mr. Podvosky work out a plan for Marciana. Initially Mr. Podvosky has some misgivings about the plan because it seems overly directive. His classroom allows choice in all activities, and he is uncomfortable trying to coerce Marciana into doing anything

(continued)

she does not want to do. The inclusion consultant expresses her concern that this might result in Marciana becoming even more isolated and disconnected from the class over time, because her preference is to be alone and engage in comfortable, highly repetitive activities. They agree to implement the plan for one month and then reassess at that time.

According to the plan, Marciana's favorite aide, Miss Chu, sits with her near the table, at a smaller table. Here they play with tubs of water. She is encouraged to put her plastic letters in the water to watch them float. Gradually Miss Chu begins to experiment with adding materials to the water. She starts with small amounts of cornstarch. She places Marciana's letters in the water and encourages her to retrieve them. As she changes the consistency of the water more dramatically by adding more cornstarch she has Marciana place her hand on top of Miss Chu's hand, while Miss Chu stirs the mixture.

Miss Chu also experiments with food coloring, dramatically changing the color of the water. Marciana became fascinated with this interesting transformation. She then demonstrates similar color transformations by mixing finger paints. Miss Chu models using just the tip of her index finger to dip in the finger paint and make a letter on the paper. Marciana loves making letters, so watching this new way of writing sustains her attention. Using a gentle hand-over-hand technique Miss Chu then begins to dip Marciana's index finger into the paint and make an *M* on the page (Marciana's favorite letter!). Initially Marciana resists touching the paint and becomes agitated. Miss Chu then places a bowl of warm water at the table, and as soon as Marciana makes her letter on the page, Miss Chu immediately places her hand in the warm water, saying "Okay, let's wash off the paint." Over time Marciana becomes so interested in making letters with different materials such as glue and glitter that her tactile defensiveness and her anxiety level significantly decrease.

Case Study Questions

1. *How do you feel about the potential conflict between the importance of child-centered environments and free choice and the more directive strategy used in Marciana's case?*
2. *What are some of the keys to success in the strategy described in this case study?*
3. *Can you think of other strategies that might have been useful in helping Marciana deal with her resistance to engaging in tabletop activities?*

KEY TERMS

90-degree angle rule representational skills
cause and effect task sequencing
picture sequence board transformations
Premack Principle

HELPFUL RESOURCES

Catalogs

Tumble Forms: for positioning, seating and mobility (#3431), and *Pediatrics: Special needs products for schools and clinics,* Sammons Preston, P.O. Box 5071, Bolingbrook, IL 60440-9977, (800)323-5547.

ARTICLES AND BOOKS

Cherry, C. (1981). *Creative art for the developing child: A teacher's handbook for early childhood education.* Belmont, CA: Fearon.

Coyle, R. (1985). *My first cookbook.* New York: Workman.

Dodge, D. T., & Colker, L. J. (1992). *The creative curriculum for early childhood.* Washington, DC: Teaching Strategies, Inc.

Ferreira, J. J. (1986). *Learning through cooking: A cooking program for children two to ten.* Saratoga, CA: R&E.

Flemming, B., Mack, D., Hamilton, S., & Hicks, J. (1990). *Resources for creative teaching in early childhood education* (2nd ed.). New York: Harcourt Brace.

Morris, L. R., & Shulz, L. (1989). *Creative play activities for children with disabilities.* Champaign, IL: Human Kinetics Books.

REFERENCES

Rainforth, B., & York, J. (1987). Position and handling. In F. P. Orelove & D. Sobsey, *Educating children with multiple disabilities* (pp 67–78), Baltimore, MD: Paul H. Brookes.

Zirpoli, T. J., & Melloy, K. J. (1993). *Behavior Management: Applications for teachers and parents* (pp 153–198). New York: Merrill/Macmillan.

10

Outside Play

Chapter-at-a-Glance

Children with disabilities often love the change in environment from indoor to outdoor play.

A daily change from inside to outside environment is essential. Many children with special needs need opportunities for learning and practicing large motor activities, which are often much easier to do outside.

- **Children with special needs often need to learn** how **to play with outside equipment.** Children may not learn how to ride a bike, catch a ball, run, or slide down the slide without specific help and repeated opportunities for practice.
- **Outside activities can provide opportunities for developing social skills.** These include negotiating turns, pretend play, and watching out for others' safety.
- **Sand and water activities may work better outside for children who have certain disabilities.** Certain classroom themes and activities can be extended to the outdoor environment to reinforce and repeat concepts, such as putting fish in the water table.
- **Special concerns and adaptations may need to be addressed for safety and access.** Children who cannot participate in large muscle activities still need activities which are appropriate for outdoors, such as being pulled in a wagon or pushed in a specially adapted swing. Use of textures and contrasting surfaces can help children with limited vision move around the playground independently.
- **A regularly scheduled discovery walk can be an excellent outdoor activity.** Careful planning for children with special needs will make this a rich opportunity for meeting children's goals.

INTRODUCTION

The importance of outside play as part of the daily curriculum cannot be underestimated. Young children (and their teachers!) need a change of environment. Opportunities for using large muscles while running, climbing, or riding bikes are usually not available inside the classroom. This kind of play may also be more limited at home for some children.

Because of limited opportunities to practice, the development of these large muscle play skills may be a particular challenge for children with special needs. This is obviously true for children who have motor disabilities. But it is also true for children who have special needs related to cognitive delay, autism, and visual impairment because they need close supervision in the outside environment.

OPPORTUNITIES FOR LEARNING IN THE OUTDOOR ENVIRONMENT

Going outside provides not only a welcome change from the classroom but also opportunities to develop large motor skills and enhance play and social skills. Several strategies and adaptations can turn the playground and surrounding neighborhood into an extension of your classroom.

Change of Environment

If you've ever been inside a classroom for three hours with a group of 8 to 12 toddlers or preschoolers, you probably understand the need to change environments! For many people, being outside has a calming effect. The natural lighting, fresh air, different acoustic characteristics, and opportunity to run and shout offer a welcome change from the classroom environment. Also, moving from the classroom to outside during the course of the day provides an opportunity for children to practice motor and play skills often quite different from the classroom.

If rain or extreme weather conditions make it impossible to go outside, teachers should still try to move out of the classroom to a different environment during the regularly scheduled outside time.

- **If the center is in a large building, take a walk through parts of the building rarely visited.** This will provide children with the opportunity to exercise large muscles while maintaining interest because of the novelty.
- **Switch classrooms with another teacher.** This will at least provide a change of environment although not necessarily meet the needs of the children to use large muscles.

- **Use a hallway or an unused room.** A space where small groups of children can throw bean bags or negotiate an obstacle course can occasionally substitute for going outdoors.

Specific planning of areas and activities will be discussed later in this chapter.

Opportunities for Using Large Muscles

Outside environments can provide the opportunity for a variety of activities for children with a range of developmental ages and abilities. These activities should be different from activities found inside the classroom. Typically, outside areas focus on large muscle or gross motor development. Due to severe motor disabilities or medically fragile conditions, a few children may not be able to engage in large motor activities. Special accommodations will be needed to provide appropriate outside activities for these children. Their participation may need to be more passive, such as being pushed in a swing, pulled in a wagon, or simply walked around the playground in a wheelchair.

Helpful Hint

Some children, such as those with *autism* or *hyperactivity disorder*, benefit from regular periods of rigorous exercise—jumping, dancing, running, and climbing. Obviously, such activity is most easily incorporated into outside time.

The following gross motor equipment should be available for children in outside areas:

- Padded rubber ground covering under climbing structures and slides
- Climbing structures (some with lower height)
- Swings (some with adapted seats, seat belts, etc. See Figure 10–1.)
- Toys that rock, such as a rocking horse or boat
- Slides of different sizes, with high rails at top
- Tricycles of various sizes
- Wheeled scooter-type toys
- Balls (many sizes, some soft) and beanbags
- Low basketball net, other containers to throw into
- Wagons to push or pull
- Pedal or foot-powered cars

Space for riding wheeled toys and throwing balls must be planned carefully to ensure safety and freedom of movement for children who are using the equipment and for those who are not.

Figure 10–1   Adapted swing.

Information about safety requirements for typical playground equipment can be obtained from the manufacturer and/or licensing agencies. For children with unsteady gaits, seizure disorders, or limited vision, additional safety measures are desirable. For example:

- Ground covering should be made of resilient material.
- Equipment should be positioned with care to avoid protrusions that may be difficult to see or which extend into otherwise clear pathways.
- Swings should be adapted with seatbelts or special seating.
- Blocks and Velcro straps can be placed on pedals of some of the wheeled toys.
- Texture/tactile cues can be designed for children with limited vision to provide contrast both visually and the way it feels underfoot. For example, a boundary between the swing area and the sandbox could be created by black and white stripes painted on rubber matting under swings, with grass or sand around the sandbox.
- Paths for wheeled toys should be clearly marked with contrasting lines. Stop signs should be placed on bike paths for safety and development of literacy.

Developing Play Skills

Some children with special needs may require assistance in learning how to play in an outside environment. For example, learning to climb up and slide

Figure 10–2 Adapting child's position to decrease fear of going down the slide.

down a slide can be a daunting but exciting challenge for many children with special needs. Figure 10–2 demonstrates an adaptation of allowing a child to go down the slide feet first, on his tummy as a first step in learning how to use the slide. This position can be safer, easier, and less frightening than a sitting position.

In addition to the obvious need to learn how to go down a slide, ride a bike, swing, climb, and play in the sand, opportunities also exist for turn-taking, playing simple games, and joining in pretend play with cars and bikes. For a few children outside time may be an opportunity for a child to have some *alone* time and recover from the often more intense enclosed classroom environment. Teachers must carefully observe young children during outside play periods to determine how much socialization and what levels of assistance they need.

Outside time may also create opportunities for learning how to negotiate conflicts among children. It is important to allow children to attempt to solve their own conflicts by carefully monitoring situations and intervening only when necessary.

Planning varying activities to supplement outside equipment can provide wonderful opportunities to develop play skills. Often, a classroom theme can be expanded during outside play. Also, art activities may be repeated outside for children who need more time to experience the process.

The accompanying box offers specific outside play suggestions that typically appeal to children with special needs.

Appealing outside play activities for children with special needs

- Bring dolls outside to feed, bathe, push in the swing, and accompany down the slide.
- Expand on a fish or animal theme and bring plastic models outside to play with in the sandbox or water table.
- Build a play house out of a large cardboard box (cut out windows and doors); include paints and brushes for children to decorate their house. Children at younger cognitive levels often love playing peek-a-boo through the windows.
- Create a garden center where children can request help with selecting and planting seeds. They can water and pull weeds in already established gardens.
- Set up obstacle courses using tunnels, balance beams, stairs, and carpet squares for children to crawl through, walk on, climb, and jump.
- Provide buckets of water and sponges for washing the outside equipment: bikes, toy cars, and climbing structures. The children have fun and learn while the playground gets a good cleaning!
- Create an art area where children can paint with a variety of tools, including brushes, sponges, fly swatters, even their hands. They can draw with large pieces of chalk on the cement or paper, experiment with drawing with shaving cream, and create *goop* from cornstarch and water. Provide aprons, water, and towels for easy cleanup.
- Teach children with special needs to play Hide and Seek. Have a peer *buddy* assist them initially. Create interesting places to hide on playground, such as tents or cardboard boxes.

Developing Social Skills

Outside environments offer some of the best opportunities for children with special needs to develop social skills. Examples of specific outside play opportunities that can help develop social skills include:

- Taking turns going down the slide
- Pulling a friend in a wagon, or being pulled in a wagon
- Negotiating around one another on trikes; playing Follow the Leader with trikes or big wheels
- Playing catch and baseball with foam balls
- Sharing toys at sand and water tables; engaging in simple cooperative activities like filling a large bucket with a cup or digging a big hole

Opportunities for Sand and Water Play

Outside time provides an opportunity for children to experience activities not easily managed inside the classroom. Sand and water play are two experiences that can also be expanded into a variety of activities and combinations.

Outdoors can be a much better setting than inside for sand and water play, especially for children with special needs. Unlike playing in the classroom with sand and water where there is always some concern for containment of the materials, playing with these materials outside allows the focus to be on exploring and expanding play schemes.

Sandboxes. Sandboxes can be built or purchased quite easily. Adding enough sand to provide a quality experience can be difficult: it is heavy and you need lots! Depending on the ages of the children, you may want to purchase sand that has been sterilized, or regular builder's sand from the hardware store, lumberyard, or garden center may be fine.

Sandboxes need to be covered when not in use. If water has been added, it is important to allow the sand to dry out before covering.

Children can play with dry sand or add water to change the texture. A variety of toys should be available for children to use during sand play (see Figure 10–3).

Figure 10–3 Sand play provides important sensorimotor experience for children with special needs.

Sand toys

Containers of different sizes and shapes

Shovels and spoons

Flour sifters

Watering cans

Funnels

Cars, trucks, dumptrucks, bulldozers, etc.

Small plastic animals and people

Water Tables. Water tables are versatile pieces of equipment that can be used with any number of materials. These tables are also excellent for encouraging social play with young children, who gather around the table to play and must stand next to each other to participate. Children with physical disabilities who may need practice standing can play naturally at the water table with typical peers.

Water tables can be used to introduce new materials to children. They may also be used to introduce small amounts of a new substance to a child with tactile defensiveness.

Suggested water table ingredients

Water with a variety of containers, funnels, scoops, and strainers

Water with food color added

Sand with a variety of containers, funnels, scoops, and strainers

Sand with water added (provide containers for children to add water and observe the changes in consistency)

Sand (with or without water) and various groups of objects, such as plastic animals, plastic fish, and shells

Cornstarch, flour, or cornmeal with containers and/or other objects

Cornstarch and water to make "goop" (food coloring may be added)

Styrofoam pieces, especially the recyclable kind that dissolves when water is added

Cups of food color when dyeing eggs (if the cup of dye spills, it's contained within the water table—no big mess to clean up!)

Dirt/garden soil (add small cups and seeds plus watering cans for planting activity)

Bubble mixture (dishsoap plus water) and bubble-making tools (commercial bubble wands in various sizes, six-pack soda plastic rings, and any other tool that can hold soap to make a bubble)

Soapy water and dolls with washcloths, sponges, and towels

PLANNING THE OUTDOOR ENVIRONMENT

Planning an outdoor environment that will meet the needs of all children by providing a variety of fun activities while contributing to the achievement of child-specific objectives can be a challenge. The following suggestions may help make the process easier.

Start with a Survey

Survey the outdoor space that is available while keeping in mind the need for several key areas.

- Safe areas for climbing, swinging, rocking, and sliding
- Tricycle paths for wheeled toys away from areas where children may be standing or playing
- Open space for ball play
- Shaded area for children who cannot tolerate exposure to the sun for long periods
- A **movable soft area** for children who may not be able to move independently (assembled using various padded mats and wedges). See Figure 10–4.

Helpful Hint

Children on certain types of medication for seizures or other types of *health conditions* may have strong allergic reactions to sunlight. Children with *physical disabilities* may be unable to move to shaded areas or communicate that need when they become too hot. Thus, teachers need to balance outdoor time between shaded and sunny areas.

Smaller containers of water or sand from water tables or the sandbox can be brought to children in soft areas who may not be able to sit in a sandbox or stand at a water table. Art materials can also be brought into the soft area for children.

- Shaded, comfortable seating areas for parents (A lawn table with an umbrella offers a welcoming place for parents and visitors.)
- Art area for easels and large paint brushes
- Sandbox
- Water table area
- Space for obstacle course

Keep the outside area as clean and dust-free as possible. Provide drinking water for the children either through an accessible water fountain or a conveniently placed cooler. And remember to keep tissues, a first aid kit, and rubber gloves available.

Figure 10–4 Children playing with indoor toys on movable soft area.

Helpful Hint

Some children have a difficult time managing large open space. For such children it may be helpful to design a more enclosed space in a corner area of the play yard. For example, the sandbox might be placed in such an area.

Selecting Materials for Outside Areas

Don't change toys and materials too often. Children with special needs require time to get used to materials, and repetition is the key to mastery!

Choose appropriate wheeled toys that meet the needs of different children. Try to have at least two of the more popular items, because young children have a difficult time with the concept of sharing.

Variety is essential in other play areas. Include as assortment of balls in the ball area: small balls, large balls, beach balls, beanbags, sponge, and ping pong balls. Change soft area toys and materials only after children achieve mastery or appear bored. This area requires careful observation as children here may not be able to initiate their choices easily.

Helpful Hint

Children who have severe *communication disorders* or *motor disabilities* that render them nonverbal can use augmentative or alternative communication (AAC) devices, such as line drawings or photographs of larger playground equipment and areas to facilitate choices.

The art area materials should not be changed too frequently. If an art area is included outside, adding different tools or materials to a basic plan can extend children's interest. It may take some children several days to choose to explore this area, so changing materials often may be more confusing than exciting.

Be sure that sandbox toys are working, in good condition, and well organized. Sand tends to clog wheels and joints in some toys. After regular inspections, line up the toys next to the sandbox for easy selection, and make sure enough containers and shovels are on hand for all children.

The water table toys need the same kind of attention. If possible, separate sand toys from water toys or have duplicates available. Water toys seem to last longer than sand toys! Check that the water table is not cluttered with too many small toys; an overabundance may affect the ability of some children to organize their play.

Leave an obstacle course assembled in the same sequence for several days. Children with special needs will enjoy mastering the course and can experience it with increasing levels of confidence. For variety, they can try it from either end or from somewhere in the middle!

SAMPLE OUTSIDE LESSON PLAN: DISCOVERY WALK

In addition to typical adventures on outside play equipment, another activity that appeals to young children with special needs is the **discovery walk.** A discovery walk need not be a walk around the neighborhood if for some reason this is difficult to manage due to traffic and safety concerns. It can be as simple as a walk around the building and out to the parking lot. To make the discovery walk a learning experience for children with special needs, consider the following suggestions.

- The walk should be a *frequent event,* preferably once a week.

Helpful Hint

While the child who does not have a disability may learn from a single walk, many children with special needs require repetition of the experience several times before they begin to learn from it.

- The route should be carefully planned and repeated until children are familiar with it.

Helpful Hint

Children with limited vision or *blindness* need the assistance of an orientation and mobility specialist to determine whether it is possible to assist them to develop independence in traveling the route.

- Once children are familiar with the route, make interesting changes and draw their attention to the change in the route: "Today we're not going to see the cars. Instead we're going to look at some very beautiful flowers."
- Include regular stopping points along the way, and label them clearly. Plan key words and concepts. For example:

"Gate. Open the gate."
"Mailbox. We can mail our letters here."
"Stop. Stop at the stop sign."
"Barking dog. This is where the barking dog lives."
"Rock. Here's that very big rock."

Helpful Hint

Encourage higher functioning children to expand on these basic labels:
"I wonder why that dog barks when we walk by?"
"Why do we have stop signs?"
"Where do you think that rock came from? What is it shaped like?"
"Who knows what happens to the mail after it goes in this box?"
For the child who has a *hearing loss* and who uses signing as the primary mode of communication, signs need to be taught for labeling key objects.

- Take bags along and collect things. You may wish to have children collect anything they find interesting. Or, on some trips collect specific things, such as stones, leaves, and sticks.
- Hide interesting treasures to be discovered along the route. Children will be thrilled to find a bag of play money or toy jewelry.
- Upon return, draw pictures representing events along the walk or make collages of items collected.
- Help children learn the route and develop a sense of direction:

"Ok, tell me where to turn."
"Which way do we turn?"

"What will we see around that corner?"
"Show me which direction we go to see the dog."

SUMMARY

Outside play can provide a wealth of opportunities to support the learning and participation of children who have special needs. The key is good planning of the outside experience and incorporating specific adaptations. Sometimes those adaptations require specially designed or modified equipment. A particularly enjoyable outside activity is a discovery walk. To make the walk an effective learning experience for children who have special needs, repeat it frequently so that children learn the route and develop expectations for what might be encountered along the way.

CASE STUDY

Creating Space for Leila

Leila is a three-and-a-half-year-old girl with Down syndrome. During the first two years of her life Leila had frequent hospitalizations and her development was significantly delayed. A major achievement for Leila was that she recently learned to walk independently, though she was still fairly unsteady and fell occasionally. Despite this vulnerability, Leila was adapting well to the classroom.

Outdoors was another matter. She was often reluctant to go outside. Once there she would only play near the sandbox. While she would not climb into the sandbox (and resisted being seated in the sand), she would sit on the outside of the sandbox and play fairly listlessly, scooping sand with a small shovel.

Leila's mother mentions to her teacher that one of Leila's favorite activities at home is swinging. However Leila's swing is a secured baby swing. The child care center has no adapted swings. Leila cannot hang on consistently so the swings are not safe for her. Leila would occasionally look longingly at the swings across the play yard from her safe vantage point near the sandbox. Because her walking is unsteady and there is a great deal of unpredictable activity between her and the swings, she never ventures out toward the swings. Because swinging is unsafe for her, the staff does not help her or carry her over to the swings.

After two months Leila shows no inclination to move away from her comfortable spot at the sandbox. Her teacher Mrs. Martinez decides to make some adaptations to enable Leila to be more of a participant during outside play. She creates a soft area with mats and wedges right next to the sandbox. Several of Leila's favorite toys from inside the classroom are placed in the soft area. Quickly, Leila begins walking back and forth between the sandbox and the soft area. This area creates a safe, demarcated zone for her. Other children frequently join Leila in her play.

Another adaptation Mrs. Martinez has implemented is to contact the physical therapist to request help in obtaining an specially designed swing seat that is safe for Leila. She encourages

(continued)

the staff to take Leila to the swing frequently. Leila begins to enjoy her treks across the play yard to the swing. Because Leila is still not ready to walk across the play yard independently, a simple picture request strategy is designed. Leila approaches an adult and gives him the picture of the swing to request that activity. Eventually, one child takes a special interest in Leila. She often takes Leila by the hand, walks with her over to the swings, and helps her give her picture request card to the nearest adult.

Gradually Leila has become much more comfortable on the playground. She is steadier and more confident in her mobility skills, and her overall energy level has increased. The picture request system is so successful that the speech and language specialist has taught the staff to use the PECS (picture exchange system) with Leila. By summer, Leila is a very different child!

Case Study Questions

1. *What are some other ways pictures could be used to increase Leila's opportunities to participate?*
2. *How would you design the "perfect" outdoor play environment for preschoolers? How would you ensure that your design supports children with a wide range of needs and abilities?*
3. *How would the design of this outdoor space differ for toddlers?*

KEY TERMS

discovery walk   movable soft areas

HELFUL RESOURCES

Articles and Books

Ebsensen, S. (1987). *The early childhood playground: An outdoor classroom.* Ypsilanti, MI: High Scope Press.

Fisher, A. G., Murra, E. A., & Bundy, A. (Eds.). (1991). *Sensory integration: Theory and practice.* Philadelphia, PA: F.A. Davis.

Miller, K. (1988). *The outside play and learning book.* Beltsville, MD: Gryphon House.

Moore, R. C., Goltsman, S. M., & Iacofano, D. S. (1987). *Play for all guidelines: Planning, design and management of outdoor play settings for all children.* Berkeley, CA: MIG Communications.

Williams, R. A., Rockwell, R. D., & Sherwood, E. A. (1983). *Hug a tree and other things to do outdoors with young children.* Mt. Rainier, MD: Gryphon House.

Catalogs

Pediatrics: Special needs products for schools and clinics, Sammons Preston, P.O. Box 5071, Bolingbrook, IL 60440-9977, (800) 323-5547.

11

Snack Time

Chapter-at-a-Glance

Some children with disabilities have very specific needs related to feeding. For others snack time provides strong motivation for learning a variety of skills.

- **For children with certain disabilities snack time provides important opportunities for learning.** Snack or meal times provide opportunities to learn social skills such as passing a dish, and waiting to be excused. Also, specific teaching strategies can be used to increase communication skills of requesting and making choices.
- **Children with motor difficulties need help learning how to feed themselves.** Learning opportunities include use of utensils, cups, and glasses. Proper positioning is a key to helping children with eating.
- **Children with special needs can learn other self-help skills.** These include pouring from a pitcher or carton, opening drink cartons, using a straw, cutting food, cleaning the table, and taking care of trash.
- **Some children will need to be fed by an adult.** They may have extreme difficulties learning to chew and swallow. The ECE teacher must obtain assistance from a specialist who has expertise in feeding problems. Snack time also provides an opportunity to model feeding techniques for parents and staff.
- **Some disabilities raise specific nutritional concerns.** Consult with parents regarding special dietary needs. Snacks can provide important nutrients for children who cannot consume large portions at a time.

INTRODUCTION

Most early childhood programs serve a snack during a specific time each day. Some serve breakfast and lunch, and others provide a mid-morning snack then lunch. Afternoon programs typically begin with a lunch and serve a mid-afternoon snack. Some programs require children to bring their meals, while other programs provide snacks or meals as part of the curriculum. Children with special needs often have specific dietary needs, allergies, or food phobias and may bring their own snacks.

LEARNING OPPORTUNITIES AT SNACK AND MEALTIMES

Children with special needs can gain a great sense of accomplishment by learning self-help and social skills related to mealtime. We will discuss strategies to encourage and support that skill building.

Self-Feeding Skills

Opportunities for learning how to eat with utensils, discriminating which foods need utensils, and drinking from a cup are available on a daily basis during snack time. Some children with special needs may require one-to-one assistance at first if they have never used a spoon or cup.

Attention should be given to *seating arrangements.* Children needing one-to-one assistance should have an adult sitting next to or behind them. Often seating a child near the corner of a square or rectangular table allows an adult to sit and assist comfortably but still be available to help other children nearby.

Asking for input from a physical or occupational therapist or a nutritional consultant may be very important if a child has severe physical disabilities that interfere with normal eating patterns. Children with severe physical disabilities may be unable to eat until they are correctly positioned; for example, their feet and trunk must be adequately supported and their head held in an upright position. Equipment such as specially designed spoons or cups may also help children eat or drink more successfully. Figure 11–1 demonstrates a simple adaptation to improve a child's position for self-feeding.

It is often necessary to task analyze skills required for self-feeding. This involves breaking the particular skill, such as eating with a spoon or drinking from a cup, into small teachable steps. The following is an example.

Steps in learning to use a spoon

1. The child grasps the spoon handle firmly.
2. She rotates her wrist to place the spoon into food.
3. She scoops food onto the spoon.

Figure 11–1 Child's position is supported by placing a phone book under her feet.

4. She rotates wrist and arm to bring the spoon to her mouth without spilling.
5. She opens her mouth.
6. She places the spoon in her mouth.
7. She closes her lips around the spoon.
8. She transfers food to her mouth.
9. She removes the spoon.

Helpful Hint

The procedure for teaching a child to eat with a spoon might be best taught using the *backward chaining* method, starting with the last step and moving backward as the child masters each step.

Some Children Must Be Fed by an Adult. Some children have such severe medical or motor disabilities that they must be fed by an adult. These children are sometimes accompanied by a one-to-one aide who performs this function. If this is not the case, the ECE teacher must work closely with the

Figure 11–2   Cut-out cup.

family and a specialist who will provide specific feeding techniques, including positioning, strategies to inhibit reflexes such as biting or gagging, and strategies to facilitate chewing and swallowing.

For a child who needs assistance drinking from a cup, Figure 11–2 is an example of an adapted cup, called a **cut-out cup,** that permits the adult to view the liquid and allows the child with severe head control or postural control difficulties to drink without tipping her head back out of alignment.

Assure Proper Positioning. If the child has a motor problem or if the child is small and chairs are too large, consult with a physical therapist to determine how to best position the child for feeding or eating.

Use of Adapted Utensils. Figures 11–3 and 11–4 picture examples of adapted bowls, cups, and spoons that make self-feeding much easier for children who have motor disabilities. Sources for obtaining this type of equipment are included in the Helpful Resource list at the end of this chapter and at the end of Chapter 3.

Modify Food Textures and Size. For some children food textures or bite size may need to be altered. Consult with parents to determine these accommodations.

Figure 11–3   Adapted bowl and spoon placed on Dycem mat for stablity.

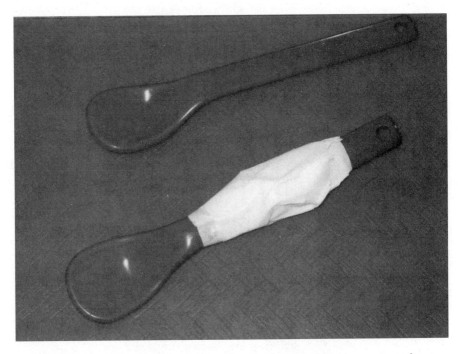

Figure 11–4   Simple adaptation of wrapping masking tape around handle makes spoon easier to grip.

Teaching Other Self-Help Skills at Snack

In addition to self-feeding, snack time provides opportunities for children with special needs to learn other self-help skills:

- Setting the table
- Pouring from a pitcher or carton
- Opening drink cartons
- Using a straw
- Cutting food
- Wiping up spills
- Cleaning the table
- Taking care of trash

Finally, some children with special needs may need help transitioning into and out of mealtime. Following a set sequence of events and providing maximal assistance for these children at first and gradually reducing that assistance is probably the most effective strategy.

The following example describes the use of a song to assist children in transitioning to a snack or meal.

Meal transition strategies

- Warn child of the impending transition: "It's time to eat in two minutes."
- Sing the same song or use the same sign to signal the beginning of the transition to the meal. One example is "Today is Monday," sung to the tune of "Are You Sleeping?"

  Today is Monday. Today is Monday.
  What shall we eat? What shall we eat?
  Today we're eating soup. Today we're eating soup.
  Yum, yum, yum. Yum yum yum.

- Follow a set routine: come inside, sing the song, set the table, wash hands, and find a seat.
- At the end of the meal, follow another routine: brush teeth, throw away dish and cup, and move to the quiet area to look at books.

Developing Social Skills at Snack

Practicing beginning social interactions during snack or mealtimes can be important learning opportunities for children with special needs because eating is often highly motivating and engaging. Examples of social skills include:

- passing food (if served family style).
- helping oneself to a single serving.

- waiting one's turn.
- requesting a second helping.
- waiting to be excused from the table.

Some children with special needs may have difficulty regulating themselves to one serving of food or waiting. They may need more direct adult assistance as they become familiar with the routine.

Over time children will begin to understand the social rules for mealtime if these rules are consistently enforced. The need for adult assistance will lessen dramatically.

Some children may need help understanding the sequence of events surrounding mealtime. Having a daily snacktime routine is helpful. Displaying the routine through photographs or line drawings may assist some children.

Developing Communication Skills

Throughout a typical day, children use some form of communication to indicate what they want or need. Some children with special needs may choose not to initiate communicating with others because they see no need to do so. However, mealtime may be a highly motivating period for some children to communicate with others because they enjoy food and are hungry. Snack periods, if well organized, may also allow staff to pay attention to communicative intent and cues that might be missed during less routine periods such as outside or free play.

Strategies for building communication and social skills during snack time
- Use family-style servings for at least part of one meal (crackers in a box, sliced fruit on a plate, yogurt in a large bowl or, juice or milk in a small pitcher) and encourage children to point, sign, or verbalize when they want more.
- Use family-style servings for at least part of one meal and let children pass the container to each other and serve themselves an appropriately sized serving with adult help as needed.
- Pretend to *not see* a preverbal child pointing to a desired food item until the child makes some type of vocalization to get your attention. Continue using this type of behavior occasionally to encourage vocalizations that begin to approximate the word you want the child to say.
- Seat nonverbal children next to verbal children.
- Direct a child who tends to look to adults for assistance to ask the child seated next to her for help. Also, make sure the second child learns the first child's cues for help.
- Set out everything for a meal—food, dishes, napkins—except spoons. Wait for the children to realize what they are missing and ask you for the utensils.

Helpful Hint

Teachers in community-based early child education settings may find these techniques in conflict with their normal snack time routine. These strategies are appropriate for a child who rarely, if ever, initiates communication, but is highly motivated during mealtime. This may be the only opportunity to encourage communicative initiation, especially if toys or other materials used during other activities are either not high preference or if there is no way to limit the child's access to create communicative need.

Demonstrating Mealtime Techniques

Mealtime for some children with severe physical disabilities may be an opportunity to demonstrate effective feeding techniques to parents or caregivers. It is important to seek input from a physical or occupational therapist or a feeding specialist on seating adaptations and feeding strategies.

SPECIAL NUTRITIONAL CONSIDERATIONS

Some children with special needs have specific nutritional needs or challenges. Some of the most common are discussed in this section.

Children with Cerebral Palsy

Ongoing communication with the child's caregiver, physician, and occupational or physical therapist is important. Food intake is often decreased due to **tongue thrust** (protruding the tongue forward), poor lip closure, **tonic bite reflex** (vigorously clamping the teeth down when the mouth is stimulated in a certain way), or **abnormal gag reflex** (either exaggerated or weak).

Frustration, fatigue, and inadequate nutrition may result from prolonged mealtimes. Be sure the child is positioned properly to reduce fatigue and encourage successful chewing and swallowing.

Foods should be selected to provide the greatest nutrient intake possible. Examples of nutritional foods that a child with cerebral palsy might more easily eat include sweet potatoes, mashed beans, and spreads made with fruits. Provide a variety of textures to encourage tongue and chewing movements. Always check with a parent or occupational therapist before offering any new food.

Be aware that abnormal muscle tone and limited physical activity increase constipation. Increasing intake of fluids and higher fiber foods may reduce this problem. Also, for some children who are not mobile spending a short period of time each day in an upright position, such as in a **prone stander** shown in Figure 11–5, may facilitate regular bowel movements.

Figure 11–5 Upright position may facilitate bowel function in children who are not mobile.

Water can be very difficult to control and swallow. If a child has extreme difficulty swallowing watery liquids, it may be helpful to thicken them with yogurt or instant baby cereal.

Children with Epilepsy (Seizure Disorders)

Ongoing consultation with the child's physician and a nutrition consultant is essential because children with **epilepsy** are often at risk for dental problems and poor weight gain. Be aware that the primary nutrition problems of children with seizure disorders are often related to the side effects of their **anticonvulsant medication** (Eicher, 1997) and the interaction of this medication with foods. Such interactions can cause poor appetite, low levels of folic acid and calcium in the blood. Swollen or tender gums caused by the drug Dilantin may cause serious dental problems and interfere with eating.

Anticonvulsant drugs may also interfere with the absorption of certain vitamins and minerals (Batshaw & Perret, 1992). Physicians may prescribe nutrient supplements to offset the side effects of medication.

Children with Low Muscle Tone

Development of the necessary skills for eating table foods and self-feeding may be delayed because of low muscle tone. Low muscle tone is a common characteristic of children who have Down syndrome. Some children with low muscle tone may have difficulty receiving adequate oral sensation or maintaining adequate muscle tension. Often this difficulty is related to excessive drooling. Children may not realize where the food or liquid is in their mouth, or they may not realize their mouth is full. This results in an increased risk for choking.

Some children may overstuff their mouth, which makes chewing even more difficult and may cause a gag reflex. Children who have a reduced gag reflex are more likely to choke.

As children with Down syndrome get older, they may be at increased risk for obesity if they are not walking or have low activity levels and low muscle tone. ECE teachers should encourage the development of the ability to engage in active motor activities, and they should help these children select foods with high nutritional value and low calories. In some cases it may be necessary to refer the family to a nutritional specialist.

Children with Autism

Some children with special needs, particularly children with autism, may show unusual preferences for certain types of food based on color, texture, or taste. They may refuse to eat certain foods and develop **food phobias.**

Sometimes children develop **food obsessions,** insisting that they will eat only one or two things. Work closely with the family to determine how best to manage these issues. In some cases where snack provides a very small portion of the child's daily nutrition, the family may opt to allow the child to eat the preferred food each day. In other cases a behavioral plan may be needed to deal with extreme or disruptive food obsessions.

Prader-Willi Syndrome

Prader-Willi syndrome is a fairly rare condition. It is included here because of its association with a severe eating disorder. Prader-Willi is a chromosomal disorder. The most striking feature of Prader-Willi is obesity, which is related to insatiable overeating caused by an abnormality of the hypothalamic region of the brain. Typical behavior patterns include constant demand or stealing of food and general patterns of impulsivity and obstinance. While children may have cognitive skills in the near normal range, the behavior disorder related to overeating is fairly resistant to treatment (Bray et al., 1983). It is extremely important that the ECE teacher work closely with specialists and parents to provide the best possible support.

Pica

In rare cases an eating disorder referred to as **pica** develops in which the child obsessively eats nonfood items such as paint or dirt. In some cases this may result from specific nutritional deficiencies. A danger in low-income neighborhoods or areas with older homes is that children with this disorder may ingest lead-based paint chips. Children who appear to crave nonfood substances should be referred to a nutritionist who is knowledgeable regarding children with special needs.

Tube Feeding

For some children oral feeding may be impossible or so insufficient that they cannot receive adequate nutrition. This may be the result of severe motor disability that interferes with basic suck and swallow functions or a tendency to aspirate food into the lungs. Children with complex medical needs are often tube fed. The most common type of tube is a **gastrostomy tube (G-tube).** This type of tube is placed through a small hole in the abdominal wall into the stomach. The child receives either a specialized formula or pureed food through the tube several times a day. Parents or a pediatric nurse practitioner are the best source of information regarding these procedures. Children who are tube fed and who are in inclusive settings may have a one-on-one assistant.

A WORD ABOUT TOILETING

Bowel and bladder control and toilet training can be significant challenges for many children with special needs. Some children simply do not have adequate neuromuscular control or adequate sensation (due to such disorders as cerebral palsy or spina bifida). Low cognitive ability, limited communication skills, and the development of fear or conditioned reactions to toileting may be other factors. For example, children who have autism may be become frightened of the sound of toilets flushing. Also, a child with a motor disability may not feel secure and in a stable position when placed on a potty, making it impossible to relax.

Space does not allow an adequate consideration of toileting in this book. However, successful toilet training, wherever it is a realistic expectation, is a critical goal for children who have special needs. Obviously the older the child becomes, the more the absence of this basic self-help skill becomes an increasing liability. Early childhood educators must work closely with specialists, possibly a behavior specialist or physical therapist, and parents to plan an intervention strategy to achieve toilet training.

SUMMARY

Children with certain disabilities may have special challenges related to eating. For example, children with severe motor disabilities may have difficulty even performing basic functions of chewing and swallowing; they need to be fed by an adult. If feeding difficulties are extreme, some children may be fed through a gastrostomy tube. Others have difficulty managing use of a spoon or drinking from a cup. Some children have food phobias or food obsessions. Snack time creates the opportunity to work directly on these problems. In addition, snack time can also provide opportunities for the development of additional self-help skills, such as pouring and clearing the table, and of social and communication skills. Toileting can present major challenges for children with special needs and may require a team approach to ensure success.

CASE STUDY

Aaron's Fruit Loops®

Aaron was a four-year-old boy with a diagnosis of autism. He seemed bright in many ways. He could read many words; he could draw cars and trucks with incredible detail. Though he wasn't social, his language structure was fairly complex. He had adjusted well to Mr. Chinn's classroom, except for one problem area: snack time. Aaron refused to join the other children at snack time. He resisted nearly all foods; yet he was obsessed with Fruit Loops®. Mr. Chinn had made several attempts to *cure* Aaron of this Fruit Loop® obsession, but had been unsuccessful in his attempts to get Aaron to eat other foods. Mr. Chinn had given up trying to get Aaron to come to the snack table. He let him wander around the room with his Tupperware® container of Fruit Loops® while the other children were at the snack table. (Mr. Chinn suspected that this might actually be a reinforcement for not coming to snack table, but it kept Aaron occupied.)

Mr. Chinn mentioned to Ms. Harris, the inclusion support facilitator for the center, that he was frustrated that he had had so little success in reducing Aaron's food obsession or in reducing his resistance of snack time. After observing Aaron at snack time, talking with his mother, and reviewing the case with Mr. Chinn and the teaching assistants, Ms. Harris and the classroom team came up with the following plan.

They would attempt to make snack time less stressful for Aaron by creating a more predictable snack routine. They decided to make laminated placemats with everyone's names on them, since Aaron loved reading words and could recognize everyone's names. Mr. Chinn assigned a specific seat for each child, placing their names on the back of their chair at the snack table. He created a mini-routine in which he signaled the transition to snack time by holding up the stack of placemats and saying, "Okay, let's get ready for snack." He handed the placemats to Aaron, who with very little prompting quickly became able to match all the placemats to the correct seats.

Aaron loved this activity. He also loved having his own placemat and quickly became comfortable sitting at the snack table. Rather than hassling him about trying new foods, Mr. Chinn would reinforce Aaron for helping and sitting down at his placemat by giving him his Tupperware® container of Fruit Loops®. Mr. Chinn was very pleased that Aaron was finally able to join the other children during this activity.

As Aaron became increasingly comfortable with this routine, Mr. Chinn noticed him looking at the other children's food. The teacher begins placing new foods on the edge of Aaron's placemat. Usually Aaron would push the food away. Mr. Chinn would simply comment, "Oh, you don't like pretzels." Occasionally Aaron would actually try the novel food, and by the end of the year he had added two new foods to his repertoire of preferred foods: goldfish crackers and raisins. While Mr. Chinn didn't exactly see this as great progress, Aaron's mother was thrilled!

Case Study Questions

1. *Why do you think Aaron would only eat Fruit Loops?*
2. *How do you think the other children in the class responded to Aaron and to the strategies that were used to get him to participate at the table?*
3. *What do you think was the most important issue in the case: the lack of participation or the food obsession? Why?*

KEY TERMS

abnormal gag reflex	gastrostomy tube (G-tube)
anticonvulsant medication	pica
cut-out cup	Prader-Willi syndrome
epilepsy	prone stander
food obsessions	tongue thrust
food phobias	tonic bite reflex

HELPFUL RESOURCES

Articles and Books

American Dietetic Association. (1987). Nutrition in comprehensive program planning for persons with developmental disabilities: Technical support. *Journal of the American Dietetic Association, 87,* 1069–1074.

Cosgrove, M. S. (1991). Cooking in the classroom: The doorway to nutrition. *Young Children, 46*(3), 43–46.

Dietz, W. H., & Bandini, L. (1989). Nutritional assessment of the handicapped child. *Pediatrics in Review, 11*(4), 109–115.

Endres, J. B., & Rockwell, R. E. (1994). *Food, nutrition, and the young child.* Upper Saddle River, NJ: Merrill/Prentice Hall.

Hahn, T. J., & Avioli, L. V. (1984). Anticonvulsant drug-induced mineral disorders. In D. A. Roe & T. C. Campbell (Eds.), *Drugs and nutrients— The interactive effects* (pp. 409–427). New York: Marcel Dekker.

Moore, M. C., & Greene, H. L. (1985). Tube feeding of infants and children. *Pediatric Clinics of North America, 32,* 401–417.

Videos

Eicher, P. M. (1997). Feeding. In M. L. Batshaw (Eds.), *Children with disabilities* (4th ed. pp 621–642). Baltimore, MD: Paul H. Brookes.

Medical issues impacting feeding and swallowing (15 minutes), Special Needs Project, 3463 State Street, Suite 282, Santa Barbara, CA 93105.

Positioning for infants and young children with motor problems, Learner Managed Designs, 2201 K W. 25th St., Lawrence, KS 66046.

Potty learning for children who experience delay (69 minutes), Special Needs Project, 3463 State Street, Suite 282, Santa Barbara, CA 93105.

REFERENCES

Batshaw, M. L., & Perret, Y. M. (1992). Good nutrition, poor nutrition. In M. L. Batshaw & Y. M. Perret (Eds.), *Children with disabilities: A medical primer* (3rd ed., pp. 171–196). Baltimore, MD: Paul H. Brookes.

Bray, G. A., et al. (1983). The Prader-Willi syndrome: A study of 40 patients and a review of the literature. *Medicine, 62,* 59–80.

Eicher, P. M. (1997). Feeding. In M. L. Batshaw (Eds.), *Children with disabilities.* (4th ed., pp. 621–642). Baltimore, MD: Paul H. Brookes.

12

Music and Rhythm Activities

Chapter-at-a-Glance

Music and rhythm activities are not only fun and energizing, but for many children with special needs it provides opportunity for total participation.

- **Music and rhythm may engage certain children with special needs in ways that other activities do not.** For example, music can be a valuable teaching tool for children with communication delays or disabilities.
- **Music can enhance physical activities.** It offers an opportunity for children to become more aware of their bodies in space as they move to various tempos and rhythm. Children with physical disabilities or mobility problems can be assisted to move in time with the music.
- **Music can hold children's interest.** Children who have difficulties paying attention may find it easier to sustain interest with music or rhythm included as part of activities. Also, songs with motions can support speech and language development.
- **Music can move active and inactive children.** Using music effectively can provide an appropriate outlet for children who are extremely active. It can also motivate children who are typically inactive.
- **Through music, a sense of community can permeate the group regardless of abilities.** Joyful, rhythmic music can create a positive shared experience.

INTRODUCTION

The value of music and rhythm activities in the early childhood setting is well documented. Different types of music can affect the overall *feel* of the

221

classroom. Music can draw children to group time or send them off for free play. Songs can signal transitions and cleanup periods throughout the day.

BENEFITS FOR CHILDREN WITH SPECIAL NEEDS

Music and rhythm activities foster a creative atmosphere in which every child can participate. Let us review the advantages of incorporating music into your classroom and the opportunities it offers for children with special needs.

Something for Everyone

The large group setting offers a variety of opportunities for reacting to music and rhythm. Children often respond in different ways to music. Some get up and dance, while others sit, listen, and observe their peers. For the child with special needs, any positive reaction to the music can be acceptable in the large group setting. When it comes to dancing and rhythmic movements, there are no rules, no *right way* to do it. The activity provides the opportunity for all children to feel successful whether they are sitting and listening, moving their head, shaking a maraca, clapping hands, or jumping up and down (see Figures 12–1A and 12–1B).

To enhance the use of rhythm instruments, children can make simple instruments themselves to create greater interest. They can paint a cardboard aluminum foil tube and hum into it, or place bottle caps in a toilet paper roll and cover the ends to make a maraca. Making their own instruments can heighten their interest in participating in the rhythm band. See Figures 12–2 and 12–3.

Building and Holding Interest

Children who have difficulties paying attention may find it easier to sustain interest with music or rhythm included as part of the activities. Music or songs used in conjunction with classroom activities requiring sustained attention, such as reading stories and learning new words and phrases, can help some children attend for longer periods of time. Also, the opportunity to move to a strong rhythm can help children prepare for a quieter task such as listening to a story or engaging in manipulative play; they can expend some of their energy prior to sitting down.

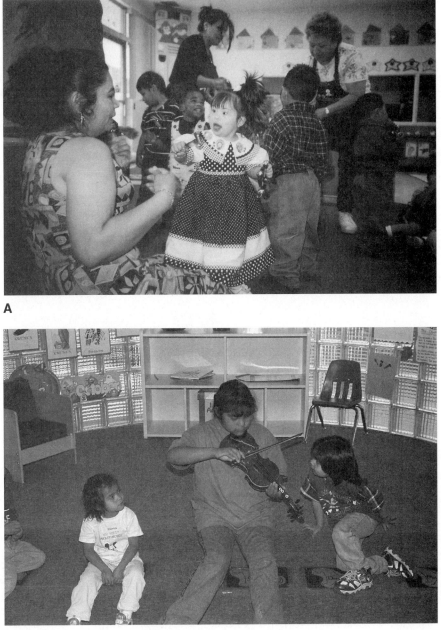

A

B

Figure 12–1   Simple rhythm activity increases participation.

Place bottle caps inside toilet paper roll and cover both ends to make maraca shaker.

Decorate empty aluminum foil tube and use as horn.

Figure 12–2 Simple ways to use cardboard tubes for rhythm instruments.

Make tambourine by sewing paper plates together with bottle caps inside.

Figure 12–3 Make a paper plate tambourine.

Jimmy

The child care teacher complained that Jimmy never sat through story time. He would stay for the first story but as soon as the teacher began the second story, Jimmy almost always began to disrupt the rest of the group. He leaned on other children, rolled back and forth on the rug, and sometimes left the group completely. One day the teacher decided to sing a song following the end of the first story. Jimmy appeared to enjoy the song and swayed back and forth while clapping his hands. When the teacher began the second story, he noticed that Jimmy was still sitting down and listening!

During the following week, the teacher carefully noted which days Jimmy sat through two stories and which days he became disruptive. Jimmy attended to the second story more when it was preceded by an active song or finger play. He was able to release some of that energy and remain more attentive throughout the second book.

Music as a Motivator

Using music effectively can provide an outlet for pent-up energy in active children and may be a motivator for inactive children. Turning on music and encouraging children to move can occur at any time throughout the day. It can happen during large group times or during free play activities. Certain types of music motivate different children to move or dance so a variety of types should be available. Repeating certain songs often may help some children engage in movement because they recognize the familiar tune and feel comfortable moving to the beat.

By giving young children the opportunity to dance and move, energy can be expelled in a highly appropriate and acceptable arena. Dancing is much more fun than being constantly reprimanded for running around the classroom for both the teacher and child! Giving children the opportunity to dance may provoke some types of movement that can hurt other children, such as falling onto other children or pushing into others. Teachers must be clear about acceptable movement and enforce boundaries for the safety of all children. It may be necessary to require overly rambunctious children to hold their teachers' hands during dancing time.

Children who may not move much, such as children with low muscle tone or children with physical disabilities, may be more motivated to move when music with a catchy rhythm is played. Teachers may need to encourage these children to move at first by holding their hands and helping them dance. Some children may need to be held by an adult to get the feeling of movement to rhythm. If it is not possible to hold children in wheelchairs, they should be moved while in their chairs so they can feel the beat and actively experience the rhythm.

Creating a Sense of Community

Through music, everyone can experience a feeling of belonging, regardless of abilities. All children can feel a sense of community when music and songs are used regularly to bring the whole group together.

Creating adaptations for children with special needs during music time so they can fully participate can contribute to a sense of community and belonging within the classroom. This is also true for staff and parents. Large group music at the end of the day brings a sense of closure and togetherness.

It is important that the music selected for these activities include songs that reflect families' culture and daily life. For example, while children from Latino neighborhoods can learn to enjoy "Twinkle Twinkle Little Star" or "If You're Happy and You Know It," more familiar music with a Latin beat and Spanish lyrics can provide a strong positive effect. Rap music can also be particularly appealing to many children (though the lyrics may need to be screened!).

Giving a child with physical disabilities the opportunity to be in control of starting and stopping the music can allow the child a feeling of control and participation. (See Debbie's Case Study at the end of this chapter.)

Encouraging Communication

Songs can be a valuable teaching tool for children with communication delays or disabilities. Using songs and finger plays to encourage language development is no new curriculum activity for early childhood teachers. Children learn how to count, use their fingers, and follow tunes while engaged in circle time music activities.

Songs with clear, simple motions that reinforce key words can be an excellent support for early development of speech and language. For example, in "Eeensy Weensy Spider" the movement of the arms up as the spider crawls "up the water spout," then down for "down came the rain," not only reinforces the child's understanding of the concept but may eventually enable the child to *say* the words.

Children with cognitive or motor disabilities can also learn through this approach as long as there are ample opportunities for repetition and the songs are relatively simple and not too fast paced.

Enhancing Physical Awareness

Music offers an opportunity for children to become more aware of their bodies in space as they move to various tempos and rhythm. Dancing, marching, shaking, stomping, and clapping are only some of the actions the body can do when music is played. As young children move their bodies to different types of rhythms, they become aware of what they can and cannot do as they move (see Figure 12–4). Most children can move some part of their body to music, and children with severe motor disabilities can be held and danced with or moved in their wheelchairs. Moving to different tempos helps young children to become aware of how to organize their body to *keep the beat,* and the tempo may actually help some children to pay more attention to what is happening around them.

Helpful Hint

For children with *hearing loss* vibrations are important. Select music that has a heavy identifiable beat and a strong bass pitch.

Making the Most of Music

Children's repertoires can be gradually expanded to experience a variety of music.

Figure 12–4 Music heightens children's affect and engagement.

Add the Opportunity to March to Music. After children have become familiar with using instruments, go on a parade throughout the classroom. Expand to the rest of the center or outside as you carry a portable tape player with you.

Helpful Hint

For children with a diagnosis of *autism* or those who have a difficult time coping with too much sensory input, using too many dissonant instruments may make an otherwise fun activity unbearable from an auditory standpoint. Observe for signs of distress if the sound is too loud or dissonant and remove children from the immediate area to calm down.

Use a Variety of Objects to Enhance Familiar Music or Songs. Encourage participation in musical activities by using toy and homemade instruments, the parachute, and puppets. The same song accompanied with different instruments sounds quite different. Using puppets to enhance songs adds novelty while offering repetition and familiarity.

USING MUSIC TO BUILD LANGUAGE SKILLS

In addition to music for dancing, songs with words and actions can support children with limited language skills. The following suggestions are made to help children with language delays participate in songs and music.

Choose Simple Songs

Stick with familiar, favorite songs and chants, and repeat them often. Then leave out key words and ask children to *fill in the blank* as you sing. Often, you don't need to give any directions to the children. Simply sing the song and stop at the word you want them to say. If it is familiar enough, they will keep singing using all words. Slowing the song down will make it easier by providing enough time for children with special needs to respond. Children without disabilities may find the slower beat an interesting twist on a familiar song.

"The eensy weensy (_____) went up the water spout.
Down came the (_____) and washed the (_____) out."

Teach or Reinforce Concepts

For example, concepts such as *stop* and *go* or *fast* and *slow* can be taught using the following strategy.

1. Play music and have all children move to the music—or play instruments; shake flags, scarves, or a small parachute; or march in place.
2. Abruptly turn off the music. Say and sign STOP.
3. Wait quietly until everyone has stopped and it is quiet.
4. Build children's anticipation, then turn on the music again and resume movement.

Helpful Hint

This approach is an excellent opportunity for a child with *motor disabilities* who has difficulty holding and shaking instruments or the parachute to be in charge of the activity by using a switch to start and stop music. Also, rhythm instruments such as maracas can be attached to the child's hand with Velcro®. Then a simple movement of the child's hand can allow the child to experience the control of restarting the music.

In addition to teaching *stop* and *go,* music and rhythm can be used to teach *fast* and *slow.*

- Teach *fast* and *slow* by using rhythm instruments or marching.
- Play music that is fast or slow and shake to that beat, or have children shake the parachute. Be dramatically fast or slow and exaggerate each concept.
- Chant or sing songs that can be sung either fast or slow.
- Select tapes of children's music that teaches concepts.

Helpful Hint

For children with expressive *language delays* or *hearing loss* who are learning to use sign language, this is a good opportunity to practice simple signs for key words with all children in a natural type of setting.

SUMMARY

The participation and learning of young children with special needs can be greatly enhanced with rhythm and music. Some tips to remember when selecting music to appeal to children with a wide range of abilities and challenges include the following:

1. Some music may need to be slowed down to enable all children to participate.
2. Select music with rhythm and repeated words and phrases. For example, "The Hokey Pokey" can be sung slowly, and its repetition allows children with special needs plenty of opportunity to master the words and the whole body movements, with assistance as necessary.
3. Music with easily performed motions that represent simple concepts (like "Wheels on the Bus") offers good learning opportunities.
4. Dance music with Latin or rock beats can create a joyful sense of participation with the group. Make sure children with special needs are assisted to move their bodies in a safe secure way.
5. Children who have difficulty tolerating the proximity of other children may need adaptations initially to feel comfortable in activities of expressive and creative dancing.

CASE STUDY

Debbie's Switch

Debbie is a three-year-old with severe cerebral palsy. She can sit in a special chair and uses her eyes and facial expressions to communicate what she wants and needs. Debbie can use her hands to press a large switch that, when connected to battery-operated or electric objects, will switch them on and off.

Debbie's teacher observes that during the course of the classroom day, Debbie usually ends up doing what someone else wants her to do. She eats when someone gives her food, she plays in whatever part of the classroom she is taken to. It is difficult for Debbie

(continued)

to move on her own so she usually relies on her mother or another child or adult to understand what she wants to do.

Debbie's mother and her teachers know she really enjoys being part of music time with the class. They often hold her and dance with her or help her move her arms and legs to the beat of the music. One day, a teacher suggests hooking up one of Debbie's switches to the tape player so she can start and stop the music with a small amount of pressure from her hand. Debbie is somewhat hesitant at first—she's not sure whether she should stop the music or let it keep going. The other children are somewhat surprised when the music stops for the first time and turn to see who did it. As Debbie continues to experiment with her control of the activity, the children begin to laugh each time the music stops and they have to *freeze*. Soon all the children are calling to Debbie to *stop* and *go* as they stop and start dancing when she operates the switch.

Case Study Questions

1. *Why was the adaptation described in this case study important for Debbie? What areas of development could be addressed by this simple switch adaptation?*
2. *How could you elaborate the activity to include other children?*
3. *What specialists might be important to using technology to assist Debbie?*

HELPFUL RESOURCES

The following are examples of available music that appeals to young children with special needs.

Cassettes and CDs

Millarg, S., & Seelsa, G. (1979). *We all live together* (Vol 3). Los Angeles: Youngheart Records. Includes:

1. "If You're Happy and You Know It," participants act out movements of clapping, stomping feet, etc.
2. "Simon Says," familiar childhood game involves many body parts.
3. "Rock Around the Mulberry Bush," participants act out, "This is the way we" make our bed, wash our face, comb our hair, etc.

Palmer, H. (1994). *Getting to know myself*. Freeport, NY: Activity Records. Includes:

1. "Feelings," vocabulary and concept development for sad, happy, sleepy, angry, funny.
2. "Touch," reinforces body parts vocabulary.
3. "Shake Something," participants move body parts up/down, bend/unbend, fast/slow, etc.

4. "Turn around," participants follow directions to close, open, wiggle, stamp loudly/softly, and shake.
5. "What Do People Do?" participants act out ways people express angry, sad, afraid, and happy emotions.

Raffi, & Whiteley, K. (1976). *Raffi singable songs for the very young.* Vancouver, BC: Homeland Publishing. Includes:

1. "Brush Your Teeth," children pretend to brush teeth following song's directions.
2. "Spider on the Floor," acting out spider moving from floor up the body to the head, using movement and facial expressions.

Scelsa, G., & Millary, S. (1987). *Kids in motion.* Los Angeles: Indian Bingo Music/Red Admiral Music (BMI), Youngheart Records. Includes:

1. "The Body Rock," by Little House Music (ASCAP), various movements of body parts to rock-n-roll beat.
2. "Animal Action I and II," movements of different animals.
3. "The Freeze," encourages creative movement until music stops and participants "freeze."
4. "Beanbag Boogie I and II," participants place beanbags on body parts as directed by song.

Videos

Kids sing along. (30 min.) Good Housekeeping Publishers. Live action contemporary versions of favorite children's songs.

Palmer, H. *Babysongs, More babysongs,* and *Turn on the Music* (30 min.) Hi-Tops Videos. Live action and animation.

Raffi. (45 min.). Shoreline. *Raffi* Live concerts.

Tickle Tune Typhoon's *Let's be friends,* (50 min.). Tickle Tune Typhoon Productions. Songs and dances performed by musicians with varying abilities.

13

Supporting Emergent Literacy in Children with Special Needs

Chapter-at-a-Glance

The use of pictures and print in the classroom can provide communication support for children with special needs while supporting emergent literacy for all children.

The development of early literacy skills can provide important advantages for children with special needs. ECE teachers should not assume that if a child cannot talk, she cannot learn to read. For some children with special needs, literacy skills can provide support for communication.

- **Some children face specific challenges in the development of literacy.** Many highly motivating strategies can be used throughout each activity of the day to encourage emergent literacy skills.
- **Pictures and print can be used to support expressive language in children who are nonverbal.** Communication boards and PECS are common ways of using pictures for communication.
- **Pictures and print can support children's language comprehension and memory.** Use of pictures can help children understand and anticipate events in the daily schedule and complex task sequences.
- **Use of pictures to help the child's understanding of daily events may reduce behavior problems.** Many children do not comprehend or cannot remember spoken language. For these children pictures, schedules, and cues for transitions are helpful.

INTRODUCTION

Historically educators have assumed that reading and writing are skills that develop after children learn to talk. Because many children with special needs have significant delays in language development, there has been a reluctance to introduce literacy activities to these children during the preschool years. However as Watson, Layton, Pierce, and Abraham (1994) point out, early exposure to literacy activities are important for *all* children, regardless of their speech and language ability.

More recently ECE programs have put renewed emphasis on the importance of including phonemic awareness activities in preschool curricula. This activity can also support specific skills of listening, sound discrimination, and speech sound production in children who have hearing loss, communication delays, and learning disabilities.

It is particularly important to realize that for some children who will *never* develop intelligible spoken language, use of pictures and print may be a critical alternative mode.

OPPORTUNITIES TO SUPPORT LITERACY

Opportunities to encourage prereading skills abound in most ECE classrooms. Let's consider a variety of simple, but interesting, ways of exposing young children with special needs to literacy.

Environmental Print

While recognition of environmental print may develop effortlessly in typical children, children with special needs may require assistance learning to recognize everyday logos, trademarks, and symbols.

- Bring in items such as napkins, paper cups, bags and wrappers with familiar commercial logos, such as McDonalds®, Kmart®, and Coca-Cola®.
- Use items with logos in pretend play activities, such as *grocery store* and *restaurant*.
- Look for matching logos in newspapers and magazines.
- Look for matching logos on walks in the community and on field trips.

Functional Print

Adults should demonstrate functional and interesting uses of print throughout the day.

- **Taking attendance.** Children recognize and count name cards.

Helpful Hint

For the child who has a *visual impairment,* attach a piece of textured material to her name card so she can identify it as her own. If the child is learning Braille, each child's name should be written in Braille on the cards so the child can learn to identify any child's name card by feeling it.

- **Sharing the lunch menu.** Write the menu on the board or chart paper. Then return to it just before lunch time to see who can *read* what will be served for lunch.
- **Assigning jobs.** Children look to see whose name is under "Setting the table," "Line leader," "Feeding the fish," etc.
- **Writing notes.** Read a note from another teacher. Write a note to someone else, and ask a child to deliver it. Write oneself a note as a reminder of something.
- **Ordering from a catalog.** Fill out the order form, address the envelope, and walk with the class to the mailbox or post office. When the item is received, read the address on the package.
- **Using labels.** Place certain play materials in similar cupboards or containers so the only way to know what is inside is to read the label.

Play Activities

Treasure Hunt. Even though children cannot yet read, a treasure hunt is a great demonstration of the function of print. Each note should be large so it can be easily shown to all the children before the teacher *deciphers* it.

Writing Letters in Pretend Play. Set up a writing table in the pretend play or library area of the classroom. Include pens and markers, envelopes, cards, and stationery. Somewhere else in the classroom or just outside the door, place a toy mailbox. Encourage children to *write* letters to each other and to family members.

Note: For children with severe *physical disabilities* who can neither manage a writing tool nor dictate a letter, one possibility is to help them select pictures and words from magazines to be mailed. More advanced children who are learning to use computerized AAC devices may have the capacity to print hard copies of messages.

Multiple Copies of Familiar Books. Children with special needs may not begin to enjoy books until the books are extremely familiar. It is helpful to include multiple copies of those storybooks that are read most frequently during circle time. These books can also be sent home for parents to read to children.

Helpful Hint

Be sure to include books with interesting textures or add textures or small objects to pages for children with *visual disabilities.* For children who are *cognitively* very young, look for books with clear drawings, simple, familiar concepts, and repeated and rhyming text.

Making Picture Albums. Making albums can be engaging for children with special needs.

- Take photos of the children and familiar people and activities.
- Let children find interesting pictures in magazines to cut out and place in the album.
- If photo albums are too expensive, children can make their own by using cardboard for the covers and clear plastic zip-lock bags or construction paper for the pages.
- Be sure to identify each picture by writing key words or a short sentence below it. Use a dark thick marker and write in big letters.
- Keep all the albums on a shelf with children's names written on the spine.
- Read the albums with children frequently. Always emphasize the print. "Now what is this picture? Let me read what it says."

Literacy Activities throughout the Daily Schedule

Each major component of the daily schedule can readily incorporate literacy activities that will appeal to children with special needs. The following suggestions are adapted from Watson, et al. (1994) and Cook, Tessier, and Klein (2000).

Arrival. As they arrive, children locate their cubbies, which are clearly marked with their name and picture. If a child arrives without a parent but has some written communication for the teacher, such as a note or parent communication book, the teacher should briefly read what it says to demonstrate to the child that this is an important form of communication.

Posting the Daily Schedule. Be sure to have the daily schedule posted in large letters. Include a photo or drawing of each major daily activity (see Figure 13–1). At various times throughout the day, refer to the schedule by reading it.

Support language and development of time concepts by asking questions, like "What comes after snack?" and refer back to the posted picture sequence representing the daily schedule.

Circle Time. Identify carpet squares or chairs with children's names and/or pictures. Take attendance using name cards.

Figure 13-1 Daily schedule board.

Helpful Hint

The process of learning to recognize and discriminate their name in print can take a long time for children with *low cognitive skills.* Including a photo of children on the cards will make it easier for them to participate. The teacher can encourage recognition of the print alone by first covering up the picture so that children look first at the print and then at the picture. Eventually children will begin to recognize the print alone. If all the children's names are accompanied by their pictures, children with low cognitive ability can also learn to recognize other children's name cards. Some children with cognitive disabilities will not be able to recognize a photo of themselves. This procedure will assist these children in understanding picture representation.

A   B

Figure 13–2 For many children with special needs, picture A will be much more difficult to process than picture B.

Identify whose turn it is to perform certain daily tasks by looking for names under job headings. Write the snack or lunch menu on chart paper. Refer to it later in the day.

Teachers can also turn calendar time into a literacy activity by *reading* the calendar with children. See Chapter 8 for a more detailed description of how to make calendar time meaningful for children with low cognitive abilities.

Have a card representing each favorite song or storybook. Include a drawing of a key element of the song and the written title. Attach the cards to a large board with Velcro® so children can take turns selecting a song or storybook for the class.

Storytime. Obviously story time is an important opportunity to help children with special needs develop emergent literacy skills. However, this activity may be challenging for children with certain disabilities, especially children with limited vision or cognitive delays.

- Pictures are often too small to see clearly or too cluttered to discriminate foreground from background. The examples in Figure 13–2 demonstrate this problem.
- The language of many preschool storybooks may be too advanced, especially if the story is told without other props or visual aids.
- The concepts and experiences depicted in the story may be unfamiliar or too complex. The trick is to find stories and illustrations that are appealing and meaningful to children with special needs.

The following suggestions can make story time a good learning context.

Repeat stories frequently. The importance of repeated stories is being increasingly emphasized, even for older children. Repetition and familiarity are critically important for children who have special needs. As children become more and more familiar with the story, they can engage in shared

Figure 13–3 Teacher reading a favorite story.

reading with the teacher (see Figure 13–3). Children who are not yet reading can enjoy participating in the shared reading because they will have memorized the story via the frequent repetitions. Children with limited language may begin to participate in a simple repeated refrain, such as "You can't catch ME!"

Include stories with developmentally simple themes. Examples of conceptually simple themes that might appeal to children with low cognitive abilities include:

- Familiar daily activities
- Familiar animals
- Family members
- Body parts and clothing
- Food
- Big and little
- Hidden objects and surprises
- Some pop-up books
- Doors and flaps that open
- Books related to familiar TV shows and movies

Make photo albums. Use photos that reflect recent classroom activities. Or cut pictures out of old magazines to reflect favorite things and activities.

Add props to stories to help maintain children's attention. Use replicas of things in the story, flannel board figures, small stuffed animals, and puppets.

Select books with rhymes and predictable phrases. Use of poems and nursery rhymes not only increases appeal and participation for many children with special needs, but will increase phonological awareness for all children.

Include books with large print. This will be especially important for children with low vision.

Place extra copies of frequently read books in the library corner. Encourage children to *read* on their own.

Encourage active participation as story is read. For example, children can act out key elements of the story. Ask children what they think will happen next before turning the page.

An example would be using the monkey puppets to accompany *Five Little Monkeys Jumping in the Tree* or the motions to the familiar song with a book based on *The Eensy Weensy Spider.*

Help children act out the story. After the story becomes familiar, have children perform a play. For example, children can take turns playing roles in *The Three Little Pigs* (see Figure 13–4).

Library Corner. Be sure the library corner is a *literacy rich* center. In addition to books with the characteristics we have described, include the following:

Helpful Hint

Children with *limited fine motor* skills need adapted writing tools. One of the simplest adaptations is a rubber tube that fits over the pen or marker. This makes the writing tool larger and easier to grip.

Pens, markers, and crayons
Stationery and envelopes
Ink stamps with letters and numbers
Stickers to use as postage stamps
Magazines (including *TV Guide*) and newspapers reflecting children's home culture
Books with cassette tapes
Cookbooks
Checkbooks
Computer software for developing prereading skills
Books with tactile and olfactory features, such as textures, flaps, pop-ups, and scratch 'n sniff

Figure 13–4 Children acting out a story.

Helpful Hint

For children with *motor disabilities* who have good cognitive skills, computer skills will be crucial to their development in the areas of both academics and communication. Ask the disability specialist for assistance in adapting the computer so children with limited arm and hand mobility can access it.

Helpful Hint

Children with *visual impairments* enjoy books with textures or with key words in Braille. (See Dahlia's case study at the end of this chapter describing the use of a simple texture book.) Ask the vision specialist to provide appropriate power magnifying lenses for children who have low vision. Children with normal vision also love looking at things through magnifying glasses.

Many of the materials in this list can also be included in pretend play, housekeeping, and dress-up areas.

Snack Time. As suggested earlier in this chapter, share a written menu with children every day. Interesting snack foods include alphabet soup and crackers, cereal, and small cookies shaped like letters and other intriguing forms.

Read labels of food containers, and follow simple recipes as you prepare a snack for and with the children. Write recipe ingredients on large chart paper. Ask children if they can read what ingredient comes next.

To provide exposure to letters and numbers, laminate block letters and numbers along with children's names on the back of placemats.

Art Activities. Children with special needs may require direct assistance drawing representations of familiar things, such as a face, flower, or ball. By showing children the object and then helping them draw it, they will learn that pictures represent real objects and experiences.

Be sure to be fairly dramatic about writing a child's name on her artwork. Use a marking pen and write in fairly large letters. Say to the child, "Shall I write your name on your artwork? Let's see, how do you spell Jane?" Then say each letter clearly as you write the child's name. This will help draw her attention to print and individual letters. Later on in the day, have the child help you look for her artwork by looking for her name. Ask if the child would like you to write something about the picture on the bottom.

Draw attention to labels on art materials. Store some materials in containers that are not transparent so their contents can only be determined by the print label.

Outside Play. Post a chart with pictures and labels of each outside play area near the door. Ask each child where he or she is going to play before going out to the playground. Label major storage areas for bikes, balls, sand toys, and other outdoor equipment.

Play "Simon Says" using picture cards. The teacher or a student holds up a card that says "Run," "Jump," "Sit," and children follow those directions.

Departure. At the end of the day, encourage children to look for their names on artwork to take home. They can also locate their cubbies and possessions by identifying their name.

Give children notes to take home to parents. Read at least part of the note to the children.

ASSISTING CHILDREN WITH SPECIAL NEEDS BY USING PICTURES AND PRINT

Many children with special needs have difficulty processing, attending to, or understanding spoken language, and many also have difficulty communicating verbally. For these children, the use of pictures can be of great assistance in helping them make sense of the world around them. In addition, pictures and symbols can provide a means of communicating their wants and needs. Hodgdon (1996) offers a detailed descriptions of these strategies.

Pictures and Print as Alternative Means of Expressive Language

Many children with special needs have delayed communication skills. Some will never be able to use spoken language. The use of pictures and print to communicate choices and basic wants and needs can be helpful for children who do not speak or whose speech is unintelligible. Also, as mentioned in Chapter 4, many behavior problems are the result of a child's inability to communicate in more appropriate ways.

Helpful Hint

Some children with *autism* prefer communicating with printed words and pictures. Occasionally a child with autism can even read and spell. Unfortunately, without intervention this interest often becomes repetitive and self-stimulatory. Thus it is important to give these children every opportunity to use print in meaningful ways.

Examples of Ways to Use Pictures and Print to Support Expressive Language. Allow children to select a song or story during circle time by pointing to or removing a picture card from a large poster board.

Make cards with pictures and key words representing things that the child will most likely need to say. If the child is ambulatory, attach the cards to a large key ring . Attach the ring of picture cards to the child's belt. Teaching assistants can help the child learn to use each card at appropriate times. Examples of helpful pictures might be:

- I need to use the restroom.
- I'm unhappy.
- I have a tummy ache/headache.
- I'd like to play with (favorite toy).
- Someone hurt me.
- Someone took my toy.

Post pictures on the wall at eye level in various areas to depict important messages for that activity. For example, in the play yard, a poster could suggest possible play choices with pictures and word labels of the sand table, slide, and balls. This would be particularly helpful for children who have limited mobility as well as limited speech.

Elena

Elena has limited mobility due to cerebral palsy. She is in a wheelchair but has not learned to move it independently. Her speech efforts are not intelligible. She loves being outside and enjoys several outside activities. However, she is picky about which specific activity she wants at any particular time. She gets frustrated if the teacher misunderstands her preference. The special education consultant suggests placing a picture board on the tray of her wheelchair. The picture board has simple drawings and words for each outside activity. Elena can *point* to the one she wants by placing her fist on the picture and thus communicate her preference clearly.

Use of Communication Boards or Picture Exchange Systems. Two picture communication systems are commonly used for children who do not have expressive language ability: **communication boards** and the Picture Exchange Communication System (PECS).

Communication board. A communication board can often serve as a precursor to development of a computerized AAC device for children with severe physical disabilities, or it can simply be used as a simple form of assistance for a child whose speech is unintelligible or a child who has no oral language and does not sign. A specialist may need to assist in the board's design (see Chapter 2 for discussion of AAC).

The communication board involves placing photos or simple line drawings on a board. The child points to a certain picture to indicate what she wants to say or do (see Figure 13–5.) In some cases it may be more conven-

Figure 13–5   Simple communication board.

ient to create several small *topic* boards and keep them in the area of the center where the child is most likely to need a particular vocabulary or set of expressions, such as in the bathroom, outside, or at circle time.

For children who are ambulatory, communication cards can be placed on a large key ring and attached to their belt.

Helpful Hint

A child with *severe physical disabilities* who cannot speak or point can use **directed eye gaze** to select pictures on a clear acrylic board. The board is held between the child and the teacher or aide, and the child simply looks at the picture representing the item she wants. It is fairly easy to discern where the child is looking if the pictures are far enough apart.

PECS. The picture exchange communication system (Frost & Bondy, 1994) has become popular in recent years. It has been used with a wide range of children with special needs who are nonverbal, particularly with children who have autism or who have little functional language. The system uses behavioral strategies to teach the child to select and exchange a picture for a desired object or activity or to make a comment. As children progress, they learn to create word combinations with the pictures as well (see Figure 13–6).

Pictures representing the high preference interests of the child are attached with Velcro® to a board or stored on the pages of a binder. Unlike the communication board, the child using PECS does not *point* at the picture but rather removes the picture and hands it to another person in exchange for the desired object or activity. Thus, PECS requires greater social interaction for the communication to be effective.

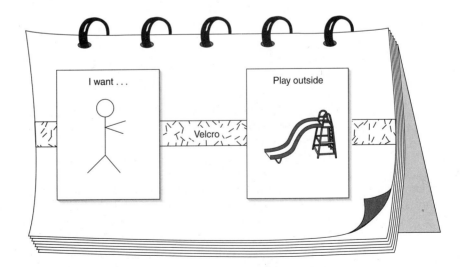

Figure 13–6   PECS cards placed on Velcro® sentence strip.

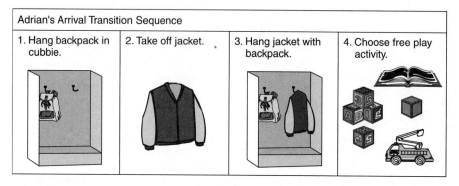

Figure 13–7   Example of a transition sequence board.

Using Pictures to Assist Comprehension and Memory

Pictures can also be used to support children with limited language comprehension and memory. Pictures can be helpful in assisting children with remembering the sequence of a task, such as hand washing, understanding and following the daily schedule, or understanding transitions from one activity to another. Behavior problems can often be significantly reduced when pictures are used to help children anticipate the next activity or understand how to do a difficult task.

Strategies for Using Pictures throughout the Day to Assist Comprehension. Post pictures at eye level above the sink to help children remember the sequence of hand washing or brushing teeth. At each transition, show the child a picture of the event that comes next or design a picture sequence board to represent the steps necessary in a particular transition, such as from arrival to free play (see Figure 13–7).

Jung Lee's Transitions

Jung Lee had a difficult time with transitions. After each activity she would wander aimlessly and become agitated if an adult tried to direct her to the next activity. Jung Lee often had difficulty engaging in typical daily activities of the center. Her greatest interest seemed to be with books and letters, which she would copy endlessly.

Her teacher decides to try to use this interest to help her make transitions from one activity to another. She makes a book with words and pictures representing each activity of the day. At the end of each activity, she opens the book to the picture of the next activity and shows it to Jung Lee. This seems to make it easier for Jung Lee to focus and anticipate the next activity.

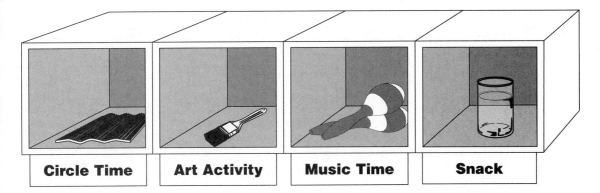

| Circle Time | Art Activity | Music Time | Snack |

Figure 13–8   An "event sequence box" can be used to represent activity sequence for children with limited vision or both deafness and blindness.

Helpful Hint

For the child who has *limited vision*—and especially if she *also has a hearing loss*—**an event sequence box** can be helpful. As in the drawing in Figure 13–8 actual objects representing each activity of the day are inserted in a row of boxes (like little mailboxes). For example, a small piece of carpet square is in the box representing circle time, a paint brush is in the box representing art activity, and a cup represents snack. The child goes to the boxes after each activity. She locates the next box with an object in it; the boxes to the left are all empty because these events have already occurred. This helps her understand what is coming next.

At beginning of free play, show the children pictures of options and ask them to indicate the activity they prefer. At the end of the day during a *recall* activity, show picture cards representing major activities of the day. Ask the child to point to photos representing the things she enjoyed most.

SUMMARY

This chapter has considered two important areas for children with special needs. The first concerns ways of supporting emergent literacy for children with various disabilities, including accommodations for children with visual impairment and children who have low cognitive abilities. Motivating uses of print throughout the day in predictable ways can help young children begin to understand written communication.

The second area considered in this chapter is how to use pictures and print to support both the expression and comprehension of language. This includes the use of picture communication systems such as PECS and communication boards for expression of communication as well as the use of pictures as an aid to children's understanding of daily schedules, task sequences, and transitions.

CASE STUDY

Dahlia's Favorite Book

Dahlia was a shy four-year-old. She wore thick glasses, and Mrs. Wang, her teacher, had been told she had extremely poor vision. As a result, Dahlia never looked at books or pictures and did not seem to enjoy story time. Mrs. Wang tried to interest her in oversized books with simple pictures, but Dahlia still had no interest.

Mr. Smith, the vision specialist, suggested that Mrs. Wang encourage Dahlia to help her make a special storybook using textures and objects. Because Dahlia had usable vision, Mr. Smith did not think she would be a Braille user. He explained to Mrs. Wang that eventually Dahlia would learn to use a variety of print-enhancing technologies. But he agreed she needed some tactile cues and accommodations to help develop her interest in books and print.

Together, Dahlia and Mrs. Wang design a book about a treasure hunt where children search for a variety of objects. In addition to a picture of each object, they include a texture or object on the opposite page to represent each of the *treasures.* On the page opposite the picture of a green sock is a small green sock. On the page opposite the picture of a red flower, they paste a dried red flower. Opposite the picture of a sponge is a little piece of sponge, and so on. Mrs. Wang writes the name of each object below it.

Mr. Smith also provides a small magnifier of the appropriate power to match Dahlia's vision with her glasses on to encourage her to look at the pictures and objects in her treasure book as well as the print in smaller books. Mrs. Wang attaches the magnifying glass to the treasure book with a piece of string. Dahlia loves this book. She *reads* it to herself and to her friends, and she takes turns with other children looking at the words and pictures with the magnifying glass. Quickly she begins using a magnifying glass to look at the print in other books.

The book eventually becomes a favorite for many of the children. As a result Mrs. Wang develops a week of activities around a real treasure hunt, and all the children make their own special books. She also provides all the children with inexpensive magnifying glasses, which are quite a hit and lead to many science activities.

Upon reflection, Mrs. Wang realizes that something that initially seemed like a problem related to Dahlia's disability had been transformed into wonderfully engaging activities for all the children!

Case Study Questions

1. *What strategies specifically address Dahlia's visual impairment?*
2. *Which elements of the adaptations would probably be effective with any child needing support in the area of literacy?*
3. *How might you simplify the strategies used?*

KEY TERMS

communication board event sequence box
directed eye gaze

HELPFUL RESOURCES

Articles and Books

Adams, M., Foorman, B., Lundberg, I., & Beeler, T. (1998). *Phonemic awareness in young children.* Baltimore, MD: Paul H. Brookes.

Beukelman, D., & Mirenda, P. (1992). Serving young children with AAC needs. In *Augmentative and alternative communication* (pp. 175–201). Baltimore, MD: Paul H. Brookes.

Mayfield, M., & Ollila, L. O. (Eds.). (1992). *Emerging literacy: Preschool, kindergarten and primary grades.* Needham Heights, MA: Allyn & Bacon.

Van Kleeck, A. (1990). Emergent literacy: Learning about print before learning to read. *Topics in Early Childhood Special Education, 10*(2), 25–45.

About or Including Children with Special Needs

Published by Redleaf Press, 450 N. Syndicate, Suite 5, St. Paul, MN 55104-4125, (800) 423-8309, fax: (800) 641-0115:

Bunnett, R. *Friends at school.* (Available in Spanish.)

Bunnett, R. *Friends together* (laminated posters).

Dwight, L. *We can do it!* (Available in Spanish.)

BOOKS THAT MAY APPEAL TO YOUNG CHILDREN WHO HAVE DISABILITIES OR DIFFICULTY SUSTAINING ATTENTION

(NOTE: While the concepts and language may be enjoyable and accessible to children with special needs, the illustrations in several of the books are problematic for many of the children, especially children with low vision, and children with low cognitive ability.)

Animal Stories

Cookie's Week, Cindy Ward
Good Dog Carl, Good Morning Chick, Mirra Ginsburg
Harry The Dirty Dog, Gene Zion
Home For A Bunny, Margaret Wise Brown
Mary Had A Little Lamb, Sarah Joseph Hale

Moo Moo, Brown Cow, Jakki Wood
The Runaway Bunny, Margaret Wise Brown
Whose Mouse Are You?, Robert Krause

Concepts (Colors, Letters, Numbers, Shapes, Sizes)

Big Bird's Color Game, Tom Cooke
Circles, Triangles And Squares, Tana Hoban
The Foot Book, Dr. Suess
Five Little Monkeys Jumping On The Bed, Eileen Christelow
Five Little Monkeys Sitting In A Tree, Eileen Christelow
Goldilocks And The Three Bears, A Golden Book
Is It Red? Is It Yellow? Is It Blue?, Tana Hoban
Little Gorilla, Ruth Bornstein
Mouse Paint, Ellen Stool Walsh
One Cow Moo, David Bennet
1,2,3,Zoo, Eric Carle
Over, Under, And Through, Tana Hoban
Round, And Round, And Round, Tana Hoban
Ten, Nine, Eight, Molly Bang
The Very Hungry Caterpillar, Eric Carle

Children's Daily Lives

Excellent books published by Redleaf Press:
450 N. Syndicate, Suite 5
St. Paul, MN 55104-4125
Phone: 1-800-423-8309

Examples:
We Can Do It!, Laura Dwight (Available in Spanish)
Friends Together, Rochelle Bunnett (Laminated Posters)
Friends At School, Rochelle Bunnett (Available in Spanish)

REFERENCES

Cook, R., Tessier, A., & Klein, M. D. (2000). *Adapting early childhood curricula for children in inclusive settings* (5th ed.). Columbus, OH: Merrill/Prentice Hall.

Frost, L., & Bondy, A. (1994). *The picture exchange communication system training manual.* Cherry Hill, NJ: PECS, Inc.

Hodgdon, L. A. (1996). *Visual strategies for improving communication. Volume 1: Practical supports for school and home.* Troy, MI: Quirk Roberts Publishing.

Watson, L. R., Layton, T. L., Pierce, P. L., & Abraham, M. A. (1994). Enhancing emerging literacy in a language preschool. *Language, Speech and Hearing Services in Schools*, 25(3), 136–145.

Part

Working with the Early Childhood Special Education Team

14

Communicating with Families

Chapter-at-a-Glance

Successful inclusion of children with special needs depends upon strong parent-professional partnerships.

- **Parents are more knowledgeable than anyone else about their child.** Parents also have a great deal of information about the disability and about effective intervention and accommodation strategies.
- **ECE personnel must establish** partnerships **with families.** It is impossible to provide optimal support to the child without this relationship with parents. The key to successful partnerships with families is communication and respect.
- **Families of children with special needs experience a wide range of stresses and challenges in their daily lives.** These daily challenges can include frustration and emotional reactions to the complex demands of obtaining and coordinating services for their children.
- **Most parents experience strong emotional reactions to the diagnosis of their child's disability.** These reactions may be similar to the processes of grief and loss.

INTRODUCTION

In recent years early childhood educators and special educators have increasingly prioritized the needs of families and have promoted parent involvement in a variety of ways. Many programs for young children do an excellent job of inviting parents to participate. They produce newsletters, establish active parent councils, and go to great lengths to support families on a daily basis. But for parents of young children with special needs it is necessary to go beyond these connections and actually seek to

253

include parents as full partners in their children's program. Early intervention programs that fully involve families through effective **parent-professional partnerships** produce better results. *It is impossible to provide optimal, effective care and service to young children with special needs without establishing a collaborative relationship with their families.*

GUIDELINES FOR DEVELOPING PARENT-PROFESSIONAL PARTNERSHIPS

The following basic guidelines should be considered when redefining the relationship between families and professionals into a partnership that will lead to successful inclusion of young children with special needs.

Development of Trust

Perhaps the most important ingredient in the process of creating a true partnership with families is the development of mutual trust. Trust will not develop unless families feel safe. Their right to privacy, to confidentiality, to ask questions, and to make choices for themselves and their children must be respected.

Parents of children with special needs—especially severe disabilities—have often spent years engaging in difficult and adversarial relationships with professionals and agencies. Their lives may have been overwhelmed by the need to interact with and seek help from a wide range of individuals. Some parents will have had many painful experiences dealing with professionals; as they enter into yet another relationship, they may initially be cautious and wary. A trusting relationship may not develop quickly. Some families need more time and more support to develop the trust necessary to enter into a true partnership. However, other families have developed partnerships with prior service providers and will expect to be fully involved.

Recognizing Parents' Knowledge and Expertise

ECE educators must recognize the knowledge and expertise that families have about their children and their special needs. Generally, families are the primary caregivers and have spent the most time with the children. They are the experts on their children's strengths, needs, desires, habits, and other relevant information. Therefore, early childhood educators must find comfortable ways to encourage families to share this information and to show that their opinions are respected. Families are, and should be, the *primary decision makers* regarding the services their children receive.

Early childhood educators must believe that most families, regardless of their background, care deeply about their children's progress and can contribute substantially if given opportunities and knowledge. Families look to

Figure 14–1   Teacher and parent teams.

professionals for affirmation of their efforts. Some families have experienced so many frustrations on the road to inclusion that their confidence may in their own judgement, and in the *system* have been shaken. Families want and deserve to be valued as essential members of the team serving their children. Only then may they realize the importance of their role in furthering their children's development (see Figure 14–1).

Parents Are the Constants in Their Children's Lives

The family is the constant in a child's life when service systems and professionals within these systems fluctuate. Recognizing that the family is the most important and most stable element in the child's life, early childhood educators have an obligation to support and strengthen the family's resources, skills, and confidence in meeting their young child's needs. We should avoid approaching the family from a **deficit orientation.** Professionals have a tendency to believe that if the family has a child with special needs, the family is also disabled. It is important to realize that these families have the same strengths that all families possess and that caring for their children with special needs and working with professionals can build on those strengths.

Making the Program Fit the Family's Priorities

ECE educators must negotiate a fit between the family's values, needs, and priorities and the program's approaches, goals, and services. The Individual

Family Service Plans (IFSPs) required by law for children with special needs provide an opportunity to ensure a good match between the families' concerns and priorities for their children and the philosophy and services of the early childhood program. The process involved in developing these plans creates the opportunity for early childhood educators to ask parents what they want or expect from services to be provided to their children. In fact, the law clearly requires that the team developing these plans actively include families and that families be given the opportunity to express their concerns and priorities for services.

Viewing the Family as a Whole. The discrepancy between what families want and what they get often occurs because professionals may focus only on the needs of children rather than on the needs of families as a whole. Families function as systems in which whatever affects one family member automatically affects all other members in some way. As systems, healthy families seek to stay in balance where life may not be perfect for each member but at least is tolerable for all. When the team focuses only on the needs of one member or on only one family function, such as education, the system can get out of balance. The critical needs of families for food, shelter, employment, transportation, and child care may have to be addressed before families can focus on the unique needs of the child with a disability. This philosophy is referred to as a **family systems approach,** which has been described in detail by Turnbull and Turnbull (1997).

Honoring the Diversity of Families. Early childhood educators usually think of themselves as knowing how to parent. This belief system is based on a combination of their own experiences and the expectations and values found in textbooks reflecting the child-rearing attitudes of middle class Euro-American culture. However, many children with special needs are being raised in nontraditional settings that include single-parent families, foster placements, group homes, grandparents, and teenaged parents. In addition, increasing ethnic diversity within the U.S. population challenges middle class values and assumptions about child rearing.

Each family system functions according to its own values and experiences. These differences influence families' attitudes and practices related to child rearing in general and the purpose of early education. In addition, families' attitudes toward disability and their attitudes toward early intervention and special education are greatly influenced by culture. For example, some families may experience a great deal of guilt and shame related to having a child with a disability. Some families may have ambivalent feelings about seeking help. (For a thorough examination of these issues see Lynch and Hanson, 1998; and Klein and Chen, 2001.)

Recognizing the Stresses Families Face

It is essential to recognize the extra stresses families of children with special needs have experienced and continue to experience in their daily lives.

Dealing with Multiple Needs and Multiple Agencies and Professionals. Families of young children with special needs have extra stresses created by their children's multiple needs and by the overall impact of those special needs on family life. These children require more frequent and more specialized medical services and therapy appointments. Families often must deal with significant behavioral challenges. Caretaking may be compounded by sleeping, toileting, or feeding problems. The following comments sum up the views of one parent:

> There are constant stresses on our family. Since one child requires more help and attention than the others, resentments build up. I find myself doing a perennial balancing act with my husband and children trying to make sure that everyone gets their fair share of me. All this is aggravated by the fact that when you have a delayed preschooler, what you really have on your hands is a child who seems to be stuck in the *terrible twos*. She is destructive without meaning to be and is forever testing us. She frequently spills her drinks, and the other day she poured a whole box of cereal all over the floor. She still isn't toilet trained. I sometimes wonder if she'll ever be fully toilet trained or if she will ever sleep through the night.

As we note in the sections that follow, some of the extra stresses that parents experience make meaningful family involvement in early childhood programs more difficult.

Increased Time Demands and the Need to Set Priorities. Families of children with special needs do have greater demands made on their time. Families simply cannot do everything and are often forced to set priorities. Early childhood educators must ensure that all contacts with their program are positive so that families want to make school/center involvement a priority. Above all, resist being critical of how families use their time. Families must often make difficult choices about how to spend their precious time. The last thing an educator should do is add stress to already stressful lives. Other suggestions for collaborating with families, even when time is limited, include:

- Call families regularly. Offer positive news. Often parents assume that a phone call must mean there is some new problem with their child. Establish a positive relationship early so that families look forward to hearing from you. Be sure to call sometimes just to see how parents themselves are doing.
- Use communication notebooks, described in a later section of this chapter.
- Create social events that accommodate all family members.

The Easter Egg Hunt

Ms. Gonzalez is the director of a large urban child care center. After months of trying to involve several families of children with special needs in the program, she came up with an activity that *broke the ice*. The center held an Easter Egg Hunt and invited all family members.

Student volunteers from the local college special education department supervised the children while parents met each other and interacted with staff. Eighty percent of the families participated, including several families of children with special needs. This was followed by an equally successful potluck dinner two months later.

UNDERSTANDING FAMILIES' EMOTIONAL REACTIONS

Individual family members may react differently to the news that their child, brother or sister, or granddaughter or grandson has disabilities. The literature on disabilities has described the reactions of parents to the birth of a child with a disability as similar to the **grief reactions** experienced when someone loses a loved one through death. This theory suggests that, in a sense, the parent may be grieving for the loss of the *hoped-for* child. While not all parents go through each stage of the grief cycle, most parents experience intense emotional reactions.

While reactions may be most intense when disabilities are first identified, *intense reactions may surface at any time* as the family moves through its life cycle. Each time a transition, such as from a home-based program to a center program, arises, long forgotten feelings may resurface. The transition into an inclusive program may highlight how different the child is from his typical peers. Families may then find themselves in need of extra emotional support as they, once again, confront the realities with which they live. The following reflections from a parent reveal one example of what can be normally expected.

I decided to place my daughter in my neighborhood nursery school part time where she was the only child with a disability. Although my daughter, who is very competent socially, adjusted fairly well, I felt lonely, isolated, depressed, and at times embarrassed. During my daughter's first few weeks there, when I stayed with her to ease her separation, I had to leave the room on a few occasions when I began to cry. Being around all those normal three-year-olds was a constant reminder of how verbal and adept little children are and how far behind my daughter was in her development.

It is important for early childhood educators to have some understanding of the typical feelings that families may experience. These reactions to the advent of a disability are described in much the same way the loss of a loved one is described in the literature on death and dying. Families may experience a strong sense of loss and grief for the child they had envisioned. They may also experience guilt, denial, anger, and depression as they work through the change in expectations that a child with special needs brings to a family.

Family members work through the process of adaptation at different rates. Just understanding possible parental reactions can help early childhood educators respond appropriately. Cook, Tessier, and Klein (2000) offer suggestions for helpful responses. Some of these are listed in Figure 14–2.

VARIOUS GRIEF REACTIONS AND EXAMPLES OF INTERVENTIONIST RESPONSES	
SHOCK & DENIAL DISBELIEF	Listen with acceptance; offer support and assistance. Connect emotionally with parents. Provide information; refer to parent-to-parent support
ANGER & RESENTMENT	Employ active listening; reflect parents' frustrations. Help parents accept feelings as normal
DEPRESSION DISCOURAGEMENT	Focus on child's accomplishments; plan for short-term future; try to encourage activity and engagement; encourage parent-to-parent support. Make referral for professional help if necessary.
ACCEPTANCE	Maintain ongoing relationship; encourage parent to reach out to others. Help parents set new goals for themselves and their child.

Figure 14–2 Possible intervention responses to family reactions of grief.

Strategies for Dealing with Families' Emotional Reactions

The following offer some general strategies for dealing with parents' emotional reactions.

Avoid Judgment. It is all too easy for educators to feel that families are in denial or being unrealistic if they are not ready to acknowledge the nature or extent of their child's special needs. An understanding of the grief cycle reveals that what appears to be denial is often a healthy approach for families to take as they take time to work through their feelings. ECE educators should *never assume* they know what a family is going through unless they also have a young family member who has a disability.

Provide Both Emotional Support and Concrete Assistance. In addition to being supportive and nonjudgmental, early childhood educators can take specific steps to provide concrete assistance for parents. Here are a few actions to consider.

- Become knowledgeable about and refer families to community family resource centers and other parent support programs or groups. (The inclusion facilitator should be able to provide this information.) These programs generally work with whole families and provide the training and support necessary to increase the ability of families to nurture their children. Most of all, they provide families with the opportunity to get to know other families who *have been there.* Families often find it comforting to know they are not alone in their experiences and their feelings.

- Get to know and develop collaborative relationships with the agencies in your community that serve children with special needs. Join an existing interagency coordinating council or help establish one in your community. You will not only become more knowledgeable about *the system*, but you will be able to assist families when they have frustrations dealing with the service delivery system. Knowing the right person to call can make a great difference when families are trying to access services.
- Become well acquainted with **service coordinators** or case managers from all the community agencies serving the children in your program. They are responsible for seeing that your families get the services they need. Building close relationships with these and other agency personnel will help ensure that all those working with the family have the same goals and objectives.
- Develop a notebook or file of community resources, such as community support groups, respite or child care providers, recreational programs, medical and dental services, adult education, and social service agencies that might assist with financial, housing, and transportation needs.
- Develop or add specific materials to a parent lending library of particular interest to families of children with special needs.
- Invite persons from community resources to assist in offering family education opportunities about such topics as the law, parents' rights and responsibilities, classroom methods and materials, IFSPs, Individualized Education Plans (IEPs), and transition to kindergarten.

Encourage Families' Participation in Support Groups or Parent-To-Parent Support. A number of parent organizations are often organized around a specific disability, such as the Down Syndrome Parents Association and the Parents of Children with Autism. These groups provide not only an opportunity to learn about the child's special needs, but to interact with many families with similar challenges and experiences.

Parent-to-parent support services provide the assistance of a parent who has been trained in peer support techniques and who has a child with special needs. This type of service is more personal and often can provide specific assistance with local services and bureaucracy. These support services are not universally welcome; especially when a disability has been recently diagnosed, parents may not be ready for this type of interaction. Early childhood educators need to respect this reaction and perhaps suggest the support at a later time.

COMMUNICATION: THE KEY TO BUILDING PARTNERSHIPS

Early childhood educators must develop effective communications skills and methods to provide information to the families of children with special needs and to encourage their input into the program. Like education, communication is a two-way process.

Providing Information

Early childhood educators readily take responsibility for communicating by providing information about their programs and services to families through orientation meetings, handbooks, special events, and newsletters. This information is essential to families whose children have been included in typical programs. These families want and deserve to become a part of every aspect of their children's program even if their children cannot participate in every activity. Early childhood educators need to make every attempt to ensure that parents *understand* the information provided.

Provide Child-Specific Communication. Families of children with special needs are likely to expect and desire specific information about their child on a regular basis. They are used to their child being assessed and reassessed. While many families become tired of their child constantly being compared to others or to criteria found on some test form, they are still interested in hearing about their child's progress from those who work with him. Families are especially interested in their child's progress in the developmental areas they hold as priorities. In addition to keen observation and comprehensive record keeping, early childhood educators need highly developed skills in personal communication and problem solving.

Communicate on a Regular Basis. Parents of children with special needs often complain that whenever they receive a phone call or message from their child's teacher, they know it will be bad news. One effective communication strategy is to set up regular meetings or phone calls in which you *debrief* one another about the child's progress as well as his difficulties. Make sure to include positive comments and amusing anecdotes, not just problems. If regular communications occur consistently, parents will eventually begin to look forward to hearing from the teacher and will use those opportunities to share information and feelings.

Use Daily Communication Notebooks. A simple but effective strategy is to send a **communication notebook** back and forth each day with the child. Both the teacher and parents may write in the book whenever they wish.

This is two-way communication in which professionals and parents not only give and receive information, but also work together in using that information to generate strategies to meet the many challenges disabilities may present.

Developing Effective Communication Skills

Let's review a few tips to increase the effectiveness of person-to-person communication between parents and professionals.

Perfect the Art of Listening. Create opportunities to give family members your full attention. Avoid trying to hold a detailed conversation with parents during arrival, departure, and other busy times. Let the *family take the lead* by asking open-ended questions if necessary to initiate the conversation. For example, you might say:

"Tell me your concerns about Jeff's progress."
"How do you think Jeff is doing here at the center?"
"How are things going at home?"

Listen with Reflection. Only if they perceive that you are listening carefully will families continue to express themselves. After reflecting on their comments you will be able to convey acceptance and concern. By responding with reflective comments based on facts and feelings offered by families, you can demonstrate understanding of what has been said. This approach helps to focus speakers and gives them a chance to acknowledge that the listener is on the right track. Here is an example of **reflective listening:**

Parent: I was wondering why Carrie still hasn't started walking after all of these months of physical therapy.
Teacher: You sound somewhat discouraged about Carrie's progress.

Such a response lets parents know you are interested in their concerns and feelings and that you want to be supportive. It gives parents a chance either to continue expressing their feelings or to seek answers more directly. This technique, also known as *active listening*, is a useful tool that all early educators should consider developing.

Avoid Jargon. Educators must be diligent to avoid using terms and acronyms that are unfamiliar to families. Many parents are reluctant to ask what such terms mean so the responsibility to offer clear communication belongs to the professional.

Phrase Negative Information Carefully. Always begin a conversation with something positive and keep the entire conversation as positive as possible. Even negative information can be phrased in a positive manner. For example, when a child continually seeks attention by blurting out and seeking to be the center of activities, the teacher might describe that challenge in this way:

> When we are doing storytelling or another child is showing us something, George just can't wait to share what he is thinking. He is so interested in what is going on that he places himself right in front of the teacher. We checked to see that his hearing and vision are normal so we are wondering how we can work together to help George control himself a bit more. What do you do at home when George wants your attention?

SUMMARY

Supporting young children with special needs demands that professionals establish close partnerships with families. Families know more about their children than anyone else. Early childhood educators need to understand thoroughly both the emotional impact of having a child with special needs and the complex day-to-day physical and time demands of coordinating the child's services. Developing support skills, the ability to connect emotionally with families, and effective communication techniques will enable the early childhood educator to support the child in the most optimal ways.

CASE STUDY

Alfredo's Mother

Alfredo Sanchez has been attending Miss Lee's child care program for several months. All in all, he is doing fairly well. When he first entered the program, he cried for a good portion of each day, especially in the morning after his mother left. His mother insisted on staying with him for more than an hour. Miss Lee believed the reason Alfredo had such difficulty dealing with separation was because his mother had such a hard time leaving him. The situation had begun to improve, but recently Alfredo had been absent frequently and separation is again beginning to be a problem.

Alredeo is small for his age and very immature. At three-and-a-half he uses only a few words. But other than the crying, he does not present much of a problem at the center. From Miss Lee's perspective, the biggest problem has been Alfredo's mother! She seems extremely overprotective and prone to keep Alfredo out of school at the slightest sniffle. She is also fairly demanding. She asks a lot of questions about health and safety policies. Miss Lee also feels that Mrs. Sanchez gives the staff mixed messages about Alfredo's social interactions with other children. On the one hand she is constantly worried about bigger, more active children hurting Alfredo. But at the same time she wants the staff to help Alfredo make friends and be involved with other children.

The child care staff has started to avoid interacting with Mrs. Sanchez because they dread her complaints. They all increasingly believe that her son would do much better if she would make sure he attends the program on a consistent basis and if she could resist being so overprotective.

Miss Lee mentions her frustrations to the ECSE consultant. The consultant realizes she has not really given Miss Lee much background information about Alfredo. She explains that Alfredo was born prematurely, at only 27 weeks gestation. He weighed less than two pounds at birth! He was hospitalized for several months, and Alfredo's physicians weren't sure whether the infant would survive. Mrs. Sanchez came every day to the neonatal intensive care unit, taking three different buses to get there. A devout Catholic, she also stopped at her church every day to light candles for Alfredo. Mrs. Sanchez clearly saw her son's survival as a true miracle and a gift from God.

In many ways Alfredo's development has also been a miracle. Despite his developmental delay and possible mild mental retardation, he has a sweet and even temperament, and he is making steady progress. The greatest challenge has been chronic upper respiratory problems, resulting in several rehospitalizations. Alfredo seems to catch cold easily, and his colds frequently result in pneumonia. The ECSE consultant explains to Miss Lee that this is a common pattern in children who are born prematurely. The consultant also shares with Miss Lee

(continued)

that Mrs. Sanchez's husband was killed in a work accident, and most of her extended family lives in Guatemala. Despite the absence of family support, Mrs. Sanchez always keeps her doctor's appointments and stays with Alfredo during his hospitalizations. Her devotion and watchful care of Alfredo is nothing short of heroic and is probably a big factor in his developmental progress.

Miss Lee appreciates this information and tells the ECSE consultant that in the future she would like to receive this kind of information prior to her first meeting with the child and parent. Miss Lee then discusses this information with her staff at the center. She explains to them why Mrs. Sanchez seems overprotective and why Alfredo is frequently absent. The information gives the staff a different perspective and a new sense of respect and admiration for Alfredo's mother.

Case Study Questions

1. *Can you think of an experience in your own work or personal life where learning more about an individual completely changed your perceptions and feelings about that person?*
2. *What do you think the mother might have done differently when she first brought Alfredo to the center that might have resulted in a different sort of relationship between her and the staff?*
3. *If you were the director of a center, what kinds of initial intake procedures would you design that might help avoid the misunderstandings and bad feelings that evolved in Alfredo's case?*

KEY TERMS

communication notebook
deficit orientation
family systems approach
grief reactions

parent-to-parent support
parent-professional partnerships
reflective listening
service coordinator

HELPFUL RESOURCES

Articles and Books

Lynch, E. W., & Hanson, M. J. (Eds.). (1998). *Developing cross-cultural competence: A guide for working with young children and their families.* Baltimore, MD: Paul H. Brookes.

McWilliam, P. J., & Bailey, D. B. (Eds.). (1993). *Working together with children and families: Case studies in early intervention.* Baltimore, MD: Paul H. Brookes.

Woods, J. J. (1995). *A family's guide to the individualized family service plan.* Baltimore, MD: Paul H. Brookes.

Organizations

National Parent to Parent Support & Information System, Inc. (NPPSIS),
Web site: <www.NPPSIS.org>
Parents Helping Parents (PHP), Web site: <www.php.com>
The Family Education Network (*Exceptional Parent*),
Web site: <Familyeducation.com/home>
The National Parent Network on Disabilities, Web site: <www.npnd.org>

REFERENCES

Cook, R., Tessier, A., & Klein, M. D. (2000). *Adapting early childhood curricula for children in inclusive settings.* Columbus, OH: Merrill/Prentice Hall.

Klein, M. D., & Chen, D. (2001). *Working with young children from culturally diverse backgrounds.* Albany, NY: Delmar.

Lynch, E. W., & Hanson, M. J. (Eds.). (1998). *Developing cross-cultural competence: A guide for working with young children and their families.* Baltimore, MD: Paul H. Brookes

Turnbull, A. P., & Turnbull, H. R. (1997). *Families, professionals, and exceptionality: A special partnership.* Englewood Cliffs, NJ: Merrill/Prentice Hall.

15

Collaborating with Disability Specialists and Paraprofessionals

Chapter-at-a-Glance

The shared expertise of several specialized educators, therapists, and paraprofessionals can enhance the classroom experience for children with special needs.

- **Early childhood special educators.** Early childhood special educators are trained specifically to provide developmental and educational services to infants and young children with special needs and their families. Increasingly they provide inclusion support for young children with all types of disabilities.
- **Speech-language specialists.** Most children with special needs have difficulty with some aspect of communication. Speech-language specialists can address disorders of speech production, expressive and receptive language delays, and pragmatic disorders, along with less common disorders of fluency and voice quality.
- **Physical therapists.** Physical therapists work with children who have motor disabilities such as cerebral palsy or spina bifida. They provide therapeutic support for the development of mobility and postural control. They may also have expertise in the use of adaptive equipment such as leg braces and wheelchairs.
- **Occupational therapists.** Although the role of occupational therapists (OTs) may overlap with that of physical therapists, generally they are more concerned with the functional use of the upper body, including arms and hands, rather than standing and walking. OTs also work to facilitate oral motor functioning for feeding. Many OTs have expertise in *sensory integration* techniques.

- **Visual impairment (VI) specialists.** These special educators are trained to work with individuals who are blind or partially sighted. They are knowledgeable about various conditions of the eye and can perform functional vision assessments. They often work as itinerants and can provide consultation related to optimal lighting, use of corrective lenses, strategies for increasing contrasts and encouraging use of the child's available vision, and use of tactile cues
- **Paraeducators.** Paraeducators are playing an increasingly critical role in supporting young children with special needs in inclusive settings. Their roles and responsibilities must be clearly defined, and they must be included as valued members of the team.
- **The collaborative intervention team.** The most effective service to young children is provided when parents, professionals, and paraeducators work together as a collaborative team.

INTRODUCTION

Including children with special needs in the ECE center-based program often poses specific challenges. The job of ECE teachers can be made much easier if they seek the help of the right specialists. A wide range of specialists may be of assistance in dealing with those children whose disabilities present significant challenges. In this chapter we will describe the roles and potential contributions of each of these specialists.

Helpful Hint

Do not assume that a specialist—other than the early childhood special educator—has expertise in working with very young children or with children who have severe and multiple disabilities. University training programs do not always emphasize training related to these populations.

EARLY CHILDHOOD SPECIAL EDUCATOR

Increasingly, early childhood special educators provide the primary support for young children with special needs in inclusive settings. Because this is a relatively new discipline, other professionals may not be familiar with their training backgrounds and roles.

The ECSE professional typically has a credential and/or master's degree and is trained to provide developmental and educational services to infants and children to age five with special needs and high-risk conditions.

ECSE professionals deal with the *whole child*. They are specifically trained to evaluate how the separate areas of development interact and influence one another. Early childhood special educators view the child within the context of the family.

ECSE professionals work with *all disabilities* across all developmental domains including:

- Language and cognition
- Motor and adaptive skills
- Emotional and social development

For children who have unique or severe challenges in specific areas, the ECSE specialist is trained to work collaboratively with specialists in those areas, such as physical or occupational therapists, speech-language specialists, and vision and hearing specialists. Many children with special needs receive one or more therapeutic services outside the center on a weekly basis. Other than parents, ECSE specialists are often most likely to be knowledgeable about these interventions.

ECSE professionals are trained to work closely with parents in a collaborative parent-professional partnership.

Traditionally ECSE specialists have worked in either home-based programs or center-based programs; they often specialize in either the infant-toddler or the preschool age range. Increasingly, as more children are placed in inclusive settings, ECSE professionals work in a consulting role to assist ECE teachers to successfully include children with special needs in the regular early childhood setting.

Role of the Early Childhood Special Educator

The ECSE consultant is likely to be the person most familiar with the child's educational goals. A young child with special needs will have an official document, either an IFSP and an IEP, listing the goals and services for the child and her family.

ECSE consultants should have a wide range of teaching and intervention strategies to address specific problems. In some cases they may work directly with the child as the child participates in the center. Other problems are more effectively addressed by discussing with the ECE staff the possible adaptations that can be made. An observation reporting form for making recommendations for possible adaptations is presented in Figure 15–1. Pull-out or tutorial models (where the consultant works with the child away from the group) are less effective. Unlike other specialists, the ECSE professional is not a therapist.

INCLUSION SUPPORT RECOMMENDATIONS

INCLUSION OBSERVATION REPORTING FORM*

Date 9-15-00   Child Joshua R.   Center Sunnydale Childcare

Teacher(s) Evelyn   Inclusion Facilitator A. Gibbs

Activity & Time	Observations (what facilitator observes)	SUPPORTS/ADAPTATIONS (suggestions for teachers that may help child be part of activities)
Arrival 8:00 A.M.	Mother leaves as soon as Josh is distracted by toys. When he notices she is gone he becomes upset. Assistant approaches him and tries to calm him. He becomes more agitated.	Establish consistent "Goodbye" routine, which includes same assistant each day.
playing at water table 9:15 A.M.	Josh pushes anyone who comes near him. Children walk away, leaving him alone at the water table.	1 Teach peers to say "stop!" when he pushes or engages in aggressive behavior. 2 Ask peers to not crowd Joshua until he is more comfortable with close proximity of others.

*Note: Above form copied on NCR paper so copies may be left for parents and staff after each visit.

Figure 15–1   Inclusion support recommendation form.

The ECSE consultant may also be responsible for monitoring the child's progress. Individual goals for the child are based on specific assessments of the child's development and skills across the developmental domains of cognition, language, motor, adaptive, social, and emotional development. Other goals may be related to health, nutrition, and behavioral management. The ECSE consultant can work with the ECE staff to determine the simplest ways to monitor the child's progress in each goal area.

SPEECH-LANGUAGE SPECIALIST

Nearly all children with special needs have some delay or difficulty in the area of communication. Speech-language specialists are trained to address the communication development of both children and adults. They are certified by the American Speech-Language Hearing Association (ASHA). Speech-language specialists are trained to address a wide range of communication disorders.

Speech Production Disorders. Children who have **speech production disorders (articulation)** are difficult to understand. The underlying causes and characteristics of speech disorders are complex. Children often have both speech and language problems. In some cases there is no other disability. Sometimes the speech disorder is related to obvious motor problems such as cerebral palsy or to more complex motor planning difficulty (Love, 1999). Sometimes the cause of the speech production difficulty is unclear.

Language Disorders. While speech production involves the motor and sequencing ability to produce sounds and syllables, *language abilities* include vocabulary development and understanding the meaning of words, as well as the rules for combining words, and the correct forms of words, i.e., *grammar.* Thus speech disorders and **language disorders** are not the same. Children who have difficulty using language in appropriate ways and have difficulty engaging in appropriate social communication are said to have problems with **pragmatics.**

Many children with special needs have difficulty learning to talk. They may not talk at all, or they may use only single words or two- and three-word combinations. Language problems may be related to a variety of factors. Often the child has a cognitive disability or delay. Occasionally the language disorder is related to severe emotional disturbance or to autism.

Some children with severe or multiple disabilities may have even more basic problems in that they have no communication system. In some instances children with multiple disabilities may not attempt to communicate, even with such nonverbal means as gestures, eye gaze, or vocalizations.

Fluency Disorders. Speech-language specialists are trained to provide therapy to children and adults with **fluency disorders** such as stuttering. They can differentially diagnose true stuttering behavior from typical early childhood language disfluency. Stuttering is a relatively uncommon disorder.

Voice Disorders. The most common type of **voice disorder** among children with special needs is hoarseness due to vocal abuse (e.g., excessive screaming or yelling) or chronic upper respiratory infections. Occasionally children may also have disorders of pitch (e.g., high-pitched voice) or loudness (e.g., a soft voice).

Role of the Speech-Language Specialist

Because communication and language are very complex processes, it is often necessary to have an in-depth assessment to understand the specific nature of the child's communication problem. Following the assessment the speech-language specialist can provide specific suggestions for intervention.

For some aspects of communication, the speech/language specialist may work primarily in the role of a consultant, collaborating with the child's teacher. This is particularly the case with children who are still in the prelinguistic stages of development or in the earliest stages of language development.

The best place to help children develop early language skills is in the context of the routine activities of everyday life, both in the classroom or child care center and at home. A variety of generic and specific strategies can support the development of language in young children. It is important that the ECE teacher obtain clear descriptions of recommended interventions.

For other types of communication disorders, such as severe articulation disorders or stuttering, a more direct intervention approach may be necessary. However, the ECE teacher should understand the goals and strategies involved and be able to support the speech/language specialist's efforts in the classroom.

Another area in which the speech/language specialist may be able to offer support is in the development of AAC for those children whose motor disabilities are so severe they cannot develop intelligible speech or for whom speech development will proceed slowly. However, it is important to realize that many speech/language specialists have *not* had training and experience in this area.

PHYSICAL THERAPIST (PT)

For children who have motor disabilities such as cerebral palsy or spina bifida, therapy and consultation from a licensed physical therapist should be provided. Physical therapists are licensed and registered by state agencies. They have had intensive graduate level training in anatomy and kinesiology, normal development of movement, and various therapy techniques for supporting the optimal development of movement and postural control. They may also have expertise in the evaluation and design of such adaptive equipment as hand splints, leg braces, and adapted seating. They can make practical adaptations in the child's daily environment that support the child's participation in activities. The physical therapist is concerned with:

- Development of postural control, including such skills as the ability to sit without support, to stabilize the head and neck, and to move from sitting to standing.
- Development of **protective reflexes,** or movements that help the child maintain balance and protect her in a fall.

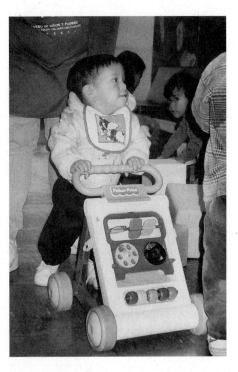

Figure 15–2   Physical therapists may suggest simple functional adaptations to support motor goals.

- Optimal development of movement of both upper and lower parts of the body. This includes the **fine motor skills** of reaching and grasping, and transferring objects from one hand to the other. It also includes the large or **gross motor skills** of crawling and walking.
- Evaluation and recommendations regarding **adaptive equipment** such as leg braces, hand splints, head and neck stabilizers, helmets, and special seating.

Role of the Physical Therapist

The physical therapist can provide critical support for children with motor disabilities. These services do not simply support the development of motor skills; certain procedures and adaptations provided by the physical therapist can make a huge difference in the child's ability to participate in the child care center or preschool program. Figure 15–2 shows a simple, functional adaptation to support child's mobility. The following are examples of services that might be provided by the physical therapist.

- Suggestions for positioning children so they can use their hands during an art activity
- Specific feeding techniques

- Practical suggestions for adapting chairs so that the child can maintain postural control and avoid excessive fatigue
- Designing hand splints so the child can grasp objects more easily
- Strategies to assist the child in learning to use a walker

OCCUPATIONAL THERAPIST (OT)

Occupational therapists are not licensed but are registered by the AOTA (American Occupational Therapy Association). Occupational therapy addresses the development of functional skills, including fine motor skills, eating, and movement of the body in space. In working with young children, the roles of the occupational therapist and physical therapist may sometimes overlap. Theoretically, the physical therapist is more concerned with the development of postural control and large muscle movements, such as sitting, standing, walking, reaching, balance, and head control.

The occupational therapist, while interested in many of the same aspects of development as the physical therapist, particularly focuses on the role of *sensation* in development. How the child discriminates, modulates, and integrates incoming sensory information is important to overall development.

Many occupational therapists are trained in the principles and intervention techniques of sensory integration. The theory and therapeutic techniques of sensory integration were developed by Dr. Jean Ayres (1973). Sensory integration therapy addresses the interrelationships of:

- The child's ability to manage and process incoming sensory stimulation
- The child's self-regulation efforts
- The development of motor skills

Sometimes children with special needs have difficulty processing or managing sensory information. The OT (or other therapists trained in sensory integration techniques) can offer therapeutic techniques and intervention activities that may be helpful for young children who have difficulty processing or integrating sensory input. Consider these sources of sensory information and examples of the kinds of sensations that some children with special needs may find difficult to manage.

Sights (visual sensation)
Flashing lights
Visual clutter
Abruptly changing visual stimulation

Sounds (auditory sensation)
Extremely noisy environments
Several people talking at once
Background music
Noisy fans or motors

Flushing toilet or running water
High pitched sounds like sirens or whistles

Touch (tactile sensation)
Feeling against the skin of clothing and other materials such as a washcloth
Reaction to being touched or grabbed by another person
Feeling of materials on the hands such as paint, glue, or foods
Sensation of various food textures in the mouth

Movement of body parts called **kinesthetic sensation** or **proprioception**
Awareness of movement of various parts of the body, including the contracting and stretching of muscles and compression of the joints
Rotating the body or the head, bending over, squatting, leaning to one side, maintaining balance while seated without support

Sensation of the position of the parts of the body
Knowing how close the body is to an object
Knowing how high to lift the foot to climb a step or step down off a curb
Knowing how hard to swing a bat

Movement of the body through space (vestibular sensation)
Sensation of the movement and position of the body as it moves through space, such as swinging, being picked up, and moving against gravity
Sensation of where the body is in space, such as awareness of losing your balance

Smell (olfactory sense) and **taste** (gustatory sense)
Strong odors like perfume or paint
Intense flavors such as spices or citrus

The OT tends to focus somewhat more on the functional movements of the *upper* body rather than lower body movements required for standing and walking. Examples include:

- Arm movements and wrist rotation involved in reaching and self feeding
- Fine motor movements of the hands involved in grasping, manipulating, and transferring objects
- Movement and control of the oral motor musculature required in chewing and swallowing

Role of the Occupational Therapist

The OT can be of assistance in a number of areas. Two common areas of assistance are feeding problems and problems with sensory integration, especially with children who are extremely sensitive to sensory input, such as children who demonstrate tactile defensiveness.

Occupational therapy techniques are highly specialized and typically should be performed by trained therapists or under their direct supervision. However, OTs may be able, through careful assessment, to help ECE teachers understand the child's motor and sensory difficulties in a more detailed way and to make general suggestions for ways of modifiying the child's sensory environment. For example, an OT may be able to provide these forms of assistance.

- How to reduce the child's resistance to messy activities and materials
- How to help the child learn to finger feed
- How to expand the child's choices of foods and textures
- How to reduce drooling
- How to help the child learn to dress herself independently
- How to help the child develop fine motor skills
- How to deal with excessively high or low muscle tone

VISUAL IMPAIRMENT (VI) SPECIALIST

Consultants in the area of visual impairment are usually special educators who have a credential in the area of visual impairment. They are knowledgeable about the nature of various eye conditions that cause blindness or limited vision. They are often trained to work as **itinerants** in school districts, traveling to several school sites. Thus they work well in a consulting mode.

Most children who have visual disabilities are not totally blind. The VI specialist can assist the ECE teacher in understanding the nature of the child's vision problem, including:

- The characteristics of the particular eye pathology
- The parameters of the residual vision. (Can the child see only light and shadows? Can she recognize objects at close range? What is the optimal distance at which the child can see?)
- A description of the child's **visual field,** or where the child can see best (such as upper left quadrant or right side only)
- The kind of lighting that is best for the child
- Colors that are most easily perceived

Role of the Vision Specialist

The following are services that can be helpful in supporting a child with a visual disability.

Functional Vision Assessment. Through a functional vision assessment the VI specialist can provide the ECE teacher with important information such as visual acuity, visual field preference, and color perception. In developing teaching strategies for young children, the information provided by the functional vision assessment is often more helpful than an ophthalmologist's or oculist's report.

Lighting. The VI specialist can suggest the best sources and angles for lighting to optimize the child's use of residual vision.

Contrast. The VI specialist can demonstrate simple ways to maximize contrast for children with visual impairments, such as placing a bowl on a contrasting place mat or covering a child's cubby with a black and white checkerboard pattern.

Use of Tactile Cues. The VI specialist can provide information on how to use tactile cues, such as textures to identify personal belongings or textures and small objects added to children's books. Touch cues can also be used to help the child anticipate transitions and different activities.

Strategies for Teaching Concepts. One of the greatest challenges for children with visual impairments is learning concepts that are visually based, such as concepts of space, size and volume. The VI specialist can provide specific teaching suggestions.

Orientation and Mobility Specialists

An important subspecialty within the field of vision is that of **orientation and mobility (O&M) specialist.** Not all states provide O&M services to very young children. Orientation and mobility specialists are concerned primarily with helping children learn to move independently and safely from one place to another and also with the ability to orient oneself in space. They may assist children in learning to use a cane, in learning **trailing techniques** (such as trailing the hand along a strip on the wall that marks the route to the bathroom), and in the use of protective strategies.

O&M specialists can teach children how to move around safely in the ECE environment. They work closely with ECE teachers to ensure that mobility skills are developed through such strategies as maintaining a consistent physical environment and providing appropriate tactile and auditory cues.

DEAF AND HARD OF HEARING (DHH) SPECIALIST

The **deaf and hard of hearing (DHH) specialist** is usually a credentialed educator who specializes in working with children who have hearing loss. Some have a subspecialty in working with infants and young children. In some cases services for young children with hearing loss may be provided by a speech-language specialist or an audiologist.

The DHH specialist has a broad knowledge of educational and developmental needs, the child's clinical needs for speech and language development, and use of the hearing aid. The DHH specialist does *not* conduct audiological assessment or hearing aid evaluation.

The DHH specialist should be knowledgeable in both manual modes of communication (sign language) and oral approaches (speech and use of residual hearing).

Role of the DHH Specialist

The ECE teacher should be able to obtain the following kinds of information and services from the DHH specialist.

Interpretation of the Audiogram. The specialist should be able to provide a functional explanation of what the child can hear, both with and without the hearing aid, by examining the child's **audiogram.** This includes an explanation of the types of sounds (e.g., high versus low pitch sounds) that are most easily heard and how the child hears various loudness levels. For example, a child may just barely be able to hear a high-pitched siren that is painful to the normal ear; another child may not be able to hear certain consonant sounds like *sh* and *f*.

Suggestions for Reducing Ambient Noise and Excessive Resonance. The specialist can analyze the acoustic characteristics of a classroom and make suggestions for simple modifications to cut down on extraneous or **ambient noise** that interferes with the child's ability to discriminate speech and important environmental sounds.

Strategies Related to the Family's Preferred Communication Mode. Children with hearing loss may be learning sign language, or families may prefer that the child concentrate more on learning speech and learning to use residual hearing; some families use both approaches. Many complex factors may determine the preferred mode of communication and the approach that is most successful for the child. The specialist can help the ECE teacher understand these different approaches and can make practical suggestions regarding teaching and communicating with the child.

Information on and Demonstration of the Use of the Hearing Aid. The specialist (and the parent) can be very helpful in explaining the basic care, battery checks, insertion, and settings of the hearing aid. If there are problems with the aid, the DHH specialist can assist in referral to the audiologist.

BEHAVIOR SPECIALIST

As we have discussed often throughout this book, children who have behavior problems can present the most serious challenge to successful inclusion. When the strategies suggested here or recommended by the ECSE support facilitator are not sufficient, it may be helpful to bring in a behavior specialist.

Behavior specialists do not represent a clearly defined professional group. In many states they are unregulated. When they are licensed or certified, there is currently little consistency from region to region on the training and competencies required. However, the development of consistent credentials may occur in the years to come.

In most cases individuals who offer their services as behavior specialists are trained in traditional *behavior modification* approaches (see Chapter 4).

Increasingly these individuals also incorporate functional behavior analysis and positive behavior support techniques.

Role of the Behavior Specialist

Typical services provided by a behavior specialist include the following.

Careful Observation of the Child Across Different Settings, Activities, and Times. As a result of careful observation and data collection the behavior specialist can evaluate the frequency and intensity of the problem behavior, and conduct an analysis of antecedents and consequences of the behavior.

Designing a Behavior Intervention Plan. Using the data from the behavioral assessment and interviews with key individuals (ideally including the parent), the specialist generates a functional analysis of the purpose and meaning of the behavior, including what triggers it and what reinforces or maintains the behavior. On this basis a specific behavior plan is drawn up. The plan may include certain changes in the child's environment, establishment of consistent ways of interacting with the child, and clear consequences for specific behavior. Behavior plans always require careful data collection and consistency.

Assistance in Implementing the Plan. Ultimately, to be most effective, the plan should be implemented by everyone who interacts with the child. One of the greatest barriers to effective use of behavior specialists is the impracticality of implementing elaborate behavior plans in programs where there are limited staff resources. Ideally, the behavior specialist will initially spend a significant amount of time demonstrating how the plan should be implemented and modifying aspects of the plan that are not feasible in a particular setting. Gradually the specialist should assist the staff in taking over responsibility for implementing the plan. The behavior specialist should also be responsible for determining if the plan is working and, in consultation with the child's intervention team, should make adjustments as needed.

OBTAINING AND USING INCLUSION SUPPORT

ECE teachers should know how to contact specialists who can be of assistance in supporting young children with special needs. Often children's needs are complex, and no one individual has all the answers. This is why a *coordinated, team-based approach* is critical to successful inclusion.

This support team is not always readily available to the ECE teacher. It may be necessary to initiate requests for support and to make the assertion that the child has the *legal* right to these services. Unfortunately, in many areas of the United States there are significant shortages of many specialists. They often carry large case loads and may work as itinerants covering a wide geographic area. Thus, ECE teachers may need to be persistent in their efforts to obtain services.

Once services have been obtained, however, another challenge often emerges. This is related to the intrusion and cumulative effect of specialists and consultants coming into the classroom. The ECE teacher must work with the ECSE support facilitator to coordinate and manage this team. Too many people going in and out the classroom will obviously become a very disruptive factor and in the end may not be effective. This list can serve as a simple guide for the ECE professional in obtaining and using inclusion support.

Suggestions for the early childhood educator for obtaining and using inclusion support

- **Identify sources of information and services:**

    Parents
    Child's service coordinator (if child is under three)
    School district program specialist or teacher
    Social worker
    Therapist
    Speech/language specialist
    Occupational therapist
    Physical therapist
    Behavior specialist
    Disability specialist
    VI specialist
    DHH specialist
    Physical disabilities specialist
    Other professional or service provider
    Information about specific disabilities (from web sites, the library, and various associations)

- **Be *assertive* about requesting information and services.** The child has a legal right to these services.
- **Establish *partnerships* with parents and support personnel.** Your input is important!
- **Ask a specialist to *demonstrate*, not just talk.**
- **Ask for *written* information and suggestions.**
- **Use one-to-one assistants *appropriately*.**

    Clarify their expectations and role.
    Discourage one-to-one assistants from isolating and overprotecting the child.
    Realize the assistant may have little or no training.

WORKING EFFECTIVELY WITH PARAEDUCATORS

Effective inclusion of young children with special needs often necessitates working with a paraeducator (or paraprofessional) to assist the professional educator in making necessary accommodations. The success of these instructional assistants depends not only on the skills and abilities of the paraeducators, but also on how well teachers and other professionals perform in the role of program managers.

Early Educators as Program Managers

Early childhood educators who are provided with the services of a paraeducator will be expected, as the classroom leader, to perform the following managerial or supervisory functions.

Develop and Provide Specific Plans for Paraeducators to Follow. Paraeducators should not be expected to plan their own involvement in the daily routine of activities. They have not been trained to create or plan activity adaptations. Too often, teachers assume that paraeducators who have been assigned to assist certain children have sufficient training. The professionals, who have been appropriately trained, are responsible for providing activity plans with clear directions to paraeducators. These plans should be well described in writing. In short, supervision demands that job expectations be well defined and clearly communicated.

Devise and Manage Intervention (Instructional) Schedules. While the daily program plan addresses the *what* and *how,* the schedule addresses the questions *when* and *where.* Successful use of paraeducators requires a detailed plan of their activities, including time and location.

Delegate Tasks Appropriately. The purpose of assigning paraeducators to inclusive programs is to free educators to do work that cannot be delegated such as planning activities, monitoring children's progress, and creating activity adaptations. No matter how many tasks the paraeducator can handle well, the ultimate responsibility for all children lies with the early educator. The professional educator is accountable for the outcomes of the instructional activities.

Cook, Tessier, and Klein (2000) offer the following list of some responsibilities that may be appropriately delegated.

- Preparing the room, including setting up centers, organizing materials needed for special projects, and locating daily supplies
- Greeting children and assisting with all routines
- Nurturing appropriate behavior, including dealing with misbehaviors acceptably and effectively
- Directing specific activities planned by the teacher
- Assisting children with eating and toileting
- Following specialists' instructions in helping to position and transport children
- Providing appropriate prompts to help ensure positive social integration

Helpful Hint

There is a tendency when paraeducators are assigned to help specific children in inclusive settings—as one-to-one assistants, for example—for the ECE teacher to avoid assuming responsibility for the development of the children with special needs. The ECE teacher should continue to interact with these children individually and in group activities.

- Preparing, cataloging, and filing educational games and materials
- Preparing materials for art activities or snack
- Helping with end-of-the-day routines, including cleanup
- Cleaning and maintaining adaptive equipment
- Recording observations of children's performance

Take Care in Assigning a Paraeducator as a One-to-One Assistant. The assignment of a one-to-one assistant exclusively to a specific child though often necessary has definite drawbacks. The ECE teacher should not assume that the assistant has been well trained to work with the child. Frequently, this is not the case. Another disadvantage is that the child often becomes very attached to the assistant because of the intensity and exclusivity of the relationship and may avoid interacting with the children and other adults.

In some cases, as with a child who runs away, who is extremely aggressive or self-injurious, or who is medically fragile and technology dependent, it is necessary to assign a one-to-one assistant—especially if the alternative is removing the child from the program.

Assess the Strengths and Needs of the Paraeducator. Once tasks are delegated by the ECE teacher and performed by the paraeducator, the teacher must observe carefully to determine the paraeducator's knowledge and skills, and the areas in which additional training may be needed. While some specific training has been developed, many paraeducators have had no formal training. Even when such formal training has been obtained, it may not have included content related to children with special needs.

On the other hand, some paraeducators, though perhaps not formally trained, may have as much experience as the teacher. These can be challenging situations. In such cases the teacher must value and use the assistant's expertise while at the same time maintaining a leadership role in the classroom. Use of a highly collaborative model will be extremely important.

In some cases paraeducators are hired because of their cultural and linguistic backgrounds. They can play a critical role in connecting to children and families.

Early educators can match their supervisory style with the qualities of paraeducators. For example, less mature or inexperienced paraeducators may need direct supervision while those with more experience might benefit from increased opportunities at self-reflection and the chance to direct their own learning.

Monitoring performance does not mean "hovering over" paraeducators as they work. Instead, the early educator can encourage independence and initiative by focusing on the outcomes of intervention rather than on perfect execution of intervention techniques and by valuing the ideas and observations of the assistant.

Create a System for Timely and Constructive Feedback. It takes time to develop skills. Paraeducators cannot learn everything at once. Early educators must have sufficient patience to allow paraeducators to practice. Feedback must focus on specific task behaviors and not on personalities. It should be descriptive, not evaluative or judgmental, and it should describe observable events or behaviors rather than being based on opinion.

Good coaches provide specific feedback providing essential information so that changes can be made. For example, it is not helpful to tell paraeducators that they must become better organized. Instead, be specific and make such statements as, "It helps to place the crayons and scissors in buckets between the children rather than placing them in the middle of the table." Coaching and modeling appropriate behavior may be needed to assist paraeducators in developing their potential.

Recognize and Reward Quality Performance. Daily recognition of quality performance is essential. Like feedback, words of recognition should be specific so the paraeducator knows exactly what actions you are reinforcing. Consider the following two statements.

1. "Mrs. Garcia, I really appreciated how you jumped in to help out today."
2. "You jumped in just in time to help the children clean up the spilled grape juice. What a mess that would have been if the children had walked in it."

Of course, both comments are positive, but the second one tells the paraeducator exactly what type of action to repeat in the future. It also lets the paraeducator know that the early educator is observant and takes responsibility for the total situation.

Words of praise not only must be specific, but they must be sincere. If they just become rote words spoken at the end of the day, their learning and rewarding value will diminish. Feedback that could be taken as negative must always be given in private away from the eager ears of children.

Early Educators as Coaches

Increasing demand for the services of paraeducators continually increases the possibility that paraeducators will have received little or no training, especially in working with children with special needs. Most paraeducators are trained on the job. Even when paraeducators have had training, there is much they must learn about the situation in which they are placed. Therefore, early educators should learn to provide coaching on a daily basis. The challenge in the case of children with special needs, especially when they have unique or intense needs, is that often early childhood educators are also just learning strategies that are effective with these children. Nevertheless, ECE teachers should do their best to pass along this information.

To do so, early educators must be skilled in the ability to evaluate the unique needs of their children and of their particular program. They must also be able to recognize the skills paraeducators bring to the job and the skills they will need to succeed.

Finally, coaching is only successful in an atmosphere of trust and experimentation. The goal of coaching is to assist paraeducators to make optimal use of their strengths and resources.

Early Educators as Communicators

Effective communication between early educators and the paraeducators working under their supervision is critical to success. Both the paraeducator and the early educator must learn to communicate their expectations and experiences.

The early educator's expectations must be consistent, clear, and realistic. Paraeducators must understand the outcomes or goals desired for each child. They should be involved in individual planning meetings. They must be instructed in which behavior management techniques are used for each student and why they are different for different children. A system can be developed so that paraeducators regularly inform the supervising teacher of unique observations they have made of children while working with them.

Meetings must Be Conducted on a Regular Basis. As early educators and paraeducators are expected to function as a team, regular meetings are needed to communicate effectively and provide for sufficient planning time. Such meetings provide the opportunity to discuss progress toward the outcomes or goals for children, plot instructional strategies, solve problems, or resolve any existing conflicts. Some programs must be creative in fitting in time for regular meetings. Use of practicum students, volunteers and parents may be helpful in providing coverage during staff meetings. Whole day programs are sometimes able to use nap time one day a week. Occasionally well-funded programs have a half day each week devoted to meeting time. Unfortunately, many programs rely on personnel giving up personal time at the beginning or end of the day to facilitate this critical communication. Despite the difficulty, the value of regular staff meetings cannot be over estimated.

Paraeducators Should Be Evaluated on a Regular Basis. Building in regular evaluation and feedback on a formal basis makes providing constructive feedback and dealing with problems a much easier task. It also provides an additional opportunity to discuss the implementation of programs

SELF-EVALUATION CHECKLIST FOR PARAEDUCATORS

How consistently do I do the following?	Rarely	Sometimes	Usually
1. Ask questions when I am unsure of my responsibility.	1	2	3
2. Observe and understand the strategies used by the teacher with specific children.	1	2	3
3. Make sure I understand the plan for the day and the details for implementing specific activities and lessons.	1	2	3
4. Offer my assistance when there is an apparent need for help, even if it is not technically my assigned role.	1	2	3
5. Observe children closely and note their likes, dislikes, strengths, and limitations.	1	2	3
6. Provide children with choices.	1	2	3
7. Praise children for their efforts and appropriate behavior.	1	2	3
8. Listen carefully to what children say, and respond appropriately.	1	2	3
9. Make sure I understand how to use children's adaptive equipment.	1	2	3
10. Use effective behavior management strategies without being negative or punitive.	1	2	3
11. Allow children ample time to respond or perform a task on their own.	1	2	3
12. Accept constructive criticism and feedback without becoming upset.	1	2	3

Things I would like to work on or learn more about:

_____

_____

Figure 15–3 Self evaluation checklist for paraeducators.

and strategies for specific children. Another helpful strategy is to encourage paraeducators to evaluate themselves. See Figure 15–3 for an example of a self-evaluation form.

EARLY EDUCATORS, PARAEDUCATORS, AND DISABILITY SPECIALISTS AS A COLLABORATIVE TEAM

One of the keys to success in working with children with special needs is the creation of effective teams. It is nearly impossible for a single individual, no matter how skilled, to meet all the complex needs of a child who has a disability. Ideally, early educators, paraeducators, and disability specialists work together as a team to provide optimum support for the child (see Figure 15–4). Parents must also be part of the team (see Figure 15–5) To function as a successful team, these educators and specialists must foster an atmo-

Figure 15–4   Teacher meets with paraeducators and inclusion specialist.

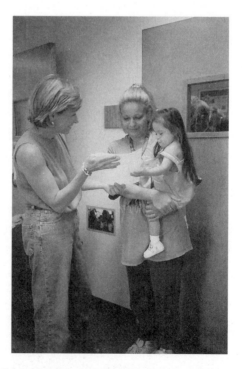

Figure 15–5   Early childhood special educator discusses inclusion support plan with parent.

sphere of respect built on trust and good communication. The following characteristics are necessary for the team to function optimally.

- The team members must view themselves as part of a team.
- The team members must view their own involvement as essential to the team's success.
- The members must be willing to work together.
- The team members must be focused on clearly defined goals.
- Team members must understand their individual role in the team effort.
- Team members must be given the opportunity to express themselves within an environment perceived to be psychologically safe.

Collaborative Problem Solving

A critical part of working as a team is engaging in problem solving. This can often be an emotional and stressful experience. Problem solving is a *skill* that requires a specific step-by-step process if it is to be successful (Heron & Harris, in press). The following is an example of a step-by-step problem solving process.

1. Clarify the issues and define the problem. *Define the problem* clearly. Often different members of the team see the problem differently. *Understand each other's perspectives.* All participants *must* define the problem as they see it. Don't assume everyone agrees with your perception of the problem. No single team member should consistently lead these discussions and share a perception first. Although it may be tempting to do so, do *not* try to generate solutions to the problem at this early stage!
2. Agree on a problem-solving process. Describe and agree upon use of the steps the team will use
3. Write down the problem. Obtain consensus from the group. Write the problem on chart paper so everyone can see it and edit it. Identify conflicts and differences of opinion.
4. Determine possible solutions. Brainstorm solutions; everyone must contribute. All ideas are acceptable during this activity. Write ideas down on chart paper or the board so group can review and edit. It is extremely important that the consultant or facilitator *not* become invested in a particular solution, even if she is convinced that it is the best one.
5. Allow the practitioner to select a solution to try. For example, to control a behavior problem the teacher may decide to begin with a careful ABC analysis. Whoever has the responsibility for implementing the plan must have the opportunity to choose which approach will be tried first.
6. Produce an action plan. What must be done to implement the solution? Who, what, where, by when? The action plan must supply this information. Figure 15–6 presents a simple action plan form.

Action Plan for Inclusion Support Team

Date: _____ **Name of Student:** _____

Team members present:

Name: _____ Role: _____

Name: _____ Role: _____

Name: _____ Role: _____

Name: _____ Role: _____

Purpose of action plan / desired outcome:

Procedure / intervention to be implemented:

What?
1.

2.

3.

4.

Who is responsible? _____

By what date? _____

Follow-up plan:

Date and time of follow-up meeting or teleconference with team if necessary

Date: _____ Time: _____ Persons:

1.   3.

2.   4.

EVALUATION: Were strategies useful? Explain below:

Figure 15–6　　Simple Action Plan Form.

7. Evaluate success. Meet together to evaluate the outcome of implementing the action plan. Try to maintain a neutral position rather than investing in a particular outcome. If the action wasn't effective, select another solution from the original brainstorming session, or come up with new suggestions. An approach that is not successful must not be seen as someone's failure.

If solution *was* effective, determine if other problems or new problems need to be addressed.

8. Recycle the problem-solving process, if necessary. Follow the same steps to address new or different problems.

SUMMARY

Oftentimes, early educators and other professionals have not been well prepared to take on their role as managers of a program team. Early educators who find themselves uncomfortable in this new role should realize that program management and team coordination are challenging areas of expertise. They will be provided with opportunities to enhance their skills in the various areas mentioned in this brief chapter.

CASE STUDY

Mark's Story

Mark's mother Amy is anxious to enroll her son Mark, a toddler, at the local child care center. However, Amy is concerned about how Mark will adjust to the classroom because he is not walking and he often chokes on table foods during mealtime. Mark has been diagnosed with Down syndrome. The physical therapist has assured Amy that he will be walking within the next year, but is developmentally not ready at the present time.

Amy calls the center's director and after discussing her concerns, they agree that Mark will need extra help in the classroom. An assistant will help him as he learns to pull to stand, cruise, and walk. The assistant will also observe him carefully during snack and mealtimes so that he does not choke on large pieces of food.

These concerns are shared with Mark's service coordinator at the agency responsible for overseeing his educational services. The team agrees that a one-to-one aide will be hired to assist Mark during his hours at the child care center.

Finding an assistant is difficult, and Mark needs to start childcare right away because his mother is returning to work. A temporary nursing assistant is hired because of Mark's problems with choking. The assistant is a good caregiver, but she knows little about the education

(continued)

of young children. She often spends long periods of time cleaning Mark after he plays with paint. She does not encourage him to play with other children, and she takes such good care of Mark that his teachers see no reason to interfere. Thus the assistant's level and type of care results in segregating Mark from his peers and teachers. On a positive note, he has no choking episodes while she is present.

Before long, an assistant with a background in typical child development is hired. At this time the team agrees that an inclusion support provider should be brought in to provide support to Mark's teachers and to supervise the training of the new assistant. The goal is to meet Mark's specific needs in ways that will allow him to participate in the child care center without placing a major burden on the staff, while avoiding isolating or overprotecting him.

Prior to the assistant's first day with Mark, the inclusion support provider asks for a meeting with the center teachers, director, the assistant, and Amy, Mark's mother. The meeting agenda includes a review of how Mark has adjusted to the classroom, how the teachers feel about having Mark in their room, what the nursing assistant's role had been, and what the teacher sees as her needs to include Mark in her classroom.

The general consensus is that Mark is adjusting well to the classroom routine, moving around independently by crawling, and enjoying the large group activities. At the same time everyone agrees that Mark had been isolated by the first assistant and not allowed to explore as much as he was indicating that he wanted to. The teachers say they felt uncomfortable approaching him because the first assistant had "always been there first." They felt they had little opportunity or reason to interact with him.

By the end of the meeting a specific plan has been developed carefully describing the specific responsibilities of the one-to-one assistant. During mealtime she will pay close attention to Mark for any signs of choking, but she should encourage independent eating. During other times she will assist Mark in moving from one place to another when necessary, but she should also encourage his interactions with other children.

The plan is successful. Teachers and children get to know Mark better and enjoy him. Mark becomes more confident. By the end of the year he is beginning to walk independently, and he no longer chokes on his food. Perhaps even more importantly, Mark develops some good friends and playmates at the center and Amy starts to relax!

Case Study Questions

1. *In a typical child care center with limited resources, what would be the challenges of implementing the team problem-solving approach described in the case study?*
2. *When a new one-to-one assistant is assigned to a child in your class, how would you orient this paraeducator to your classroom? What would your own preference be in how the assistant would function in your classroom?*
3. *What steps would you take to clarify the roles and lines of communication for the one-to-one aide, yourself, and the regular assistant?*

KEY TERMS

adaptive equipment
ambient noise
audiogram
deaf and hard of hearing
(DHH) specialist
fine motor skills
fluency disorders
gross motor skills
itinerants
kinesthetic sensation

language disorders
orientation and mobility (O&M) specialist
pragmatics
proprioception
protective reflexes
speech production (articulation) disorders
trailing techniques
vestibular sensation
visual field
voice disorder

HELPFUL RESOURCES

Working with the Intervention Team

Bruder, M. B. (1994). Working with members of other disciplines: collaboration for success. In M. Wolery & J. S. Wilbers (Eds.), *Including children with special needs in early childhood programs* (pp. 45–70). Washington, DC: NAEYC

Gallagher, P. A. (1997). Teachers and inclusion: Perspectives on changing roles. *Topics in Early Childhood Special Education, 17*(3), 363–386.

Heron, T. E., & Harris, K. C. (In press). *The educational consultant: Helping professionals, parents and mainstreamed students* (4th ed.). Austin, TX: Pro-Ed.

Zipper, I. N., Weil, M., & Rounds, K. (1993). *Service coordination for early intervention: Professionals and parents.* Cambridge, MA: Brookline Books.

WORKING WITH PARAEDUCATORS

Doyle, M. B. (1997). *The paraprofessional's guide to the inclusive classroom.* Baltimore, MD: Paul H. Brookes

Giangreco, M. F., Edelman, S. W., Luiselli, T. E., & MacFarland, S. Z. (1997). Helping or hovering? Effects of instructional assistant proximity on students with disabilities. *Exceptional Children, 64*(1), 7–18.

Jones, K., & Bender, W. (1993). Utilization of paraprofessionals in special education: A review of the literature. *Remedial and Special Education, 14*(1), 7–14

Pickett, A. L., & Gerlach, K. (1997). *Supervising paraeducators in school settings.* Austin, TX: Pro-Ed.

Skelton, K. (1998). *Paraprofessionals in education.* Albany, NY: Delmar.

Striffler, N. (1993). Current trends in the use of paraprofessionals in early intervention and preschool services. *NECTAS Synthesis Report.* Chapel Hill, NC: National Early Childhood Technical Assistance System.

REFERENCES

Ayers, J. (1973). *Sensory integration and learning disorders.* Los Angeles: Western Psychological Services.

Cook, R., Tessier, A., & Klein, M. D. (2000). *Adapting early childhood curricula for children in inclusive settings* (5th ed.). Columbus, OH: Merrill/Prentice Hall.

Heron, T., & Harris, K. C. (In press). The consultation process. In *The educational consultant: Helping professionals, parents and mainstreamed students* (4th ed.). pp. 1–36. Austin, TX: Pro-Ed.

Love, R. J. (1999). *Childhood motor speech disability* (2nd ed.). Boston: Allyn & Bacon

Appendix A

Blank Recording Forms

DAILY CLASSROOM SCHEDULE

(Indicate which IEP objectives are targeted in each daily activity)

NAME _____ DATE _____

IEP OBJECTIVE	CLASS SCHEDULE					

INCLUSION SUPPORT RECOMMENDATIONS

INCLUSION OBSERVATION REPORTING FORM*

Date _____ Child _____ Center _____

Teacher(s) _____ Inclusion Facilitator _____

SCHEDULE	OBSERVATIONS (what facilitator observes)	SUPPORTS/ADAPTATIONS (suggestions for teachers that may help child be part of activities)

*Note: Above form copied on NCR paper so copies may be left for parents and staff after each visit.

INCLUSION ACTION PLAN

GOAL _____　　　Child _____　　　Teacher _____　　　Date _____

ACTIVITIES	EXPECTED OUTCOMES	PERSON RESPONSIBLE	TIME LINE	EVALUATION

A QUICK LOOK AT THE IEP

Child _____ Date _____ Teacher(s) _____

Goal #1 _____

Objective(s)
a)

b)

c)

d)

Goal #2 _____

Objective(s)
a)

b)

c)

d)

Goal #3 _____

Objective(s)
a)

b)

c)

d)

Goal #4 _____

Objective(s)
a)

b)

c)

d)

Goal #5 _____

Objective(s)
a)

b)

c)

d)

Goal #6 _____

Objective(s)
a)

b)

c)

d)

Child's Name _____ **Week of** _____

LEVEL OF PARTICIPATION IN DAILY ACTIVITIES

ACTIVITY	Monday	Tuesday	Wednesday	Thursday	Friday
Free play					
Circle					
Outside play					
Snack					
Toileting					
Centers					
Computers					
Good-bye circle					

X = Participation refused
A = Needed assistance
I = Participated independently

ROLES AND RESPONSIBILITIES FOR INCLUSION

Child's Name _____ **Date** _____

RESPONSIBILITIES — **WHO IS RESPONSIBLE?**

	Child Care Teacher	Special Education Teacher	1:1 Aide (as needed)	Administrator
Developing child's goals				
Assigning responsibility and supervising 1:1 aide				
Adapting environment and/or curriculum				
Implementing lesson plans				
Monitoring child's progress				
Communicating with parents				
Consulting with other service providers				
Arranging and coordinating team meetings				
Other?				

CODE:
P = Primary responsibility
S = Secondary responsibility
E = Equal responsibility
I = Has input in decision-making process

OBJECTIVE BY ACTIVITY MATRIX

Child's Name _____ **Date** _____

OBJECTIVE

ACTIVITY						

SPECIAL ACTIVITY PLAN

Child's Name _____ **Date** _____

ACTIVITY	STRATEGIES
Description:	Peers:
Purpose & objective(s):	
	Adults:
Materials:	

EVALUATION
Outcomes:
Suggestions for future activities:

INDIVIDUAL SUPPORT SCHEDULE

Child's Name _____ Date _____

Teacher _____ Center _____

Inclusion Consultant _____

SCHEDULE	SPECIFIC SUPPORTS/ADAPTATIONS (what staff will do for child that will help child be part of activities)
Arrival	
Morning activities (free play)	
Cleanup	
Toilet/Handwash	
Snack	
Circle time	
Small group (work time)	
Outside play	

ACTIVITY/STANDARDS INVENTORY

Child's Name _____ Date _____

Situation	Peer Behavior How do peers participate?	Target Child Behavior	Barriers to Participation

POSSIBLE MODIFICATIONS FOR EFFECTIVE INCLUSION

PERSONNEL
_____ No extra support necessary
_____ Part time extra support (specific parts of day)
_____ Full time extra support (1:1 aide)

PHYSICAL ASSISTANCE
_____ No physical help necessary
_____ Physical help as needed
_____ Partial physical help
_____ Full physical help

CURRICULUM
_____ Adapt for lower cognitive level
_____ Adapt for vision impairments
_____ Adapt for hearing impairments
_____ Adapt for physical handicaps

PACING AND AMOUNT OF TIME PER ACTIVITIES
_____ Same pace and time as all other children
_____ Less time than other children (e.g., less attention)
_____ More time than other children (e.g., goes slower)
_____ Slower pacing necessary for understanding (e.g., more wait time for comprehension and/or action)

HIERARCHY OF PROMPTS
_____ Full physical help to complete activities
_____ Partial physical help to complete activities
_____ Direct verbal reminders to complete activities (e.g., "Sit down")
_____ Indirect verbal reminders to complete activities (e.g., "What do you need to do?")
_____ Gestures to complete activities (e.g., pointing)

ENVIRONMENT
_____ Seating adaptations (e.g., chairs too high, child does better sitting next to specific peers, etc.)
_____ Reduce/minimize distractions or stimulation
_____ Define limits (e.g., physical and/or behavioral)

BEHAVIOR
_____ Define limits (e.g., physical and/or behavioral)
_____ Use positive reinforcement
_____ Determine behavior plans through use of ABC (antecedent, behavior, consequences)

Appendix B

Detailed Descriptions of Three Tabletop Activities

While almost any activity *can* be made interesting for children with special needs, this section presents detailed descriptions of activities that are particularly engaging for children with a wide range of skills. While we usually think in terms of adapting the activity for the child with special needs, it is often easier to identify an activity that easily engages the child with special needs and adapting that activity for the *typical* child by adding complexity and variety.

Variations on these activities and lists of other activities that have a high probability of success with children with special needs are also provided in this section.

CORNSTARCH AND WATER (GOOP)

This is a messy, fun activity. Inclusion of children with motor disabilities and difficulties with impulse control may significantly increase the messiness of this activity. Leave extra time for cleanup! This is a good activity to try outside or inside with children standing around an empty water table. Consider how the children are grouped, whether sitting at small tables or standing at a water table. Be aware of how much adult support is available and group children according to their need for adult help, including motor support, language help, and behavioral considerations, for this activity.

One of the advantages of this activity is it's simplicity. There is no right way to implement it and it allows for creative exploration and sensation at all developmental levels.

Materials
Cornstarch (one box per small group of four to six children)
Water
Trays or similar surface that can get MESSY
Child-sized containers for pouring water
Aprons or similar cover-all for children, if needed
Water in large containers or sinks for clean up

305

Optional materials

Food coloring
Spoons
Scraper-type instruments

Environment

Outdoors
Indoors around water table
Indoors around tables on flooring that can be easily cleaned

Strengths of activity for children with special needs

- This sensory motor experience provides a pleasurable tactile sensation that feels good for many children, though some children with tactile defensiveness may resist. (Even with these children, you can start with dry cornstarch and add water slowly at their pace.)
- Children can observe changes in texture as water is added (cause/effect).
- This activity follows a simple sequence: start with dry cornstarch, add water, make goop.
- Colors can be added to the goop (more cause/effect).
- The goop is not an unpleasant texture and can be warmed up in an adult hand before the child touches it.
- The activity has many opportunities for language development via use of key words: dry, wet, soft, crunchy, goopy, push, hold, squeeze, pour, mix, etc. Children can ask or sign for "more water" or "more cornstarch" as needed.
- Socially, this activity lends itself to children sharing the fun by handing goop to each other or adults, showing others what they can do with it (dribble, push, pour), and asking for ingredients from nearby friends.
- Self-help skills are addressed by following directions ("pour the water"), helping to clean up ("put your goop in the bowl"), and washing hands.
- The activity is good for developing motor skills while playing with the goop: holding it, dribbling it, pouring water, and mixing.

MAKING PUDDING

This small group activity provides an opportunity for young children to take turns, cooperate, and begin to understand how to sequence an activity. This type of activity also results in dramatic changes to the ingredients as they are combined, guaranteeing children's interest! Fine and gross motor objectives, such as opening and emptying a box, pouring milk, and stirring, can be taught. The activity is rich with language, and children can create—and taste—their end product.

This activity is ideal for inclusion of young children with special needs because of its appeal to a wide range of ages and interests. Making and eating dessert can be a high preference activity for anyone—from toddlers to grandparents!

Materials

Damp paper towels or warm water for hand washing

Boxes of instant pudding (at least one for each small group of three to six children, but you may want to have choices of flavors as well)

Milk in small pitchers

Medium-sized bowl

Several large spoons (in case spoon *slips* into someone's mouth during the mixing process!)

Small cups or bowls (one for each child and adult)

Spoons (one for each child and adult)

Trays or shallow boxes to place all materials within teacher's reach

It is crucial to have all materials ready for each group of children. This activity can be fun only if adults are well prepared!

Objectives

A variety of individual objectives for children with special needs may be met via this activity, including:

Cognitive/preacademic (sequencing, measuring)

Fine and gross motor (opening box, stirring)

Communication (making choices, requesting turns)

Social (turntaking)

Self-help (eating, pouring)

Key Words

wash	in
hands	pour
pudding	mix
empty	stir
all gone	thick
milk	eat
spoon	good

Step-by-Step Description of Activity

For many children the sequence of events in the activity will be easier to comprehend if a picture board is used, with pictures displayed from left to right representing each of the major ingredients and processes.

1. Give brief introduction to children and show materials.

   "We are making pudding today. We will open the box and pour the pudding in the bowl. We will pour the milk in the bowl and mix it all up with the spoon. Then we can eat the pudding."

2. Briefly demonstrate the sequence or use a picture board as you introduce the materials.

3. Separate the large group of children into smaller groups of three to six (if you need to have two or three small groups, prepare the multiple sets of materials ahead of time).
4. Help children wash hands with towelettes if they haven't washed before sitting down.
5. Ask children what should happen first. Prompt them if no one initiates.
6. Pass around the sealed box of pudding. Ask children to shake it. Ask children what we should do with it (again, prompt if no initiation).

Helpful Hint

At this point in the activity you do not need to have every child participate each time. Some children can be exploring the empty box, while others are helping to pour the milk. If every child needs to wait for a turn during each step, you will lose them!

7. Have children help you open a box.
8. Have children help shake pudding mix into a bowl.
9. Pass around the empty box (say and sign "all gone").
10. Show children the milk in a pitcher. (Premeasuring makes this activity easier.)
11. Let children take turns pouring the milk into their bowl.

Helpful Hint

Encourage children with severe visual disability to smell and feel the pudding mix and milk.

12. Show children how to stir the pudding mixture.

Helpful Hint

For children with severe motor disabilities, provide hand-over-hand assistance, as needed, stirring the pudding.

13. Go around the group with all children taking turns stirring, then passing the bowl to next child. This *is* an important step for all children to have a turn so they can experience the feel of the pudding as it changes from liquid to solid. If the group is large, or this turn taking is too slow, divide the pudding into two different bowls and have another adult assist with the turns.

14. Label what they are doing and what is happening to the pudding: "You are stirring—around and around. Look—the pudding is getting thick." Be sure to *sign* and say key words directly to children with *hearing loss.*
15. Foreshadow: *"Soon we can eat some pudding."*
16. When pudding has thickened, serve in small paper cups with spoons and distribute to children for eating. Again, label the experience: *"Good pudding." "Yummy!"*

Helpful Hint

This is an excellent opportunity to motivate children with special needs to use a spoon. If the pudding is placed in a paper cup, it is very difficult to get it out without using a spoon!

---

17. Allow time for children to ask or sign for more.
18. Assist children with cleanup.

Extending the plan

Once you have made pudding several times, you can introduce variations:

- Offer choices of types of pudding: "Do you want chocolate or vanilla?"
- Use a picture board for children to predict sequence: "What do we do first?"
- Let an older child *lead* the activity.
- *Forget* a step and wait for children to remind you. For example, leave out the milk.
- Delay eating until lunch and serve the pudding as part of the meal: "Remember, we made the pudding? Now we can eat it."

Variations

- Make a microwavable cake for a child's or teacher's birthday.
- Make tortillas using masa harina and water (use an electric frying pan where the children can watch but not touch).
- Mix fruit or milk shakes using blender and frozen fruit or ice cream (use an adapted switch for children with motor delays to operate the blender).
- Make jelly sandwiches by letting children spread jelly with plastic knives and "build" a sandwich (great for sequencing).

MAKING FACES

Typically, the early childhood classroom curriculum emphasizes the *process* of using art-type materials rather than the *product.* However, some young children with special needs may never learn to recognize and produce simple representations of familiar daily images without assistance. Thus it is important that some art activities provide the opportunity for children to learn that familiar images and objects can be represented graphically and that they can develop this ability.

This type of activity can meet a range of developmental levels and objectives. If repeated often with minor variations, teachers may begin to see children shaping this particular activity into a product as familiarity with the process is combined with cognitive growth. The activity should be repeated often enough to allow children to understand it and learn, but not to the exclusion of the many important art experiences that emphasize creative process and sensory experiences.

Materials

Large paper cut in circle or with circle drawn (circles for eyes, nose, and mouth can also be drawn or left until after the activity is repeated several times)

Many pieces of paper cut or torn into small pieces

Bowls (to put small paper shapes in)

Bottles of glue (squeeze type, with holes in cap adjusted as needed)

Markers (for writing children's names on their artwork; adapt as necessary depending on children's motor skills)

Objectives

Children will experience textures and properties of glue and paper.

Children will develop fine motor skills necessary for school readiness, including holding and squeezing glue, tearing paper, and scribbling with markers.

Children will learn sequence of events to create a paper collage: first glue, then paper, etc.

Children will create representational *faces* with eyes, nose, and mouth.

Children will create faces to use during play or song times as a mask or prop.

Skill areas and developmental domains

Cognitive/preacademic: picture representation, sequencing, use of art materials.

Language: labeling body parts and art materials.

Fine motor: cutting, squeezing, gluing.

Key Words

glue	circle
stick	eyes
sticky	nose
paper	mouth
on	face

Step-by-step description of activity

1. Gather all materials needed prior to start of activity.
2. Demonstrate both collage idea and face idea to children, stressing sequence of use of materials.
3. Distribute large paper and bowls of smaller pieces of paper with an individual bottle of glue for each child.
4. Encourage assisting adults to allow children to freely explore textures and properties of glue and paper. If children want to squeeze out lots of glue, allow them to do so.
5. Model sequence of applying glue, then adding paper for children as they become more aware of both glue and paper.
6. As children become more spatially aware of the large paper and smaller pieces, model how individual pieces of paper can be glued to the larger piece.
7. As children begin to initiate gluing pieces of paper separately, model how small papers glued over predrawn shapes can create a specific pattern.
8. Model creating a face with predrawn eyes, nose, and mouth and gluing paper over these shapes.
9. Encourage children to make their own faces with no predrawn shapes.
10. Label appropriate body parts as children become more deliberate in creating a face.
11. Write children's names on their paper and let them watch you doing this to encourage awareness of names. Ask "Where should I write your name?" to make sure the child is attending to your writing.
12. At end of the activity period, help children clean up.

Helpful Hint

It may be a challenge to make this activity meaningful for children with severe visual impairment. The following may be helpful:

1. Use different textured materials for face parts, including three-dimensional objects, such as half of a small rubber ball for the nose.
2. Be sure the face parts are highly contrasting with the color of the paper.
3. Have the child touch his own face parts, then have him touch your face parts. Say, "These are your eyes, Johnny's eyes. These are my eyes, teacher's eyes." (Children with visual impairments may have special difficulty understanding the pronouns *I, me, my, you, and your.*) Describe the process step by step with comments such as, "Now we're going to put eyes on the mask."

Helpful Hint

When working with children with motor disabilities, it is helpful to tape the paper onto the table to keep it from moving around. This leaves both hands free to manipulate markers, glue, and small bits of paper.

Extending the plan

- Repeat this activity often in conjunction with other parts of the curriculum: making pumpkin faces at Haloween, jolly Santas at the holidays, and animal and character faces for plays, songs, and games. Bring in examples of masks from other cultures, such as native American Indian and African masks
- Use paper plates to create a *face*. Encourage children to add yarn hair and a large stick as a holder at the bottom of the plate mask. Cut eyes in the face so that children can look through it.
- Cut paper into specific shapes or use specific colors for eyes or nose or mouth. Draw matching shapes or use the same colors on large paper and have children *match* the shapes or colors as they create a face.
- Provide markers and crayons for children to add their own scribbles and marks.

Variations

- Help children learn to draw rather than construct faces.
- Use the same process with other familiar representations such as:
  A car or bus, with wheels, window, door, etc.
  Shapes of bodies on larger paper with cut-out shapes of shirts, pants, and shoes
  Simple house with windows and door (Use the house when you say good-bye to children: "You're going home.")
  Place mat with shapes of plate, spoon, and cup (laminate for use at snack times)

Glossary

90 degree angle rule   An informal rule of thumb that suggests that good positioning and body alignment is with feet, knees and hips positioned at 90 degree angles.

AAC   see *augmentative and alternative communication*.

ABC analysis   Method of observation and evaluation of a problem behavior that describes the *antecedent, behavior,* and *consequence.*

abnormal gag reflex   The forward and downward movement of the tongue and extension of the jaw, often caused by hypersensitivity or by difficulty swallowing.

accommodations   Assisting a child with special needs to allow for full access and participation in typical early childhood settings.

activity area   An area of the room which is designed for a particular activity such as the art area or block area.

activity / standards inventory   Analysis of the discrepancy between the participation of nondisabled peers and the participation of the child with special needs, and identification of the barriers responsible for the lack of participation.

adaptations   Special teaching techniques or equipment that enable the child with special needs to participate in an activity.

adaptive equipment   Physical devices designed or modified to support the independence and participation of a child with special needs.

aided hearing   Hearing that is augmented by amplification via wearing a hearing aid.

ambient noise   Surrounding, extraneous sounds in an environment.

anecdotal record keeping   Monitoring child behavior and progress by writing narrative descriptive notes, rather than by recording the duration or frequency of specific behaviors.

anticonvulsant medication   Drug that prevents or lessens seizure activity in the brain; antiepileptic drug.

asymmetric tonic neck reflex (ATNR)   A reflex in which turning the head to one side causes the arm and leg on that side to extend and the limbs on the opposite side to flex. Normal in infants up to six months. May persist indefinitely in children who have severe motor disabilities such as cerebral palsy.

athetosis   Slow, involuntary writhing movements typical of some types of cerebral palsy.

audiogram   Graphic representation of an individual's hearing thresholds, plotted by pitch (frequency) and loudness (intensity).

auditory cues   Speech or environmental sounds presented with, and which the child learns to associate with, specific events.

augmentative or alternative communication (AAC)   Method of communicating that uses assistive devices or techniques, such as signs, picture boards, and computers; assists children who do not have intelligible speech.

aversive   Unpleasant stimulus.

backward chaining   Teaching the steps of a task in reverse order; teaching the last step in the chain first.

behavior chain   A sequence of behaviors.

behavior modification   Systematic, consistent efforts to modify a specific behavior by manipulation of antecedents and consequences.

behavior specialist   A professional who assists teachers and parents in understanding effective techniques of behavior management.

blindness   Lack of vision due to damage to the eye or to the vision centers of the brain. Legal blindness is a corrected visual acuity of 20/200 in the better eye (which means the person can only see at 20 feet what a person with normal vision can see at 200 feet) or a visual field of 20 degrees or less in the better eye.

call and response   A routine in which the teacher provides a familiar "call" such as "How are you today?" and the group responds with a routine refrain, such as "Fine, thank you!" Or a highly practiced group refrain to a rhyme such as "No more monkeys jumping on the bed!"

cause and effect   Understanding that specific actions create specific effects.

circle time   Gathering children together in a group to share an activity directed by an adult, such as singing or listening to a story.

communication board   Board displaying pictures that a nonverbal child can point to express wants and needs.

communication notebook   Augmentative communication technique used with a nonverbal child in which picture cards depicting important communication topics and key words are arranged in a notebook. Can also refer to parent-teacher communication in which notes are written back and forth in a notebook which is sent home with the child each day.

communicative function   Communicative value or purpose of a specific behavior.

conductive hearing loss   Hearing loss caused by obstruction in the transmission of sound to the cochlea due to obstruction in the ear canal or the middle ear, which may result from otitis media or a perforated ear drum.

consequence   What happens immediately following a specific behavior.

cortical visual impairment   Visual impairment resulting from an inability of the occipital lobe of the brain to process visual stimuli. The eye itself may be normal.

cut-out cup   A flexible plastic cup with a semicircular piece cut out of the rim. Adult can monitor flow of liquid while holding cup and allow child to drink without hyperextending the neck.

data recording   Recording, usually in writing, the frequency and/or duration of a specific behavior through direct observation.

deaf and hard of hearing (DHH) specialist   Person trained to provide educational and communication services to individuals with hearing loss.

decibel   Unit used to measure the intensity or loudness of sound.

deficit orientation   Viewing families (or children) as having deficits and problems to be solved, rather than focusing on their strengths.

diplegia   Weakness or paralysis, usually associated with cerebral palsy, which primarily affects the legs.

directed eye gaze   The purposeful use of eye gaze as a communicative act by looking in the direction of a desired object or symbol.

discovery walk   Early childhood activity in which a walking route is planned with the goal to discover and collect interesting things.

discrete trial   A behavioral teaching strategy, most often used with children who have autism, characterized by direct, one-to-one instruction of specific behaviors, such as saying a certain word or making eye contact. Training consists of intense repeated practice of specific, discrete trials consisting of a *stimulus* (e.g., "What is this" and presentation of an object), a *response* (e.g., the child says "ball"), and a *consequence* (either a reinforcer, or if the response is incorrect, a negative consequence).

Down syndrome   Genetic disorder caused by a chromosomal abnormality; associated with a constellation of physical characteristics, including certain identifiable facial features and some degree of mental retardation.

Dycem mat   Piece of non-slip plastic material that is slightly sticky. Often used as placemat for dishes or other objects to keep them from sliding around on a table surface.

epilepsy   Recurrent seizures caused by abnormal electrical activity in the brain.

event sequence box   A row of small boxes in which actual objects are placed to represent the sequence of activities of the day.

expatiation   Caregiver responds to a child's utterance with a more complex version of the child's utterance with new information added.

extinction   Reducing the strength or frequency of a particular behavior by eliminating the reinforcer following the behavior. A common example would be extinguishing an annoying behavior by ignoring it.

family systems approach   The family is viewed as a dynamic interactive unit; what affects one family member affects all.

fine motor skills   Skills, such as drawing and picking up small objects, that require the coordination of the small muscles, particularly muscles of the hands and fingers.

floor time   Approach developed by infant psychiatrist Dr. Stanley Greenspan for young children with problems with self-regulation and characteristics of autism; focuses on the interactive relationship between the child and caregiver and attempts to enhance and increase turn taking and emotionally responsive interaction cycles through play activities.

fluency disorder(s)   Speech disorder such as stuttering that affects the rate and rhythm of speech production; characterized by frequent repetitions, prolongations, and blocking of speech sounds.

food obsessions Craving of certain foods, often to the exclusion of most other foods.

food phobias Obsessive avoidance of certain foods or textures.

frequency Pitch of a sound measured in cycles per second extending from low to high. Also referred to as "hertz" (Hz).

freeze game Any game in which children are moving in time to music, then they must immediately stop when the music stops, listen for music to start again, then resume movement.

functional behavior analysis Behavioral analysis technique that seeks to determine from the child's perspective the *function* or value of a problem behavior by carefully observing and recording the antecedents, consequences, and frequency of the behavior. Intervention consists of finding a more appropriate behavior and/or changing the environmental contingencies that trigger or maintain the behavior.

gastrostomy tube (G-tube) Feeding tube inserted directly into the stomach through a surgically created opening in the abdominal wall. Used when the child is unable to receive adequate nutrition orally or if the esophagus is blocked; may be temporary or permanent.

goals General statements in a child's IEP that state the desired outcomes for a child with special needs, such as "Carla will be able to eat independently."

grief reactions Normal emotional processes in response to a loss, such as the death of a child or the birth of a child with a severe disability. Family members experience such reactions as shock, denial, anger, depression, and acceptance.

gross motor skills Skills that require the coordination of large muscles, such as sitting, walking, and throwing a ball.

hand-over-hand guidance Adult places own hand over child's hand to guide the child to explore or to manipulate an object.

hand-under-hand guidance Child puts hand on top of adult's hand to experience the adult's hand movements.

hemiplegia Weakness or paralysis on one side of the body.

high-incidence disabilities The most common disabilities, including learning disabilities, speech and language disorders, and mild mental retardation.

high-preference inventory Identification of a child's most preferred and least preferred activities, objects, and people, determined through caregiver interviews and careful observation of child's likes and dislikes; information can be used to identify ways of motivating, engaging, and reinforcing a child who has a severe disability.

hypertonic Characterized by increased tone (stiffness) in the muscles.

hypotonic Characterized by decreased tone or floppiness in the muscles.

inclusion support Assistance provided by a special educator that supports the achievement of developmental or academic goals and the successful participation of a child with a disability in a typical setting (either a community-based early childhood setting or a regular education classroom).

Individualized Educational Plan (IEP) Written educational plan for a child with special needs who qualifies for special education services.

Individualized Family Services Plan (IFSP) Written statement of the child and family services needed to support an infant or toddler who has special needs during the first three years of life.

insistence on sameness Term used to refer to tendency of many children with autism to become anxious when certain daily routines or features of the environment are changed.

internal state Individual's state of arousal or alertness, such as asleep, drowsy, quiet awake, active awake, and agitated; usually used in reference to infants, but may also be useful in understanding children with multiple disabilities.

itinerants Professionals who provide specialized services in a variety of settings, traveling from site to site; frequently use a consultation model of service delivery.

kinesthetic cues Movement cues that stimulate the child's *kinesthetic sensation*, the awareness of the movement and position of one's body or limbs in space.

language Symbolic, rule-governed system of communication that may be written, signed, or spoken.

language disorder Inability or difficulty with expressing, understanding, or processing language.

language skills Vocabulary development and the mastery of a system of rules governing the sequencing of words into sentences and the forms of words (syntax and morphology), as well as the effective use of language.

learned helplessness Development of a pattern of nonresponse or lack of effort because of a lack of opportunity to experience the success and efficacy of one's own behavior and initiative.

learning disability Difficulty processing spoken or written language, which interferes with academic performance and results in a significant discrepancy between academic achievement and intellectual ability.

low-incidence disabilities Disabilities that occur fairly infrequently, including sensory impairments (visual impairment, hearing loss and deafness, and blindness), motor disability such as cerebral palsy, severe mental retardation, autism, and multiple disabilities.

low vision Corrected visual acuity of less then 20/70 in the better eye; children can learn to use residual vision, often with the assistance of optical aids such as magnifiers and special lenses.

manipulatives Small toys and objects that encourage use of the hands and the development of fine motor skills.

manual approach Use of manual signs as opposed to speech production (oral approach); the mode of communication preferred by many deaf individuals. Most commonly preferred manual sign system is ASL, American Sign Language.

mapping language onto experience Language strategy in which the adult carefully uses words and sentences to describe the activities in which the child is engaged.

mastery motivation   Intrinsic drive to master a skill or behavior

mild to moderate disabilities   More recent term used to refer to *high-incidence disabilities.*

mini-script   A short scripted play routine in which certain key words and phrases are used within a repeated play scenario; can provide an excellent teaching context for children with special needs.

mobility   The ability to move about in one's environment.

motor control   The ability to voluntarily engage muscles in purposeful movements.

movable soft areas   Outdoor or indoor play surfaces and structures that are soft and portable; can be used to create play spaces for children with severe motor disabilities or for developmentally young children.

muscle tone   A muscle's level of tension and resistance while at rest; abnormal muscle tone may be either *hypertonic* or *hypotonic.*

objectives   Behaviors and skills the child will learn en route to the achievement of long-term goals. Objectives are specific and measurable. For example, "Kathleen will walk 10 steps with adult holding her hands" and "Kathleen will walk a distance of five feet, unassisted" are objectives moving toward the goal of independent walking.

objectives-by-activity matrix   Chart that displays each activity of the day and the specific IEP objectives to be addressed during each activity.

olfactory cues   Cues that stimulate the sense of smell, such as encouraging a child who is blind to smell the paint before beginning an art activity.

one-to-one aide   Adult assigned to shadow a specific child and provide specific kinds of support, such as physical support and mobility assistance, behavioral management, or medical assistance when needed.

oral approach   Communication approach preferred by some individuals with hearing impairment that focuses on auditory training and learning to understand and produce speech; (As contrasted with the *manual* approach which advocates for the primary use of signs.)

orientation and mobility (O&M) specialist   Professional who provides training in both orientation skills (such as the use of all available senses to help children who are blind orient themselves in relation to their environment) and mobility skills (use of aids such as a cane and strategies such as trailing).

pacing   The speed at which a caregiver performs an activity or moves from one activity to another; the rate of speech, and amount of time the child is given in which to respond.

parallel play   Children play independently, along side one another.

parent-to-parent support   Parent support model that links experienced parents of children with special needs to parents who are new to the experiences and services related to having a child with special needs.

partial sight   Refers to an individual with *low vision.*

phonemes   The smallest units of speech sound which can be combined to produce words, *ship* has three phonemes, sh-i-p.

pica   Craving to eat nonfood substances, such as dirt or chalk.

picture exchange communication system (PECS) System of communication training often used with children who have autism who do not use functional speech; they select a picture card representing a desired object or activity and hand it to an adult as a request.

picture sequence board Display of pictures (photos or drawings) representing the sequence of steps in a complex task.

positive behavior support Behavioral technique that focuses on *prevention* of problem behaviors and providing support for more positive behaviors by identifying the *function* of the problem behavior and teaching the child a *replacement* behavior that is more acceptable. The technique also identifies the antecedents of problem behaviors as clues to the possible "triggers" or causes of the behavior and attempts to modify or eliminate them.

postural control Ability to assume and maintain an upright balanced position; ability to control and stabilize the trunk.

Prader-Willi syndrome Chromosomal disorder associated with obesity, low tone, mild to moderate mental retardation, and severe feeding disorder (food cravings).

pragmatics Ability to use language effectively in different situations; pragmatic rules govern how language is used in different types of interactions and for different purposes.

Premack Principle Children's performance can be enhanced by allowing them to engage in a highly reinforcing activity immediately following a less preferred or more difficult activity. For example, scheduling outdoor play immediately following story time would be beneficial for a child who has difficulty sitting quietly and maintaining attention.

progressive matching Matching the child's vocalization or word with a similar utterance, which is slightly more complex or elaborated. For example, if the child says "ba" for bottle the adult responds "bottle": if the child says "bottle" the adult responds "want bottle", and so-on.

prone stander Padded board that enables a child with severe physical disabilities to be positioned upright. Properly aligned standing position allows the child to engage in certain activities while developing head and arm control.

proprioception Body's awareness of its position in space. Proprioceptors in the inner ear, muscles, and tendons provide feedback that supports posture and balance.

protective reflexes Automatic reactions to loss of balance, such as extension of arms and/or legs to protect oneself in a fall or extension of one arm to the side when sitting balance is lost.

punishment Behavioral term referring to a negative consequence that decreases the strength of a behavior.

quadriplegia Weakness or paralysis of both arms and both legs, usually involving the head and trunk as well; can be caused by spinal cord injury or neurological disorder such as cerebral palsy.

reflective listening Comments made by the listener that let the speaker know he or she has been heard and understood. Effective reflective listening gives back to the speaker both the ideas and the feelings perceived by the listener.

reinforcer Any consequence of a behavior that increases the strength or frequency of the behavior.

replacement behavior Behavior that the child can be trained to use in place of an unacceptable behavior. For example, a child may be trained to use the sign for "Stop" rather than hitting other children.

representational skills The understanding that a picture or symbol can represent reality, and the ability to demonstrate such representation, for example, a dog can be represented by the spoken word "dog", by a picture of a dog, or by the written word "d-o-g".

request-for-more strategy A simple, but effective, strategy for increasing the participation and initiation of a child with severe disabilities in which a pleasurable activity is interrupted and the child is taught to use a particular response to request the activity to resume (e.g., swinging) or to request more of something (e.g., a drink of juice).

residual hearing The degree of usable hearing without amplification.

scaffolding Adult's provision of just the right cues and supports necessary to assist children to perform a task they cannot yet do independently.

security object Familiar object with which a child seeks to maintain contact, particularly when experiencing stress or new situations.

self-stimulatory behavior Repetitive behaviors produced by a child that provide sensory stimulation to self-calm or to block out other stimuli, which the child experiences as painful or uncomfortable. Self-stimulatory behaviors include visual self-stimulation (e.g., spinning a wheel), tactile (twirling one's hair or head banging), kinesthetic (rocking), or auditory (constant humming).

semantic extension Adult language response to child that not only expands on the structure of the child's utterance but also adds additional information, e.g., child says "coat" and adult says "That's *Mommy's* coat."

sensorineural hearing loss Permanent hearing loss resulting from damage to the cochlea in the inner ear or to the auditory nerve, which interferes with the transmission of neural impulses to the brain.

sensory integration Ability of the central nervous system to receive, process, and learn from sensations, such as sights, sounds, movement, and the pull of gravity.

sensory integration therapy Technique that applies the theory of sensory integration to help children who have tactile defensiveness, poor motor planning, attention deficits, and poor body awareness.

separation An infant or young child's removal from or lack of access to an attachment figure.

service coordinator Individual identified in the IFSP who will be responsible for coordination of services specified in the early intervention plan.

specialized teaching techniques Specific strategies designed to assist the learning of children with certain disabilities, such as visual impairment or autism; specialized techniques that would not typically be used with children who do not have special needs.

speech Oral production of language; the representation of language via speech sound sequences (phonemes).

speech production (articulation) disorder Condition that interferes with the production of speech; includes articulation disorders (such as difficulty producing speech sounds or coordinating the oral musculature), fluency disorders (stuttering), or voice disorders (hoarseness).

speech skills Refer to the ability to produce the sounds, or phonemes, that make up words.

spinal subluxation Partial dislocation of the upper spine; occurs in 15 percent of children who have Down syndrome but becomes symptomatic in only 1.5 percent. Can lead to spinal cord compression. Symptoms of spinal cord compression include head tilt, increase in motor clumsiness, and weakness in one arm.

switch-activated Battery-operated toys or other electronic devices (such as a tape player) that are adapted so they can be easily turned on by a simple motor movement such as pressing the hand on a large switch.

tactile cues Signals provided by an adult that stimulate the sense of touch; especially useful for children who are blind or deaf and blind. Cues accompany or precede an event, such as touching the child's hand with a washcloth before washing the child's face and hands (also referred to as an *object cue*) or touching the spoon to the child's lips before beginning feeding.

tactile defensiveness Abnormal sensitivity to touch resulting in a child's avoidance or resistance to being touched or to handling certain materials; occurs commonly in children who have autism, children who are blind, and children with severe sensory integration difficulties.

task analysis Breaking a task into a sequence of steps to determine which components of a task the child can already perform and which need to be trained. A task analysis also suggests the order in which steps should be taught.

task persistence The extent to which a child will persist at accomplishing a difficult task: also related to concept of *mastery motivation.*

task sequencing Understanding and carrying out the behaviors and events in a task that has multiple steps, such as toothbrushing or making pudding.

TEACCH Program For Treatment and Education of Autistic and Related Communication Handicapped Children, this educational program is designed for children with autism to create a highly structured classroom and specifically adapt the environment and activities to reduce those factors that interfere with learning and to support the development of communication and academic skills.

threshold (auditory) The intensity (loudness) level at which an individual can just barely detect a sound.

time out Behavioral consequence for unacceptable behavior. The child is removed from the group or from an activity to a quiet place for no more than five minutes. Time out should not be used to frighten or punish the child, but to provide an opportunity for the child to gain self-control and then to reengage in the activity in a more appropriate way.

tongue thrust Strong reflexive protrusion of the tongue; interferes with eating and dental development.

tonic bite reflex Teeth clamp shut as a result of jaw closure, which occurs reflexively when gums or teeth are stimulated; normal in infants from one to eight months of age; may persist in children who have cerebral palsy.

total communication Approach used with children who are hearing impaired that consists of using multiple modalities in communication, including facial expression, manual signs, finger spelling, lipreading, speech, writing, and AAC devices.

traffic management Arrangement of space and materials to encourage efficient movement of children from one area of the room (or playground) to another; avoids cross traffic, considers access and mobility needs of children with disabilities, and places materials so they are accessible in the areas where they will be used.

trailing techniques Technique used to assist children who are blind with the development of independent mobility; involves following along a surface (such as a wall) or edge (such as the edge of a countertop) with the hand extended at a 45 degree angle to the side. For example, a preschool child may learn to trail along a wall to find the bathroom.

transformations An interesting, clearly noticeable change in the characteristics of some object or substance, e.g., adding green food coloring to white frosting, or inflating a balloon.

transition The process of moving from one event or activity to another (e.g., from circle time to recess), from one setting to another (e.g., from home to children's center), or from one program to another (e.g., from preschool to kindergarten).

transition strategies Techniques designed to assist children in their movement from one activity to the next. Also refers to a transition from one program to another such as the transition from preschool to kindergarten.

trial-and-error exploration Typical behavior of a child in the sensorimotor stage of development, characterized by purposeful exploration of objects and search for novel effects by systematically engaging in trial-and-error type manipulation. For example, a child seated in a high chair drops Cheerios® from different angles and positions and watches where they land.

tunnel vision A condition in which the visual field is constricted, allowing only straight ahead vision; effect is similar to looking through a tunnel.

vestibular sensation The vestibular system is located in the inner ear and responds to the position of the head in relation to gravity. This sensation enables people to maintain balance.

visual field Total area that can be seen while looking straight ahead, without moving the head or eyes.

voice disorder Conditions that affect the quality of the voice, such as pitch, loudness, and resonance; includes such disorders as hoarseness and excessive nasality.

zone of proximal development (ZPD) Level of ability or performance a child can exhibit while interacting with a significant adult but cannot perform independently.

Index

Blocks, 69, 137, 144–146
    development stages of block play, 145
    and language, 138
    types of, 145
Body movement through space
        (vestibular sensation), 275
Body parts movement (kinesthetic
        sensation or proprioception), 275
Body position sensation, 275
Books, 71–72, 149–151, 235–236
Boredom, 187
Boundaries, 67–68, 184
    case study, 75–76
    fluid, 67
    space, 141
    see also Physical environment
        arrangement
Bowel movements, 214–215
    see also Toilet training
Braille, 149, 161, 235, 241
Bristle Blocks™, 142, 151
Brown Bear (Martin), 150
Bubbles, 143, 151, 158
Building area, 69
Busy boxes, 147

Calendar time, 162–164, 238
Calendars, 162–164
"Call and response" participation, 149, 161
Candles, 147
Canes, 277
Cardboard blocks, 145–146
Carle, Eric, The Very Hungry Caterpillar, 151
Carpet squares, 160–161, 165, 236, 247
Case studies
    autism, 218–219
    behavior intervention plan, 98–99
    blindness, 132–133
    boundaries, 75–76
    cerebral palsy, 177–178, 229–230
    communicating with families, 263–264
    diplegia, 152–153
    down syndrome, 17–18, 205–206,
        289–290
    low vision, 248
    tactile defensiveness, 189–190
    toilet training, 117–118
    vision impairment and cerebral palsy,
        55–56
Catching, 152, 198
Cause and effect, 180, 185
    toys, 143, 147–148
Cerebral palsy, 23–24, 33–40, 180, 272
    case study of, 55–56
    characteristics of children with, 33–37
    definition of, 33
    and Follow the Leader, 177–178
    and music, 229
    and picture boards, 244
    and snack time, 214–215
    teaching strategies for children with,
        37–40
    and toileting, 217
Chalk boards, 142
Challenging behaviors. See Behavior
        challenges; Behavior management
Change, tolerance for, 162
Chewing, 207, 275
Choking, 73, 151, 216, 289

Christelow, Eileen, Five Little Monkeys, 151
Chromosomal condition, 24, 216
Circle time, 76, 130, 149, 235, 236, 243
    activities, 158–159
    case study, 177–178
    definition of, 156
    Follow the Leader activity, 174–176
    good-bye, 128–129
    learning opportunities during, 156
    making the most of, 156–158
    parachute activity, 170–173
    prototype of, 159–165
    variable features, 158
    What's in the Box? activity, 166–169
Clapping, 226
Clean-up song, 131
Clear boundaries, 68
Climbing, 195
Climbing structures, 75
Clutter, 66, 83, 86, 238
CMV. See Cytomegalovirus
Coaching, 283–284
Coca-Cola®, 234
Cognitive disabilities, 5, 24, 147, 181
    and books, 236
    and delayed reinforcers, 91
    in Down syndrome children, 24–27
    and music, 226
    and play, 140, 143
    and storytime, 238
    and water activities, 148
    and What's in the Box?, 168
Cognitive level
    cerebral palsy, 35–36
    and hearing loss, 50–51
Cognitive skills
    developing, 185–186
    and hearing loss, 50–51
    and name cards, 237
Collaborative intervention team, 268,
        285–288
    action plan for, 287–288
    step-by-step problem solving, 286–287
Collecting, 204
Color perception, 276
Communication
    behavior problems as, 92–97
    and cerebral palsy, 36
    child-specific, 261
    eye level, 126–127
    with families, 126, 253–265
    family's preferred mode of, 278
    and hearing loss, 50
    and music and rhythm, 226
    the need to, 14–15
    and paraeducators, 284–285
    skill development, 213–214, 261–262
    strategies for, 12–15
    visual for autistic children, 32
    see also Parent-professional
        partnerships
Communication boards, 244–245
Communication disorders, 271
    and alternative communication (AAC)
        devices, 203
    and behavior challenges, 82
    see also Speech-language specialists
Communication notebooks, 261
Community-based settings, 4

Complex sentence structure, 15
Comprehension, 246–247
Computers, 142, 147
Conductive hearing loss, 49–50
Consequences (following a behavior),
        88–89
    see also ABC analysis
Consistency, 87
    of materials, 69
    and transitions, 131
Constipation, 214
Contact paper autumn collage, 165
Contrast, 44, 277
Control procedure, 91
Conversation, turn-taking, 15
Cookie cutters, 146
Cooperation, 140
Coordinated, team-based approach,
        279–280
Cortical visual impairment, 42, 43
    strategies for working with children,
        45–46
Crayons, 72
Creative boundaries, 67
Crowd tolerance, developing, 140–141
Crying, 81
Cubbies, 123, 128–129, 236, 277
Cues, 10, 52, 188
    acoustic, 139
    auditory, 43, 277
    difficult-to-read, 5
    kinesthetic, 43
    multiple, 131
    olfactory, 43, 139
    sensory, 43
    tactile, 43, 268, 277
    texture/tactile, 196
    touch, 187
    transition, 130–132
Cupcake tins, 147
Cups, 208
Cut-out cups, 210
Cytomegalovirus (CMV), 49

Daily activities, level of participation
    in, 116
Daily schedules
    for autistic children, 32
    and literacy activities, 236–242
    predictable, 16, 18, 86
    see also Schedules
Dancing, 159, 177, 225–229
    and cerebral palsy, 229
    see also Music and rhythm activities
Dancing song, 177
Data recording, 107–117, 279
    see also Individualized education
        plan (IEP)
Deaf and hard of hearing (DHH)
        specialists, 277–278
    role of, 278
Deaf-blind, 247
Decibels, 46–47
De-escalating behavior, 87–88
Deficit orientation, 255
Delays
    cognitive, 55, 147
    motor, 149
    speech and language, 24, 54, 70, 267